DATE DUE		
JAN 1 3 1981	DEC 1 4 1992	
MAR 3 1 1981		
FEB 1 8 1986	JAN 1 6 1995	
SEP 8 1984	MAR 1 9 1995	
DEC 3 1985	DEC 1 9 2000	
OCT 3		
SEP 2 8 1998		

Policy Studies and the Social Sciences

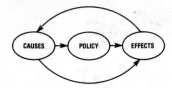 **Policy Studies
Organization Series**

Policy Studies and the Social Sciences

Edited by
Stuart S. Nagel
University of Illinois

Lexington Books
D.C. Heath and Company
Lexington, Massachusetts
Toronto   London

Library of Congress Cataloging in Publication Data

Main entry under title:

Policy studies and the social sciences.

"Based on symposia coordinated by the Policy Studies Organization."
    Includes index.
    1. Policy sciences—Addresses, essays, lectures. 2. Social sciences—Addresses, essays, lectures. I. Nagel, Stuart S., 1934- II. Policy Studies Organization.
H62.P59   1975b   309.2'12   75-2293
ISBN 0-669-99531-2

Published simultaneously in Canada

Printed in the United States of America

International Standard Book Number: 0-669-99531-2

Library of Congress Catalog Card Number: 75-2293

**Dedicated to the application
of social science
to important policy problems**

Contents

Introduction

This is the second book in a series of policy studies volumes being published by Lexington Books based on symposia coordinated by the Policy Studies Organization. Each of these symposia is either devoted to a specific policy problem or to a general approach to analyzing policy problems. This particular volume on *Policy Studies and the Social Sciences* has the general theme that meaningful research on the causes and effects of alternative governmental policies often requires appropriate knowledge from a variety of social sciences and sometimes other fields of knowledge as well.

This volume, like the others in the series, deals with social problems mainly from a political science perspective which emphasizes the relevance of governmental involvement in resolving the problems discussed. This perspective is in conformity with the primary purpose of the Policy Studies Organization, which is to promote the application of political *social* science to important policy problems. In light of that perspective, many of the chapters address themselves to the question of what a specific social science can contribute to the research and teaching of political scientists interested in governmental policy problems. Some of the chapters are written by political scientists who have acquired an expertise in another social science. Other chapters are written by non-political scientists who have acquired an expertise in the relevance of their social science or field of knowledge to the work of political scientists.

Although all of the chapters authored by political scientists recognize that interdisciplinary knowledge is important, they differ in the degree of importance they place on going outside of political science. Some political scientists, like Duncan MacRae, argue that primary concern should be placed on developing interdisciplinary structures for doing policy studies research. Other political scientists, like Theodore Lowi, argue that primary concern should be placed on internal development within political science. The debate is a little like the one over whether world socialism must come before or after socialism in one key country, but fortunately without the purges that were associated with the development of left-wing socialism. Also fortunately, *intra*disciplinary policy-oriented developments are going on within each social science, while *inter*disciplinary developments are going on among them. The key within-discipline events relate to the growth of sub-discipline organizations, periodicals, courses, and books that take a policy orientation. The key across-discipline events relate to team research, interdisciplinary periodicals, combined degree programs, much self-teaching, and possibly an interdisciplinary policy studies organization operating like or within the Social Science Research Council or the National Academy of Sciences.

The chapter authors also differ on how important certain aspects of a specific social science may be to policy studies work. Political scientist Larry Wade finds considerable value from the application of economic reasoning to policy studies in his chapter, but political scientist James Levine questions how much utility there may be in the rational utility analysis of the economists. Likewise, political philosophers John Ladd and Martin Golding emphasize the importance of philosophy, but philosophical political scientist Eugene Meehan finds some defects in the relevance of philosophy as it has currently developed. These differences of opinion add to the liveliness of the analysis. The scholarly qualifications of the authors, however, keep the liveliness on a reasonably high intellectual level.

Although there are differences of opinion on the relevance of various social sciences for policy studies research and teaching, there seems to be agreement on some of the basic aspects of what each social science may have to contribute to policy causal analysis and policy evaluation analysis. Sociology, for example, has developed a substantial amount of factual knowledge and theory in broad fields like social control, socialization, and social change which can be helpful in understanding the effects of alternative policies and the behavior of policymakers and policy appliers. Sociology has also concerned itself more so than other social sciences with the specific policy problems of race relations, family problems, and criminology.

Of all the social sciences, the field of economics has clearly developed the most sophisticated mathematical models for synthesizing normative and empirical premises in order to deduce means-ends policy recommendation. These mathematical models relate to the optimum allocation of scarce resources, the optimum level at which to pursue a given policy which has a curvilinear relation with net benefits achieved, and the optimum strategy to follow when the net benefits achievable are dependent on the occurrence of a contingent event. Institutional economists have been especially relevant in discussing the role of economic class structures, ownership systems, and technology in determining policy choices. Economics has also concerned itself, more so than other social sciences, with the specific policy problems of union-management relations, consumer problems, unemployment, and inflation.

Psychology is the social science that has probably done more to develop techniques of statistical inference, cross-tabulation, survey research, and multivariate analysis, at least with regard to the kinds of variables with which political scientists deal, unlike the more monetary statistics of the econometricians. Psychology also provides an important focus on the role of the individual or small groups (as contrasted to sociological institutions), especially with regard to attitudes, perceptions, and motivations. Psychology also has special relevance to social problems dealing with alcoholism, suicide, drug addiction, and related mental health problems.

Anthropology, geography, and history provide a broader perspective over space and time than the other social sciences do. That kind of cross-cultural and historical perspective can help to make policy analysis less culture-bound and less time-bound. The theoretical and practical findings of policy studies thereby become more broadly meaningful when dealing with the causes and effects of alternative public policies. Anthropology also has a special relevance to policy problems that affect present or former preliterate peoples. Geographers are becoming increasingly concerned with the optimum location of various facilities or districts. Historians by extrapolating trends or analogizing to the past can add a futurism element to policy studies.

Without philosophy, especially normative social philosophy, policy studies might tend to lack direction with regard to what they are seeking to achieve. Indeed, one of the major criticisms of quantitative policy analysis is that it is too capable of being used to maximize socially undesirable goals as well as socially desirable ones. Philosophy, in spite of its contemporary emphasis on positivism, is still the leading discipline for discussing what is socially desirable on a high level of abstraction. Philosophy also provides a high level of abstraction with regard to discussing ultimate-type causes as to why societies make certain basic policy choices. In addition to its normative and causal components, philosophy provides the most developed principles of logical and semantic analysis on which the more narrow social sciences can build.

Without the quantitative and computer science tools that are ultimately associated with mathematics, policy studies might tend to overemphasize evaluative gut reactions, armchair speculation, and isolated historical anecdotes. Mathematics provides the basis for both an empirical statistical approach to policy studies and a deductive syllogistic approach. Through the mathematics of algebraic equations and the calculus of change, the syllogistic premises can take on a much greater precision than is provided by the kind of dichotomous reasoning that is normally associated with symbolic logic. Physical and biological science to some extent provide models to emulate in the development of mathematically scientific laws, provided one always considers the differences in the behavioral instability of people as compared to physical or biological objects. Natural science is also quite relevant substantively to certain specific policy problems like environmental protection, energy development, and population control.

The field of law has important social science elements when it involves studying why the law is what it is or the effects of alternative laws, as contrasted to studying what the law is and how to use it as a lawyer. As a social science, the legal field is close to the heart of policy studies because virtually all policy problems are capable of at least attempted resolution by legislatures, courts, or law-making administrative agencies. Legal literature can be helpful in (1) generating policy hypotheses, (2) providing large quantities of data especially with regard to policy decisions, and in (3) providing a better understanding of the societal rules which relate to the problems of such institutions as the family, the economy, and the criminal justice system. The legal orientation usually emphasizes a civil liberties orientation of free speech, due process, and equal protection rather than a more technocratic orientation, but not necessarily, as illustrated by Frederick Beutel's chapter.

Since policy studies particularly refers to the study of the causes and effects of governmental policy, one would expect political science to be especially relevant even though political scientists may be very dependent on other social sciences for a variety of relevant methodological tools and substantive knowledge. Political scientists have traditionally devoted much of their intellectual resources to analyzing how governmental policy gets made, with special emphasis on the role of interest groups and more recently on the role of individual decisionmakers. Political scientists are now turning more toward the analysis of specific policy problem areas (like welfare and taxation) rather than more abstract studies of the policy-making process. Along with this concern for specific policy problems, political scientists have shown increasing concern for studying the impact of various policies such as those in the civil liberties field. Along with civil liberties, the subject matter of political science has made the discipline especially relevant to policy problems related to reform of elections, legislatures, courts, administrative agencies, and reform of other governmental institutions, as well as relevant to problems of international relations and foreign policy.

From this collection of social sciences, one can readily perceive that the study of governmental policy problems is clearly an interdisciplinary activity, at least in the sense that many disciplines have something to contribute to the study. For any political or social scientist, it would be too much to acquire an expertise in all the relevant perspectives. Indeed, it is too much to become an expert in all the sub-fields within one's own social science. Nevertheless, there probably is a consensus among the authors that if one is interested in developing competence in policy studies work, he should be familiar in a general way with the potential contributions and drawbacks of the various social sciences. Such familiarity will at least enable him to know when to call upon a fellow social scientist or a treatise in another social science, the way a layman has a general idea of when to call upon a doctor or a lawyer and a general idea of the meaning of what the doctor or lawyer says. With those caveats and considerations in mind, the Policy Studies Organization in cooperation with Lexington Books hereby presents this interdisciplinary volume on *Policy Studies and the Social Sciences*.

Part I
General Social Science

1

From Social Science to Policy Sciences: An Introductory Note

Daniel Lerner

Policy relevance has been at the core of social science from the beginning. Indeed, the emergence of new policy needs stimulated the development of each of the social sciences in turn. In this introductory note, we shall look briefly at: (1) the historical retrospect; (2) current alternatives in policy studies; (3) futurism and the policy sciences.

Historical Retrospect

A glance at the evolution of the social sciences over the past three centuries might—if one's glance is focused on policy relevance—yield a table that looks approximately like Table 1-1.

Demography developed in England in the late eighteenth century because of the dramatic increase in human mobility. Traditional methods of "keeping tabs" on populations—such as parish registers of birth, marriages, and deaths—no longer sufficed when increasing numbers of people were no longer wed or dead where they had been born. A "national census" was needed to know how many people (by sex, age, occupation, etc.) were living where at any given time. To foresee needs in housing, schooling, public works of all kinds, governments also wanted reasonably accurate projections of future trends in human mobility. In response to these new policy needs, such scholars as Sir William Petty and John Graunt initiated studies which evolved into the science of demography. What happened first in Britain, in demography as in subsequent initiatives, was followed rapidly in the Old Continent and the New World.

Indeed, it was Britain's maritime prowess that led directly to modern economics. This hinged on the simple discovery that one could "turn a shilling" by loading one's ships with cheap natural resources everywhere and then processing them for resale in one's factories at home. It is likely that the French, who accepted the Physiocrats' priority on land values, were rapidly outpaced by the British as a result of Britain's option for manufacturing. The initial heroes of this weighty policy decision were Adam Smith and Ricardo. (It is probably fortunate that the United States, in this case, followed Hamilton's "Report on Manufactures" rather than Jefferson's preference for plantation and land economics.)

The policy of manufactures led to the rapid growth of urban factories

3

Table 1-1
Evolution of the Social Sciences

Approx. Time Period	Social Science	Policy Issue
1700-1750	Demography	Human Mobility
1750-1800	Economics	Industry & Commerce
1800-1850	Sociology	Urban Poverty
1850-1900	Anthropology	Imperialism
1900-1925	Psychology	Human Resources (Public Health)
1925-1950	Political Science	Democratic Planning
1950-1975	Communication	Globalism

with the concomitant growth of a new class of urban poor. From the very start, urban poverty has been the core problem of sociology. In France, Frederic Le Play devoted forty years of his life to the study of the urban poor in his own country, in most of Europe, and in much of Asia. His studies led directly to reform legislation designed to improve the dreadful lot of the urban industrial worker. A similar sequence was enacted in Britain by Charles Booth, whose monumental *Life and Labour of the People in London* led to major reform legislation. Indeed, Booth himself was named to the Royal Commission on the Poor Law. The work of both these European pioneers was subsequently taken up in the United States. Booth's method of direct systematic observing and reporting was translated directly in the *Hull House Maps and Papers* (1895) and became a building block for the famous "Chicago School." Le Play's instruction for study of the family was translated in the *American Journal of Sociology* (1897), which remarked that there had been no significant advance in this area for forty years.

By the latter half of the nineteenth century the British Empire had grown to such unprecedented proportions that a new systematic method of acquiring knowledge about the diverse people under British rule became essential. Its early efforts appeared in the Indian *Gazeteer* and in the British *Field Notes in Ethnography*. These became the basis for the science of anthropology.

With the turn of the century, the problems of urban work and living had become so intense that a fledgling social science called psychology emerged. It was responsive to two separate but related sets of policy issues: (1) the problem of maximizing human resources; (2) the problems of public health in urban environments. The first led to a school of "industrial psychology" symbolized by "Taylorism," an epithet for the type of "time-motion studies" initiated by Henry Taylor. The second led to studies of congestion and crowding, noise and speed, in urban settings. The early work of the outstanding German experimental psychologists focused on such problems as these. As we know, psychology developed rapidly and spread widely thereafter. The "Army Alpha" tests diffused into every conceivable variety of psychological testing. The concern with urban health, given further impetus by Dr. Freud, developed into the vast areas of psychiatry and mental health.

World War I, in line with the developments just noted, produced an overall concern with the shaping of a truly democratic polity. Boys just back from the war demanded a "square deal" (Theodore Roosevelt) and a "new freedom" (Woodrow Wilson). Urban industrial workers everywhere were organizing to demand their rights. By 1926 Britain was in the grip of a general strike, and a few years later was under the government of the Labor party (Ramsey MacDonald) for the first time in its history. Clearly, the old preoccupation with formal institutions in academic government departments could no longer meet these new policy issues. Largely under the leadership of Charles E. Merriam, who chaired the first presidential commission on social needs and resources, a new political science developed rapidly with a focus on democratic planning—a focus which Lasswell has characterized as a "concern with the shaping and sharing of all values."

Deriving from the experiences of World War II, the past quarter century has developed a new social science which, for want of a more widely accepted term, we call communication. Although this originated in the propaganda efforts of both world wars, it went far beyond psychological warfare during the course of World War II, which was both "global" and "total." Where wartime slogans focused on "the man behind the man behind the gun," a dimension of concern for maintaining "morals" on the home front took equal priority with "demoralizing" the enemy. In the American armed forces, which numbered some twelve million men and women by 1945, care for the attitudes of these citizen-soldiers had to be given high priority.

Much of what we are here calling communication originated in the wartime *Studies in Social Psychology* led by Stouffer, Lazarsfeld, Hovland, and others. Social psychology was indeed the home base in the early development of communication as a field. But as the war receded, "globalism" remained. During the most intense years of bipolarization known as the Cold War, major governments considered it essential to understand the attitudes of people with whom they were dealing all around the world. Accordingly, anthropology soon came to supplement social psychology in building the communication field via the studies of "culture and personality" by such pioneers as Ruth Benedict and Clyde Kluckhohn and the studies of "national character" by Margaret Mead and Alexander Leighton.

Throughout its brief career, communication has been continuously concerned with issues of national and global policy. It is taught in virtually every major social science department, and nowhere more vigorously than in the new political science. Let us now turn briefly to what all this work has produced in terms of current alternatives in policy studies.

Current Alternatives in Policy Studies

Since this volume is mainly concerned with identifying, explicating, and advocating our major current alternatives, I can be very brief here. At the risk of appearing too cavalier in treating this important topic—and pleading only that other, wiser, observers will deal with it more carefully in the rest of this book—I shall look only at two major variants of policy studies that are currently in vogue.

The first is based on the conception of "applied social research" developed by Lazarsfeld and Merton at Columbia and subsequently reproduced in most regions of this country and many developed countries abroad. The core of this approach is to take an existing policy issue and subject it to systematic empirical observation. Early classics produced by this approach are the *voting* studies by Lazarsfeld and his associates. The policy issue here was the individual voter's decision on how to cast his ballot and one of its intended by-products was the improvement of pre-election forecasting through sample surveys. Similar efforts have been made in economics and market research, following the early work of Rensis Likert and George Katona.

A second major array of approaches may be grouped together under the rubric "policy studies." In some instances the issue studied is a single national policy decision. Good examples of this approach are Bernard C. Cohen's study *The Japanese Peace Treaty* and W. P. Davison's *The Berlin Blockade*. The latter was done under the auspices of the RAND Corporation, which has been a leader in policy studies of this type. Beyond single national policy decisions, many RAND studies have dealt with policy processes, and indeed with the process of decision-making itself. One example is Nathan Leites' *The Operational Code of the Politburo*. Another is the illuminating series of papers by Hans Speier, particularly those dealing with "nuclear blackmail" that are contained in his books *Social Order and the Risks of War* and *Force and Folly*.

Studies of both types mentioned above have exercised wide influence among social scientists and continue to produce studies of great value on issues of national and world policy. We would like to close, however, by referring to a third conception of policy studies pioneered by Harold D. Lasswell, which is only now beginning to make its importance known to social scientists everywhere.

Futurism and the Policy Sciences

Futurism has captured public attention by focusing on such dramatic projects as "the year 2000." It has produced such widely acclaimed products as Daniel Bell's *Toward the Year 2000* and *Hawaii 2000* by George Chaplin and Glenn Paige. It has enlisted such first-rate minds as Bertrand de Jouvenel who, as a high priest of futurism, has been among the first to explain that its present techniques are largely related to *The Art of Conjecture*.

Somewhat more rigorous techniques have been developed in connection with that specialized branch of futurism known as "Technological Forecasting." Important as much of this work is, however, we are obliged to recognize that it has developed mainly where it has been able to formulate technological variables in quantitative terms. As compared to these conjectural and specialized versions of futurism, we refer to the future and policy orientation of the policy sciences.

What Lasswell proposed under the heading of policy sciences is a comprehensive conception of the present as a movement from the past to the future with a central tendency and a determinate direction. One form which work along these lines may take is the "developmental construct." Lasswell has both explained and exemplified the procedure for building such a construct in his classic paper on "The Garrison-Prison State" (1937).

Since this early effort, Lasswell has systematically laid out the basic groundwork for the policy sciences. He has identified and specified the eight base and scope values which are comprised in any social system. He has identified and operationalized the five intellectual tasks to be performed by the policy sciences. For those who want a guide to Lasswell's thinking, the most concise summary is presented in his *A Pre-View of Policy Sciences*.

Lasswell's seminal thinking over the decades has begun to produce ripe fruits. There is now a *Policy Sciences Book Series*; there is a quarterly journal entitled *Policy Science* under the editorship of Garry Brewer; the RAND Corporation now offers a Policy Sciences Program for its postgraduate students.

I believe that further articulation and implementation of Lasswell's conception is greatly needed. I believe that policy sciences may turn out to be the most productive form of policy studies for the decades ahead. I commend it to your attention.

2

Evaluation Research and Public Policies

Howard E. Freeman and Ilene N. Bernstein

The boundaries of the field of public policy analysis are elusive, and the outlooks and styles of individuals and groups involved in policy studies vary markedly. There is virtual agreement, however, that an integral part of the policy analysis activity is the evaluation of the conduct, efficacy, and efficiency of human resource programs. It is important to assess both the many on-going public and quasi-public programs in the health, education, welfare, public safety, and environmental arenas and the numerous innovative and experimental efforts to better the human condition.

Today, evaluation research is a robust activity with a large number of persons in universities, nonprofit groups and profit-making corporations engaged in the assessment of established and innovative programs. From the standpoint of the social sciences, evaluation research has a considerable history. In a little known article some forty years ago, A. Stephen Stephan (1935) pleaded for the experimental evaluation of Roosevelt's "New Deal," and substitution of Kennedy's "Great Society" slogan would have made his paper timely in the 1960s. The Nixon Administration was much too busy erasing tapes and defending themselves in court to develop a catchy phrase to describe their human resource and social welfare programs, and the Ford Administration is sloganless too. But the theme of Stephan's paper is applicable now as well. The message is clear. Unless policymakers, social planners, and the public know the consequences of efforts at planned social change and innovation, broad-scale action programs cannot be judged rationally.

The Evaluation Research Endeavor

There is no commonly accepted definition of evaluation research. In its broadest context, evaluation research can be seen as a force for social change, as a set of actions in which social-science trained researchers participate in order to improve the human condition. Underlying this general view, however, there is considerable variation and difference of opinion on what constitutes evaluation research.

From one standpoint, any information or assessment that allows one to reach decisions on programs, treatments, and interventions can be considered to be evaluation research. Much of what takes place under the guise of evaluation research only can be classified as such in terms of a broad definition. There are many agencies and programs in which evaluation research consists of what may be regarded as the application of conventional wisdom or "common sense." For example, if it is repeatedly observed that large number of children in some schools do not bring their lunch and a school lunch program is initiated and the children eat the food, the latter fact becomes the "common sense" evaluation.

It is important, of course, not to make too strong a case about the inappropriateness of "conventional wisdom evaluations." In the first place, in many cases they are right; in the second, given the resources, methodological difficulties, and time pressures, often this is all that can be done. The problem is, however, that many such efforts, one knows from experience, oftentimes lead to faulty conclusions. For example, take the case just noted: if the parents of the children are indeed desperate for funds and consequently provide inadequate diets for their families, knowledge that their children are receiving a meal in school can result in a redistribution of the food provided family members at home, such that a school lunch program is not over the long run supplementary to normal diets, but rather just a substitute for what they would have received at different hours of the day at home.

A second type of activity often referred to as evaluation research is the assessment of the merits of whether or not certain activities, treatments, and interventions occur in conformity with generally accepted professional standards. Evaluations of many medical care and social welfare programs are so conducted. For example, an evaluation of a school health program might include information on whether or not the child was given, either in or out of the school, an annual physical examination. This idea has been promoted by the medical profession for considerable time. In a mental health counseling program, the question of whether or not the social worker took a detailed case history is information used to judge a program. Of course, many professional practices operate on the basis of data that clearly point to the desirability of usual practices, such as the importance of clinical tests before the administration of particular psychopharmaceutical drugs, since the side effects from them are not the same in all persons. But many practices go on because of tradition and professional values with no knowledge of their utility. This is, for example, the case with the example first cited here. The evidence, at best, is equivocable that children between the ages of six and twelve are benefited by annual physicals in terms of future health, morbidity or the detection of disease. Yet this generally accepted professional practice is a criterion even today in evaluating school health programs, and heavy fiscal commitments by local, state, and federal government are made to encourage health examinations.

A third category of activities often regarded as evaluation essentially consists of clinical, impressionistic judgments of programs. Again, it is important to point out that sometimes this is the only feasible or possible approach. Thus, for example an experienced educator may be called upon to review the value of a newly-prepared set of testbooks by sitting in a classroom and observing students' and teachers' performance, and judging whether what takes place is better than, worse than, or the same as what he regards as "usual" on the basis of his experience. Clinical assessments often are seriously defective for a number of reasons, two of which are perhaps important. First, there is great variation in clinical judges, as well as in the criteria that are used to identify the judge as an expert. Second, in general, clinical evaluations operate with relatively small units of analysis, whether they be people, groups, organizations or some other unit. Clearly if one makes an assessment of a program on a basis of judging a few units, problems of sampling bias enter into the conclusions.

Without disputing the sometime need for implementing the kinds of activities described in the above three categories, many advocates of evaluation researchers do not regard such work as competent evaluation research investigations. The difference lies in the commitment to utilizing the principles and approaches of research in undertaking assessments; it is the difference between what Suchman (1967) called *evaluation*, a procedure for judging the worthwhileness of some activity and *evaluative research,* the use of the tools of science to make the judgment. There is thus a qualitative difference in orientation between individuals who accept the rules of science as a guiding philosophy in their work, and those for whom they are either unknown or unimportant. Also, in addition to the overlay of a philosophical nature, to our minds, the evaluation researcher needs to be a person who is knowledgeable about the techniques required to undertake rigorous, empirical evaluation studies. Thus, for example, he or she should not only be concerned about developing a particular and systematic way of measuring a dimension or variable, but should know about and have the capacity and competence to carry through the necessary reliability and validity studies. In brief, an evaluation investigator needs to have the technical repertoire and competence to develop and execute a rigorous design by himself or herself, or by consulting with experts, or through some combination of both mechanisms. From this standpoint, evaluation research is similar to all social research in that it depends upon both the orientation of the individual undertaking the work and the technical repertoire that allows the task to be well done. Evaluation research is the application of social science methodology to the assessment of programs in a way that allows one empirically to assess their implementation and efficacy.

There are numerous volumes (Freeman and Sherwood (1970), Caro

(1971), Rossi and Williams (1972), and Suchman (1967)) that go into detail regarding the appropriate criteria for deciding whether or not an evaluation study is well done in terms of the perspective advanced here. Here it is important, however, to discuss only the general outlines of evaluation research.

Process Evaluation

Fundamentally, there are two questions that one is concerned with in doing evaluations. The first is whether or not a particular program intervention or treatment was implemented according to its stated guidelines. This type of evaluation usually is referred to as "process evaluation." The process evaluation generally centers on two questions (Freeman and Sherwood 1970):

1. Whether or not the program has been directed at the appropriate and specified target population or specified target area.
2. Whether or not the various practices and intervention efforts were undertaken as specified in the program design or derived from the principles explicated in that design.

The reasons for evaluating processes are obvious. In the first place, from the standpoint of the administration of human resources programs, it is critical to know that what presumably was paid for or deemed desirable was actually provided. Second, there is no point in being concerned with the impact or outcome of particular programs unless one has knowledge that they indeed did take place, and did so with the appropriate target group. Many programs fail to be implemented and executed in the ways originally designed for a variety of reasons: sometimes because personnel and equipment simply are not available, and sometimes persons engaged in the program are prevented by political and value reasons for undertaking what they intended. Also, individuals who are part of the program staff may not have the motivation or know-how to carry out their tasks as outlined. Finally, there are instances in which the intended targets of programs are either non-existent in the numbers required or cannot be identified precisely or, cooperation from them is not possible. For example, in certain suburban communities, funds have been provided for various types of programs in which the target populations are children with past histories of juvenile delinquency. There are instances in which, after such studies have been started, it is found that there are simply very few delinquents in the communities, or that the police and courts are not willing to cooperate in providing identifying data on them, and they cannot be located by the investigators, or the juveniles concerned simply will not participate in the treatment programs.

Impact Evaluation

The second aspect of evaluation research is what may be referred to as impact evaluation. Here the concern is with gaging the extent to which a program effects a change in the desired direction. It implies that there are a set of pre-specified, operationally-defined goals and criteria of success, and measured impact refers to movement or change toward the desired objectives. These objectives may be social-behavioral such as reduction of parole violation and decline in the rate of admissions to hospitals; they may be community measures, such as the frequency of crime reported to the police or reported in sample surveys of community members; or they may be physical changes such as the amount of carbon monoxide in the air or the number of buses that succeed or fail to conform to a planned time schedule.

In terms of impact evaluation, a design is required that allows the investigator, in a persuasive way, to demonstrate that the changes that occur are a function of the particular program intervention and treatment and not accountable for in other ways. Oftentimes a variant of the classic experimental design, in which there are control and experimental groups that receive different treatments, is utilized; it is also held (Campbell 1969) that a variety of other means are possible for approximating the conclusions from experimental designs such as the use of longitudinal designs with comparisons over time. In general, most evaluation researchers take the position that experimental designs, or when not feasible, quasi-experimental designs, are the most appropriate way of measuring impact since they provide known means of controlling external biases.

Comprehensive Evaluation

The term comprehensive evaluation is restricted to studies that, in fact, do include both a process and an impact evaluation. Ideally, all evaluations should contain both process and impact components. That is, the position taken here is that for purposes of policy determination, as well as for contributions to basic social science knowledge, the most appropriate evaluation is one that includes the study of both process and impact. A comprehensive evaluation is one in which appropriate techniques and ideas have been brought to bear so that it is possible (1) to determine whether or not a program, intervention or treatment is carried out as planned, and (2) to assess whether or not the program resulted in changes or modifications consistent with the intended outcomes.

The importance attached to undertaking comprehensive evaluations that include measurement of *both* process and impact is questioned by some researchers and policymakers. Clearly, there are cases where it is foolish to invest in studying impact when there is good reason to believe programs are not being undertaken as planned or where programs are known to be inconsistently implemented. In such cases, it may be strategic to devote resources to studying process *first*. Then, too, there are cases where either programs are so cut and dry or where there is a body of evidence on their implementation available that most of the resources can be devoted to impact evaluation. But impact evaluation in the absence of knowledge of what took place can fault a vital program and result in poor policy decisions without reason; just as huge expenditures of public funds may continue indefinitely because the program is implemented as planned and responsible officials regard this as satisfactory evidence of worth.

Advocating comprehensive evaluations should not imply that partial ones, either solely process or impact, are not useful. There are times when they are strategic in program planning and development and may serve important management functions. From the standpoint of public policy, however, it is comprehensive evaluations that hold the most promise.

The application of evaluation research can have one out of three different important purposes. First, evaluation research—like much of social research—functions to destroy popular myths. Because we all live in groups and communities, every man and woman thinks of him or herself as a social scientist and policy analyst. Thus, it is obvious that better housing makes better people, or was until Wilner et al. (1962) found out that quality of housing has little impact in persons' life circumstances and outlooks. Professional groups also have their myths transmitted from one generation of practitioners to another. Evaluation studies, such as the Kassebaum et al. (1972) study which voids the belief that psychotherapy really helps penal offenders, thus are important in reshaping our social reality. Both popular beliefs and professional commitments often are challenged, and occasionally confirmed, by competent evaluation research.

A second important function of evaluation research is to provide measures of public accountability and to allow the spotting of undesirable situations in the provision of various services and treatments. Acting on behalf of the public has been much more as a responsibility of persons like Ralph Nader than of card-carrying social scientists and policy researchers. But there is an important need for evaluations, repeated evaluations, to be undertaken in order to protect and improve activities in the public domain. These evaluations can range from measuring the waiting time in public health clinics and the outcome of services provided there to the availability of coin telephones in various areas of a city and the rapidity of completing telephone calls.

But the most promising use of evaluation research is as part of a rational effort to plan and implement new social resource programs, and to modify and refine social policies. Although the fields of policy analysis and social planning are far from mature, and lack rigor and specificity of procedures, there is general agreement on the major elements involved in developing social programs. Rational policy and program development is required in all human service fields. The current interest in evaluation research and its political sponsorship is, we would like to believe, a forerunner of a move toward wider acceptance of systematic policy development and planning, in which evaluation research is only a part.

The Current State of Evaluation Research

With the growth of evaluation research activities and increased respectability of such studies within the social science academy, a number of persons have begun to probe systematically the status of evaluation research. Wholey et al.'s report (1970) on federal evaluation programs clearly indicate major defects in the enterprise and the lack of utility of many recent studies. The consistency of views, on the one hand, about the potential of evaluation research but the limited availability, on the other, of systematic knowledge about what is actually taking place in the field led us, with Russell Sage Foundation support, to undertake an analysis and critique of evaluation studies directly supported by the federal government.

We developed (Bernstein and Freeman 1975), via a mail questionnaire, information on the scope and methods employed in evaluation studies that succeeded in obtaining information on somewhat over 80 percent of all federal studies that had research budgets of over $10,000. During the design and data collection phases of our research, we had an opportunity to gain additional, first-hand knowledge about evaluation research undertaken with federal support, and about a very complex evaluation research industry.

Naturally, only a few fragments of this study can be touched on here. Some descriptive information may be of interest. In fiscal year 1970, we estimate that between $45 million and $50 million were expended directly by the federal government for evaluation research. Indirect expenditures of federal funds through state and local agencies might double this figure. Probably, now, direct expenditures for evaluation research total about $75 million to $100 million per year; $150 million for direct *and* indirect federal disbursements may be a conservative estimate.

Virtually every federal agency undertakes evaluation research studies by means of contracts and grants. These contracts and grants vary greatly in dollar amounts, with about one-half of them being over $100,000. In time allowed for completion of the research, they take somewhere over two years on the average. An array of university, non-profit groups and for-profit groups participate in the evaluation research enterprise. There are also a variety of arrangements with respect to the relationships between the persons undertaking programs and those who evaluate them; sometimes both action people and evaluators are at work in the same organizations; other times they are close collaborators although in different units; and still other times, they are entirely separate from each other, and indeed funding agencies may require that they maintain their distance.

Funding agencies also differ in both the processes that are used in awarding contracts and grants, in the way these studies are monitored, and in the extent that the federal sponsoring group is research-oriented or not. Naturally, the persons who do the work differ in training, in years of experience, and disciplinary orientation.

These characteristics of the evaluation research endeavor are systematically related to each other. For example, service-oriented federal agencies, such as the group in the Department of Labor charged with job training, are likely to award contracts rather than grants, and these contracts are likely to go to profit-making organizations, be of short duration, and undertaken by persons without doctoral training. Research-oriented federal groups, such as the National Institutes of Health, are likely to award grants based on the recommendations of outside review committees, with these grants going to universities, being of longer time duration, and generally undertaken by persons with doctoral-level training.

In addition to gathering descriptive information, we were interested in trying to understand the relations between such characteristics as those just noted and the quality of evaluation research undertaken. Admittedly, via a mail questionnaire, it is possible to obtain only a gross measure of quality. But with some confidence, we obtained information on sampling, data analysis, statistical procedures, design characteristics, and the like of evaluation efforts.

Our data confirm earlier estimates of the sorry quality of evaluation research, at least in terms of the perspective we have advocated regarding what evaluation research should be. Of the 236 studies on which we have information for the fiscal year 1970, 84 are not comprehensive, that is, they do not include procedures to measure both process and impact. Of the 64 percent of evaluations that do measure process and impact (152 studies), *less than 20 percent* follow consistently generally accepted procedures with respect to design, data collection, and data analysis. We are not the only ones that decry the state of affairs. In addition to the work of Wholey et al. that we have noted, Wilkens (1969) and Whyte and Hamilton (1964) conclude that the art and practice of the field are deficient. Rossi and Williams (1972) preface their collected readings on evaluation with the statement that they hope their volume assists in raising the methodological quality of evaluation research, which they find wanting. So, too, Stromsdorfer (1972) criticizes the poor condition of work in the field.

We found, in our study, that it is possible to explain a significant part of the variation of quality of evaluation research by the characteristics of the persons who do the research, the organizations they work for, and the groups they sponsor and whose studies they support. The evaluation research endeavor has the same strains, albeit in perhaps an exaggerated form, as the entire field of policy studies. As we found out in our study, responsiveness to the needs of policymakers, the taking on of an activist, social change posture, often requires a style of activities that inhibits the highest quality social science research. It is to a discussion of this matter that we wish to turn.

Styles of Evaluation Research

The evaluation research enterprise is characterized by diversity, from the beginning of the process—awarding and initiation of the study—to its termination—the dissemination and implementation of findings. But, as noted, there are systematic relations between different properties of the enterprise.

Academic and Entrepreneurial Research

Our findings suggest that, at the extreme, there are two types or styles of work—the academic and the entrepreneurial. We use these terms not only to differentiate researchers by place of work and level of training but to distinguish the relations between sponsors of research and groups who do the work, as well as between different types of awards and contractual commitments. In Table 2-1, the differences between the polar styles are highlighted. The *academic style* is consistent with the way so-called basic social science research is undertaken, supported and disseminated; the *entreprenaurial style* is similar to the research and development activities that take place in many fields that have an underlying scientific base.

Research Style and Research Quality

In order to examine the quality of evaluation research, it was necessary for us to take a stand on which procedures were best used to measure and analyze process and impact in evaluation research. Our position should be clear from the comments in the earlier section of this chapter. We believe that quantitative data, gathered by systematic sampling procedures, and analyzed by sophisticated statistical procedures yield the most definitive

Table 2-1
Characteristics of Evaluation Research Endeavors

Funding Agency

Academic

Has the support of research as a predominant part of its mission; staff involved in research activities, including planning, negotiations, and monitoring of awards; staff made up of persons with social science and related training and experience. View researchers as colleagues, and funding staff have academic persons as their reference group. Agency staff often identify themselves as members of particular social science disciplines, belong to and attend meetings of social science associations, and sometimes are engaged in own research and publication activities.

Entrepreneurial

Primarily concerned with operational programs; staff tends to be dominated by persons with administrative and program experience. Staff engaged in planning, negotiations, and monitoring of awards generally do not have advanced training and research experience themselves. View researchers as contractors and emphasize the importance of conforming to award specifications including submission of reports on time, performance consistent with specifications, and so on. Tend to identify themselves as professional employees within the federal establishment rather than as persons who have a disciplinary reference group.

Award Process

Academic

Awards are grants that have been judged by peer-review groups of persons affiliated with academic-type organizations. Awards are made in competition with other proposals in the same area which have different problem foci. Proposals are initiated by investigators who are often interested in carrying out their line of research for extended periods. Peer judges and agency staff often have personal knowledge of investigator and his (her) organization and technical expertise to judge past work and design aspects of proposals. Investigators submit proposals to meet deadlines three or four times a year, time to develop proposals is often lengthy, and the award process takes from six months to one year.

Entrepreneurial

Awards are contracts provided to organization or individual after competition to undertake advertised need for research contractor. Competition is between potential contractors who have submitted proposals to undertake a specified piece of work. Specifications usually include requirements regarding time period of study. Agency personnel have much more participation and influence in decision-making about who receives support. Often lack technical expertise to judge past work and design of proposal, which may require use of outside consultants. Usually contractors have short period between advertisement of proposal and submission data for consideration. Overall award process short.

Elements in Study

Academic

Generally study has formulated frame of reference and theoretical underpinnings. Studies tend to deal with more specified, less complex designs by sites investigated, populations studied, and so on. Generally studies are for extended periods of time, usually two years or more. Most studies include graduate student assistants while the investigator is engaged in personal writing and teaching and spends only part-time on project. Studies generally are under $100,000.

Entrepreneurial

Generally study is developed in ways consistent with an advertised set of specifications. Likely to have been developed in response to legislation or the pressures from congressman or executive department administrators and policymakers More likely to test "service model" idea than theoretical notion. Studies tend to be more complex because of the action programs being evaluated. Most studies represent the major time commitments of the investigator; infrequent use of graduate students and more frequent use of regular technical staff. Studies are large in budget, short in time for completion.

Table 2-1 (continued)

Research Organization

Academic	Entrepreneurial
Generally part of university although may be independent non-profit organization devoted to social research. Activity is seen as furthering the research interests of investigator and colleagues and supplementing and supporting educational program of institution.	Generally a profit-making group. Some are small and with relatively short life spans and low volume of research. Others are large and do consulting and advising for government and industry as well. Activities are oriented to maintenance and expansion of organization and toward profit-making.

Research Investigator

Academic	Entrepreneurial
Usually a Ph.D., most often in psychology although sociologists are also common. Investigator's career trajectory is academic.	Usually a non-Ph.D. Quite frequently a person with limited graduate training in economics or other related social science disciplines. Careers generally are in non-university-type organizations.

Monitoring and Reporting

Academic	Entrepreneurial
Investigator given wide latitude by funding agency. Generally flexible in time extensions, modification of research design, and so on. Only fiscal auditing, with final reports more often than not a formality. Encourages publications in journals and public reporting via monographs and funding-agency publications. Decisions on conduct of research usually made independent of funding agency.	Investigators often have specified reporting requirements. Limited flexibility in time extensions, modification of time specifications, and so on. In addition to fiscal auditing, program reports often required for payments to support research. Generally final report is regarded as the "product." Limited encouragement for professional publication which may require funding-agency permission. Decisions on conduct of research may require participation of funding agency.

Audience

Academic	Entrepreneurial
Peers in research and academia are seen as a major audience.	Funding agency and sometimes program personnel are seen as primary audience.

results. Further, that impact of programs should be measured by developing an experimental or quasi-experimental design so that "exposed" and "unexposed" groups can be compared. Our view that evaluation research requires rigor, that we opt for the "hard-nosed" type of evaluation is not necessarily shared by all in the field. But it clearly is the "majority" position.

When we examine the relations between properties of the evaluation research endeavor and quality, at least as we define it, there is an amazing fit with one differentiation between academic and entrepreneurial types of research styles. High-quality work is most often undertaken by psychologists with Ph.D.'s who are based in universities. The studies of high quality most often have an underlying theoretical framework, are longest in duration (over three years), are funded by research-oriented federal groups, and are planned with an academic audience in mind.

Studies of poor quality most frequently are contracts given to profit-making corporations by service-oriented government groups. Funding is for short periods and are atheoretical investigations that are carried out by persons without doctoral level training, most commonly B.A.'s or M.A.'s in economics.

There is considerable literature in the sociology of science (examples are Hagstrom 1965; Kornhauser 1962; and Ben-David 1960) that lead credence to our findings. At the present time, there is every reason to predict that the best evaluation research from the standpoint of methodological quality is that which approximates our description of "academic-type research."

Research Quality and Characteristics of Evaluation Researchers

Although a number of dimensions reflecting the funding, organization, and implementation of studies are important determinants of the quality of evaluation research, the disciplines and levels of training of evaluation researchers were found to be of major factors in the quality-ranking of studies. As in the case of participants in other policy science activities, evaluation researchers are drawn from a variety of basic social science disciplines. The largest group of investigators come from psychology, followed closely by persons with backgrounds in economics and sociology. But even so, persons with these disciplinary backgrounds constitute only about one-half of the cadre of investigators—project directors trained in education, medicine, social work, law, public health and management also are found in significant number in the evaluation endeavor. Investigators also vary in their levels of training; somewhat less than one-half hold Ph.D.'s, the other one-half are dominated by persons with masters level education and degrees from professional schools.

These two characteristics of investigators—discipline and level of education—are both related to the quality of the work performed under their direction. Psychologists predominate as the directors of projects rated high in quality followed by persons with backgrounds in sociology and economics. At the same time, persons with doctorates are over-represented as the directors of high quality studies in comparison with those whose training is at a lower level. The relations between discipline and educational level to quality are complicated by the differences in organizational settings with which persons of different levels of training are affiliated. Persons with Ph.D. degrees are most often associated with universities and non-profit research groups and those with less training are found in profit-making and public-service organizations. Almost one-half of evaluation researchers who serve as project directors and who hold only bachelor degrees are affiliated with profit-making groups, as compared with but 20 percent of Ph.D.'s; almost one-half of the Ph.D.'s are found in universities as compared with only 10 percent of those with a bachelor degree and 20 percent of those with a master's degree.

The data of our study strongly suggest that not only level of training, that is the completion of a doctoral program, is typically a requisite for high quality work, but that project directors trained in disciplines where research rigor and quantification are stressed are most likely to be associated with high quality studies. The importance of those characteristics are explainable in terms of a set of selection and contextual factors.

First of all, length of training obviously provides increased exposure-time for advanced technical training, and thus the aquisition of a wider range and deeper level of skills to be used in evaluation research. But it is more than technical skills that are acquired at a doctoral level; it is a very special kind of socialization that includes being critical of past work, "keeping up" with developments in the field, the idea that one's work will be subject scrutiny, and a sense of responsibility to a broad community of peers who are engaged in the research endeavor.

Second, doctoral level work in certain fields emphasizes research training of major relevance for evaluation research. For example, it is practically impossible to earn a Ph.D. in psychology without course work in experimental design and instrument construction. Doctoral training in economics usually includes extended exposure to statistical methods and the analysis of large data-sets. Thus, as a general rule, the selection of persons with doctoral-level training to direct evaluation research studies (particularly those from fields that emphasize rigor and quantification such as psychology and economics) is most likely to result in the production of studies of high quality.

But to leave the explanation there would be an oversimplification. Ph.D's in the evaluation field are usually found in academic settings that undertake evaluation studies because they often are committed to careers in universities. Many such persons had aspirations for an academic career or they would not have pursued doctoral training in the first place. Further, the three, four or more years of graduate training orient the uncommitted and reinforce the committed in this direction.

Moreover, university positions, particularly when they include teaching and faculty status, are pretty much confined to persons with doctorates. Thus, persons with Ph.D.'s select and are selected for academic positions and those without these credentials are pretty much limited to other evaluation research settings. Salary differentials (which often are not as great as one may suppose) foster career mobility and other rewards which may be offered by the non-academic research organization simply are not sufficient to lure many persons with doctorates to non-university jobs.

Perhaps most important, however, not only are the best trained persons most likely to be found in university settings but once there they have opportunities to do high quality research because of the tangible and intangible assets of universities as research environments. Certain kinds of resources are simply more accessible. These include, for example, access to libraries and oftentimes better computer and data analysis services, and to a broad range of colleagues who are available as consultants and "sounding-boards."

But it is perhaps the intangibles that are the key to explaining why differences in context are important. The university sets norms regarding the performance of faculty and research staff that are associated with high quality research. For example, persons in academic settings are expected to publish their research in journals that accept and reject articles, at least a large extent, on the basis of conceptual and methodological sophistication. Unlike the profit-making sector, the university does not stress satisfying the "client" as much as it does satisfying the community of research peers. Promotion, tenure, and day-to-day recognition to a large extent are achieved on the basis of the individual's personal reputation as an investigator, not what he or she does for the firm.

Certainly, the differences are not always clear-cut. Some non-university settings do emphasize the same norms as university settings. Some have the same tangible assets as universities. Also, university-based persons are rewarded in many cases for the same reasons as those working in commercial enterprises, such as having secured a large volume of grants and contracts and for having a large number of persons working under them. But the differences are real, with the context of the university much more conducive to high quality research of all types—including evaluation studies—than the other sectors of the research enterprise.

At the same time that the employment of persons with Ph.D. training in one of the more rigorous social science disciplines in university settings is conducive to the conduct of high-quality research, there are reasons to be concerned with advocating a "back to the university" and "back to the basic social sciences" point of view. The issue not only is one for evaluation research but for the entire field of policy research. Typically doctoral level training in the basic social sciences does not prepare persons for the breadth of activity involved in policy-related work and for moving across disciplinary and substantive boundaries. The emphasis of graduate training in the basic social sciences that result in becoming a sophisticated researcher may discourage contacts and opportunities for relationships with persons in policy and other influential community roles, and limit sensitivity to identify problems and undertake work on relevant social issues. Moreover, there are liabilities to universities as work settings, including their ability to respond rapidly to the need to address important issues within a short time-frame. Moreover, the culture of the university and its reward system often fails to acknowledge activities which cannot be conducted in ways completely consistent with the expectations of how the world of research and scholarship should operate. Thus, for evaluation research, as for the policy sciences in general, the matter of who does the work, how they are trained, and the settings most amenable to high quality output represent unresolved challenges.

Implications for Policy Research

Our findings pose perhaps the major dilemma for policy research. The solution for improving research quality by having all studies undertaken in academic centers, by professors with Ph.D.'s in psychology, who are committed to publication in social science journals after spending extended periods on work sponsored and monitored only by research-oriented funding groups, who have highly trained staffs is a foolish strategy. As Coleman (1973) has indicated, if the findings of quality studies are not available, work of questionable quality—or none at all—will be utilized by policymakers. Moreover, turning policy research, including evaluation research, back to traditional social scientists presumes they will accept responsibility for studying matters of national priority and engage in the necessary dialogues with policymakers. For these and other reasons, the solution of arguing for the existing academic model does not make sense.

One of the possible outcomes of the emerging policy sciences is a movement toward meeting the demand for relevant research, available *before* policy decisions are firmed—studies undertaken by well-trained investigators socialized to undertake high-quality work embedded in theoretically-grounded frameworks but who at the same time plan and conduct studies in ways that make them attractive and useful in the policy arena. Such a development requires restructuring the training in the social science disciplines that are provided both graduate and undergraduate students, revising the reward system that affects persons in research roles including academic investigators, and bringing closer together individuals who are located in various work settings including those in universities, non-profit groups, government, and profit-making corporations.

With respect to evaluation research in particular, and perhaps to policy research in general, however, we do not believe the general state of affairs will change dramatically or rapidly enough without a clear national policy that is developed collaboratively by public officials in policy roles and policy researchers in various academic and non-academic settings. In the monograph from which most of the information in this chapter is drawn (Bernstein and Freeman, 1975) we recommend a variety of innovations to speed up the time required to complete studies, to increase the lead time between the planning and implementation of studies and the time of decision-making, to place research activities closer to the loci of decision-making, to improve the mechanisms that surround the funding of studies, to make the monitoring of projects by sponsors more effective, and to develop a variety of social control mechanisms in order to insure quality research.

To the extent that the policy sciences represents a social as well as an intellectual commitment, it is critical that a comprehensive effort is initiated to develop or rather restructure the research endeavor, not narrow fragmented attempts at improving the state-of-the-art. At least in the case of evaluation research, an activity of considerable promise must not continue to produce defective work. Rather, evaluation research, indeed the entire policy science research movement, must emerge as a strong and rigorous scientific field, lest it lose its supporters and an opportunity to contribute to the improvement of the human condition.

References

Bernstein, Ilene N. and Howard E. Freeman. *Academic and Entrepreneurial Research*. New York: Russell Sage Foundation, 1975.

Ben-David, Joseph. "Scientific Productivity and Academic Organization in 19th-Century Medicine." *American Sociological Review* 25 (December 1960): 828-843.

Campbell, Donald T. "Reforms as Experiments." *American Psychologist* 24 (April 1969): 409-429.

Caro, Francis (ed.). *Readings in Evaluative Research*. New York: Russell Sage Foundation, 1971.

Coleman, James S. Speech delivered in December 1972, American Association for the Advancement of Science, Washington D.C. Reported in *Footnotes 1* (March 1973): 1.

Freeman, Howard E., and Clarence C. Sherwood. *Special Research and Social Policy*. Englewood Cliffs, New Jersey: Prentice-Hall, 1970.

Hagstrom, Warren O. *The Scientific Community*. New York: Basic Books, 1965.

Kassebaum, Gene, David Ward, and Daniel Wilner. *Prison Treatment and Parole Survival*. New York: Wiley, 1972.

Kornhauser, William. *Scientists in Industry: Conflict and Accommodation*. Berkeley: University of California Press, 1962.

Rossi, Peter H., and Walter Williams. *Evaluating Social Programs, Theory, Practice, and Politics*. New York: Seminar Press, 1972.

Stephan, A. Stephen. "Prospects and Possibilities: The New Deal and the New Social Research." *Social Forces* 13 (1935): 515-521.

Stromsdorfer, Ernst W. *Review and Synthesis of Cost Effectiveness Studies of Vocational and Technical Education*. ERIC Clearinghouse on Vocational and Technical Education, Ohio. Washington, D.C., 1972.

Suchman, Edward. *Evaluative Research*. New York: Russell Sage Foundation, 1967.

Wholey, Joseph, et al. *Federal Evaluation Policy*. Washington, D.C.: The Urban Institute, 1970.

Whyte, William, and Edith Hamilton. *Action Research for Management*. Homewood, Ill.: Dorsey Press, 1964.

Wilkins, Leslie T. *Evaluation of Penal Measures*. New York: Random House, 1969.

Wilner, Daniel, et al. *The Housing Environment and Family Life*. Baltimore: Johns Hopkins Press, 1962.

3

The Social Scientist as Methodological Servant of the Experimenting Society

Donald T. Campbell

Societies will continue to use proponderantly unscientific political processes to decide upon ameliorative program innovations. Whether it would
be good to increase the role of social science in deciding on the content of
the programs tried out is not at issue here. My emphasis (Campbell 1969,
1971) is rather on the more passive role for the social scientist as an aid in
helping society decide whether or not its innovations have achieved desired
goals without damaging side effects. The job of the methodologist for the
experimenting society is not to say *what is to be done,* but rather to say
what has been done. The aspect of social science that is to be applied is
primarily its research methodology rather than its descriptive theory, with
the goal of learning more than we do now from the innovations decided
upon by the political process. I argue that even the conclusion drawing and
the relative weighting of conflicting indicators, should be left up to the
political process (1967, 1971).

This emphasis seems to me to be quite different from the present role as
government advisors of most economists, international relations professors, foreign area experts, political scientists, sociologist of poverty and
race relations, psychologists of child development and learning, etc. Government asks what to do, and scholars answer with an assurance quite out
of keeping with the scientific status of their fields. In the process, the
scholar-advisors too fall into the overadvocacy trap (Campbell 1969) and
fail to be interested in finding out what happens when their advice is
followed. In such planning, there is detailed use of available science but no
use of the implemented program as a check on the validity of the plans or of
the scientific theories upon which they were based. Thus economists,
operations researchers and mathematical decision theorists trustingly ex-
trapolate from past science and conjecture, but fail to use the implemented
decisions to correct or expand that knowledge. Certainty that one already
knows precludes finding out how valid one's theories are. We social scientists could afford more of the modesty of the physical sciences, should
more often say that we can't know until we've tried. For the great bulk of
social science where we have no possibility of experimental probing of our
theories we should be particularly modest. While the experiments of the
experimenting society will never be ideal for testing theory, they will

This paper borrows in part from Campbell (1971), and Raser, Campbell, and Chadwick (1971).
Its preparation has been supported in part by NSF Grant GS30273X.

probably be the best we have, and we should be willing to learn from them even when we have not designed them. More importantly, measuring the effects of a complex politically designed ameliorative program involves all of the problems of experimental inference found in measuring the effects of a conceptually pure treatment variable—all and more. The scientific methods developed for the latter are needed for ameliorative program evaluation. With the most minor of exceptions, it can be said for the United States that none of our major ameliorative programs have had adequate evaluations (Schwartz 1961; Hyman and Wright 1967; Etzioni 1968; Rossi 1969; Campbell 1969a; Wholey 1970; Campbell and Erlebacher 1970; Caro 1971). There is general agreement among these authors that the prospectively designed experiment offers the best possibilities of evaluation.

The distinction is overdrawn. It reflects my own judgment that in the social sciences, including economics, we are scientific by intention and effort, but not yet by achievement. We have no elegantly successful theories that predict precisely in widely different settings. Nor do we have the capacity to make definitive choices among competing theories. Even if we had, the social settings of ameliorative programs involve so many complexities that the guesses of the experienced administrator and politician are apt to be on the average as wise as those of social scientists. But whatever the source of the implemented guess, we learn only by checking it out. Certainly in the experimenting society, social scientists will continue to be called upon to help design solutions to social problems, and this is as it should be. Perhaps all I am advocating in emphasizing the role of servant rather than leader is that social scientists avoid cloaking their recommendations in a specious pseudo-scientific certainty, and and instead acknowledge their advice as consisting of but wise conjectures that need to be tested in implementation.

The servant-leader contrast is overdrawn in other senses also. The truism that measurement itself is a change agent is particularly applicable to the experimenting society. Advocating hardheaded evaluation of social programs is a recommendation for certain kinds of political institutions.

Interaction-ridden Social Science and the Problem of Generalizing

The most important justification of the emphasis on method and on the need for confirming in practice the efficacy of social ameliorations, comes from the fact that our experience in generalizing social science findings shows that higher order interactions abound, precluding unqualified generalization of our principles, not only from laboratory to laboratory, but especially from laboratory to field application.

It is most convenient to explain this proposition in terms of a statistical method called *analysis of variance* which is much used in experimental psychology and agriculture. In this approach one uses multiple dimensions of experimental variation, A, B, C, D, etc., each of which occurs in several degrees of strength, with (in the simplest of design) each combination of strengths being employed. (Thus if there were four dimensions, A, B, C, and D, each of which had three levels, the total number of different treatment packages would be 81.) In addition to these treatment or independent variables, there is at least one dependent variable in terms of which the results of the treatments are measured, let us call this X. For our present purposes, two major types of outcome need to be distinguished: *main effects* and *interactions*. If a main effect for A is found on X, then we have what could be called a *ceteris paribus* law: B, C, D being held constant at any level, the same rule relating A to X is found, e.g. the more A, the more X. Where *interactions* are found, the relations are complexly contingent. For example, in an A-B interaction, there may be a separate rule relating A and X for each different level of B (e.g. if B is high, the more A, the more X, but if B is low the more A, the less X). Much more complex (higher order) interactions can also occur, such as an A-B-C interaction in which the A to X rule is different for each combination of B and C.

Interactions, where they occur in the absence of main effects, represent highly limited and qualified generalizations. It is typical of the history of the physical sciences that many strong main effects were found —generalizations conceivably truly independent of time and place and the status of other variables. While eventually in fine detail the laws were found to be more complex than this, nonetheless there was a rich nourishment of "laws of nature" which could be stated without specifying the conditions on the infinitude of other potentially relevant variables.

There is no compelling evidence so far that the social sciences are similarly situated. If we take the one social science that uses the analysis of variance approach, experimental social psychology, the general finding is of higher order interactions in abundance, and main effects but rarely. Even where we get main effects, it is certainly often due to the failure to include dimensions E, F, G, etc., which would have produced interactions. We rarely are able to replicate findings from one university laboratory to another, indicating an interaction with some unspecified difference in the laboratory settings or in the participants.

If such multiple factorial experiments be regarded as experiments in generalization, they give us great grounds for caution, particularly when we generalize the expectation that had we included in our experiment dimensions E, F, G, and H, or Y and Z, the A-X relationship might well have shown interactions with some or all of them too. The high rate of interactions on the variables we have explored must make us expect such for the many unexplored ones.

A given experiment may be regarded as holding constant at one particular level every one of the innumerable variables on which no experimental variation is introduced. It is like a single level of a potential experiment in which two or more levels of this variable were systematically employed. We can guess with confidence that the farther apart the two values of B (or E or Z), the more likely B will interact with the A-X relationship. (An empirical exploration of this might well be worth making. Data from complex experiments using 3 or more levels of a given treatment could be reanalyzed as two level experiments, some as wide range, using the two extreme levels and disregarding the intermediate, others as narrow range, using adjacent levels from the original experiment.)

In anticipation of the outcome of such studies, and in common with the intuition of most scientists, let us assume as a general rule that the larger the range of values on the background variable, the more likely are these variables to have strong interactions with the A-X relationship under study. Or to put it more simply, as scientists we generalize with most confidence to applications most similar to the setting of the original research. When generalizing from our laboratory based theory to a real-world social-ameliorative program, the values on all dimensions are extremely different and new interaction effects, as yet unexplored, become extremely likely.

This must give us great pessimism in the relevance of our theory for applied settings. It makes it extremely important to revalidate any recommendations in the setting of the policy application itself. This revalidation requires the methods of science, of experimentation and quasi-experimentation. This technology, rather than our disciplinary knowledge, is what we social scientists have to offer to the social policy process.

References

Campbell, D. T. "Reforms as Experiments." *American Psychologist* 24, 4 (April, 1969):409-429.

Campbell, D. T. "Methods for the Experimenting Society." Duplicated draft of a speech delivered to the American Psychological Association, September 5, 1971, Washington, D.C. To appear, revised, in the *American Psychologist*.

Campbell, D. T. and Erlebacher, A. "How Regression Artifacts in Quasi-Experimental Evaluations Can Mistakenly Make Compensatory Education Look Harmful." in J. Hellmuth, (ed.). *Compensatory Education: A National Debate*. Vol. III of *The Disadvantaged Child*. New York: Brunner/Mazel, 1970, pp. 185-210. Reply to the replies, pp. 221-225.

Caro, F. G. "Evaluation Research: An Overview." In F. G. Caro, (ed.). *Readings in Evaluation Research*. New York: Russell Sage Foundation, 1971, pp. 1-34.

Etzioni, A. "'Shortcuts' to social change?" *The Public Interest* 12 (1968): 40-51.

Hyman, H. H., and Wright, C. R. "Evaluating Social Action Programs." In R. F. Lazarsfeld, W. H. Sewell, and H. L. Wilensky, (eds.). *The Uses of Sociology*. New York: Basic Books, 1967.

Raser, J. R., D. T. Campbell, and R. W. Chadwick. "Gaming and Simulation for Developing Theory Relevant to International Relations." *General Systems*, 15 (1970):183-204.

Rossi, R. H. "Practice, Method, and Theory in Evaluating Social Action Programs." In J. L. Sundquist (ed.). *On Fighting Poverty*. New York: Basic Books, 1969, Chapter 10, pp. 217-234.

Schwartz, R. D. "Field Experimentation in Sociological Research." *Journal of Legal Education* 13 (1961):401-410.

Wholey, J. S., J. W. Scanlon, J. Fukumoto, and L. M. Vogt. *Federal Evaluation Policy*. Washington, D.C.: The Urban Institute, 1970.

4

Programming, Planning, and Evaluation: A System for Assessing Social Policy

Paul M. Wortman

"H.E.W. Preparing a Welfare Plan" proclaimed a recent front page headline in the *New York Times*.[1] Although certainly a policy-relevant item in the continuing saga of welfare reform, it would not have caught the social scientist's eye had it not been for one remarkable fact. The secretary of HEW in arguing for this new program cited the findings of a recently completed social science experiment sponsored by the government. To methodologists in economics, education, law, political science, psychology, and sociology, who are those primarily involved in the rigorous evaluation of social policy, this represents an encouraging milestone—the planning, execution, and utilization of a randomized, field experiment in the policy formation process.

In the past decade a growing number of social scientists have advocated the application of more rigorous scientific methods as the appropriate procedure for evaluating social program innovations.[2,3] While this concern has led to an emerging discipline called evaluation research, it is, in reality, a multidisciplinary approach involving the joint expertise of economists, psychologists, sociologists, and others. These evaluation researchers have correctly pointed to the methodological inadequacies of such early large-scale program evaluations as Headstart[4] to make their case. However, even while this controversy concerning the proper procedure for policy assessment and inference was raging, new policies such as the negative income tax approach to welfare and more sophisticated program evaluations such as the New Jersey Income Maintenance Experiment[5] were being initiated. This program incorporated many of the most important features—stratified sampling; random assignment of participants to treatment programs; and systematic, parametric variations in the treatment variables—advocated by the new breed of evaluation methodologists. Although this evaluation has not escaped criticism on a number of points (e.g., its limited three-year duration may have been too short to affect real-life decisions), nonetheless the "internal validity," the possibility of alternative explanations, of this policy experiment has not been questioned. It would be easy to conclude, therefore, that a new era of higher-quality policy evaluations is upon us. Unfortunately, this does not appear

The work on this chapter was supported by Grant No. T01-MH12981-03 from the National Institute of Mental Health and Contract No. C-74-0115 from the National Institute of Education.

to be the case, as similar programs in housing and education have not maintained this high standard.[6]

In light of the hopeful, although inconsistent, status of policy assessment involving program evaluation a number of salient questions emerge. What is the relationship between policy formation and program development? And what is the relationship between various programs and evaluation methods? The remainder of this chapter is concerned with explicating these relationships in the belief that such an understanding will improve the policy-making process. It will deal with the political and philosophical bases for various policies, the types of programs established to implement these policies, the techniques for evaluating such programs, and the political constraints influencing these evaluations. Obviously, many and probably most programs are tailored to the political realities of the communities that adopt them. But prior to such specific problems in implementation there are general philosophical and methodological constraints that account for the basic framework of the programs and evaluations. Wherever possible, specific examples of policies, programs, evaluations, and different disciplinary approaches will be presented to illustrate these points.

The Policy Formation Process

In a recent psychological analysis of the evaluation process it was suggested that policy formation originates with the values of the policy maker and society.[7] Similar psychological models based on the primacy of values have been advocated by other researchers as a means of demonstrating the differences in political philosophies.[8] Although this approach typically encompasses multiple categories or sets of values, it is the two ends or goal values of "freedom" and "equality" that have been viewed as comprising the basic dimensions of political thought. Major political ideologies have been shown to differ according to the importance they assign these values. Thus liberals, humanists, and socialists initiate policies that emphasize these values, while fascists, on the other hand, assign little if any importance to either value. Whereas the former would undertake policies to protect minority rights and prohibit the excess consolidation of power, for example, the latter would reverse these policies. In addition to consistent positions on these values, it is possible to endorse one of them and not the other. This is the case with conservatives who value freedom quite highly, but harbor no such feelings for equality. In direct opposition to this, one finds Communists who emphasize equality but not freedom.

This analysis indicates that any reform policy where equality played a salient or dominant role would create substantial political friction between liberals and conservatives. The conflict that surrounded and finally undermined the Nixon Administration's attempt at welfare reform—the Family Assistance Program (FAP)—is a case in point. The primary goal of this program was a more equitable distribution of income to end poverty for both the poor and the near- or working-poor.[9] Although the legislation twice passed the House of Representatives, joint attacks upon it by both liberals and conservatives kept it buried in the Senate Finance Committee. Liberals attacked the bill for not providing enough economic equality in the "basic guarantee" or income floor for the poor, while conservatives viewed it as a threat to the free-enterprise system by destroying the incentive to work and hence interpreted "reform" as the elimination of welfare abuses by those able to work (i.e., free to compete). These value-derived differences in perspective and emphasis created enough opposition to kill the bill in committee. As a result of this debate, a number of methodologically sound experiments, including the recently completed New Jersey study, were designated to test the effects of such "income maintenance" on the incentive to work in both urban and rural settings before any final policy decision was reached.[10] Although the timeliness of these experiments may have been somewhat fortuitous, the need for such an unambiguous and rational mechanism to resolve political conflict was quite apparent.

In this discussion, policies have been viewed as the instruments of rather fixed value orientations. If this is the case, can these values possibly be changed by evaluation research findings? Rokeach has found that it is indeed possible to change values,[11] but only when they are inconsistent with actual behaviors. Since policies (i.e., plans for behavior) are assumed to be consistent with values, the impact of evaluation research findings on theoretical and political views appears likely to be minimal. Moreover, given the many ways in which an evaluation can be criticized, it seems probable that other research elements such as the particular program derived from the policy, the experimental design, choice of goals, and statistical procedures could be challenged and altered many times before a comparable change in values or philosophy would be either merited or considered. For example, studies indicating that pornography does not increase, and may in fact decrease, sexual crimes[12] have been ignored by conservative policymakers holding the opposite views. Similarly, liberal students and faculty members have often proven intolerant and inhospitable hosts to scientists expounding genetic theories to account for racial differences in intellectual achievement. Thus, while values seem to affect the research to be evaluated, the results of such research also appear to have little impact on these values. From a policy standpoint, however, perhaps the most important question is not whether policymakers will change their values, but whether the results of evaluative studies will affect the policies they initiate. The answer to this question is not known, but the congressional response to the new welfare reform program noted above should begin to clarify the issue. Certainly, there should be other policies or programs derived from the same policy that are considered in the absence of supportive results from a social experiment.

Policy and Programs

Not only do values characterize differences in political thought, but recent events have made it clear that they can lead to entirely different classes of social-action policies. Implicit in the usual notion of experimental evaluation is the concept of a treatment or ameliorative "service" program. The service strategy represents a conscious attempt to redress the balance and achieve equality between the advantaged and disadvantaged (e.g., Headstart). However, as Moynihan has pointed out,[13] there is an alternative set of policy-derived programs to this service strategy approach—namely, an "income strategy." That is, instead of establishing a middle-class bureaucracy to tend the needs of the disadvantaged, cash grants can be provided directly to those who need them without a costly and cumbersome intervening organization. This, of course, formed the point of departure for the FAP plan as noted above. Poor families were to be given money or cash grants directly instead of social welfare services, food stamps, and ancillary programs.

The service strategy, on the other hand, assumes that the remedial action programs are necessary to achieve equality and the organizational talent to provide them is either unavailable or too costly to be provided by the economy at a price many can afford. In this situation, the policymaker is caught in a dilemma by assuming a somewhat elitist (unequal) posture in order to achieve equality. This dilemma arising out of the clash among values, goals, and power is not confined to politicians alone nor is it limited to the highest organizational levels, but is present in all parties involved with the program including those evaluating it. Thus the desire for methodological sophistication in the form of a true experimental (i.e., randomized) design with the appropriate dependent measures may move the evaluator to seek more control and leadership in a community than is politically tolerable. This, in turn, may create hostilities that undermine his chances for completing the evaluation properly.

Which strategy is correct? On the face of it, there is no definite answer but certainly it is an empirical question assuming that there is consensus on the need for a new policy. The record of service programs to date is quite tattered and notable for the absence of many successes at the very time that useful techniques for evaluating such programs are finally becoming available. For each reform there is usually either an income or service approach available. Moreover, for each strategy there are many programs that could be established. For example, in education equality can be enforced through quotas, busing, location of new schools, and the like, or by a "freedom of choice" income approach incorporating "educational vouchers" where every family has the same amount of money to spend on a child's schooling and gives this voucher to the school of their choice. Many social critics and program administrators have been demanding such increased freedom through the "deinstitutionalization" of educational and penal systems.[14] In this context, it is important to note that a single program only reflects a general policy and is not equivalent to it. Thus these different classes of policy strategies or approaches may entail numerous programs that reflect the policy in various ways.

From an organizational systems point of view, Moynihan also argues that the income approach is better since it is more "parsimonious" and less complex than a service approach.[15] Moreover, it is often difficult, if not impossible, to subject large, dynamic organizations to the type of control needed for a systematic, experimental scrutiny. This points to an important distinction between the two strategies concerning the nature of the programs derived from these policy orientations. In an income approach the treatment program is the money (or, more abstractly, the choice) given to respondents and not the services they receive. In fact, there is no fixed standardized service in this scheme since those programs are under the control of private entrepreneurs who are presumably offering a wide variety of approaches tailored to individual needs. The income strategy is thus restricted to outcome, as opposed to process, variables (i.e., the effects of the money, the specific choices, etc.). Thus in the income maintenance experiment the amount of money guaranteed was systematically varied as was the negative taxation rate. The effect of this on employment (hours worked) was examined.

In sum, given the plausibility of the parsimony argument and the ability of reforms in the system of taxation to equalize economic opportunity and change the rules of competition, it seems reasonable to consider such a strategy first before resorting to the more unwieldy service strategy with its attendant entrenched bureaucracy. In this sense, the value conflict between liberal and conservative action-programs reduces to the priority of strategies—categories of policy-derived programs—with rigorous evaluation possible in either case. The continuing conflict over national health insurance is illustrative of these differences. While both liberals and conservatives agree on the need for such a program, they differ on the details. Conservatives want to involve the free market system that already exists and use the insurance companies to handle the program. Liberals feel this would be too costly and unresponsive, and would like a public corporation to handle the programs.

Programs and Evaluations

In recent years a number of income policy programs have been initiated in education, health, and housing. As was mentioned earlier, the evaluation methods now being employed in these cases are not as satisfactory as the techniques used in the New Jersey experiment. Although the policy basis for these income-based programs appears identical, it would be premature and incorrect to conclude that the specific evaluation designs should also coincide. In the Alum Rock educational voucher demonstration, for example, the concept of freedom of choice in education program selection is being evaluated. Each family is free to choose from among the various schools and programs participating in the demonstration project. While parental, student, and also teacher satisfaction are perhaps the major outcomes to be evaluated, it was not possible to select these individuals on a random, unbiased basis since a school's participation determined who was eligible and the schools themselves volunteered (by staff vote) for the program. Thus the unit of analysis in this program was not the individual as it was in New Jersey. Moreover, since the public school district has a monopoly on the service or educational programs offered (i.e., California law prohibited private and parochial school participation), it was necessary that diverse programs be created in order to make freedom of choice meaningful.

Unlike the income maintenance program, then, the voucher program is concerned with the relationship of income and specific services. This presents a more complex policy problem since the existence, quality, and effects of the educational services must be monitored and measured. If one were to adopt the Jencks' position that schools do not account for much of the variability in student performance,[16] then this aspect of the study would not be essential. However, diversity of choice and quality of educational programs are crucial. Without such information it is probable that other school districts would not be interested in participating in this project. With such large units of analysis (e.g., school districts) it becomes harder to support many different "participants" and thus to generalize the findings. This is true of the housing experiment also where whole cities—two cities are involved—are the relevant units. It should be added, though, that other voucher sites are currently being solicited. In those circumstances involving self-selected, administrative units one is forced to collect information at regular intervals both before and after the programs are established in order to make accurate inferences concerning the utility of the policy. These so-called "time series designs"[17] require reliable data collection and archiving over numerous observations to be properly analyzed. They are most appropriate for evaluating school programs. Legal or administrative reforms based on such archived information as crimes,[18] and other reforms of activities where information is typically collected on a continuing, consistent (i.e., without changes in tests or measuring instruments), and regular basis are most suitable for time-series analyses.

If such data are not available, then other approaches or designs for evaluating the policy must be found. One approach is to introduce some systematic variation into the program. For example, in Alum Rock the value of a voucher varies depending on income. Those students qualifying for the free lunch program are given a "compensatory voucher" worth a third more than the regular, basic voucher. Does this affect satisfaction? Student performance? This can be evaluated through a statistical analysis involving the regression of these observations on the type of voucher. If there is an effect, it will be reflected in a break or "discontinuity" in the regression line.[19] Such an analysis has been proposed and will be conducted on the voucher data.

While it is hard to categorize policy-derived programs into specific evaluation schemes, the above discussion offers some broad guidelines that are useful to follow. Clearly, if the target of the policy or treatment unit is small (e.g., an individual), then a randomized experiment of the New Jersey type should be feasible and conducted. When larger units such as schools, hospitals, cities, and even states are involved, a time series analysis is recommended where periodic information can be and has been collected. If this fails, then some variation in the program (or treatment) should be considered along with a regression analysis. However, it must be added that in income-related policies where individual choice is being instituted, the individual is the appropriate unit of analysis. In the Alum Rock voucher program, students and parents are selecting schools. To evaluate the program using time series data from schools as was recently reported[20] is to ignore this crucial element of choice. Such an analysis mistakenly assumes student continuity in schools before and after the start of the voucher program. A more sensitive analysis would focus solely on those students who remained in the school system before and after the voucher program was instituted.

Some Political Aspects of Planning Social Experiments

It should be obvious that action programs containing ameliorative policy innovation are not free of the political controversy surrounding their implementation. Glennan has observed that social experimentation is "a political act."[21] This implies that the projects and persons involved with them are thereby subject to the same political pressures already enveloping the issue. Moreover, he has explicated some of the practical issues and problems involved in assessing social policy through social experiments by developing a taxonomy of "organizational roles" for the personnel participating in the policy process. In addition to the more basic issues in evaluating and assessing the validity of social experiments noted above, he has pointed out a number of organizational problems: staff continuity, competence, integrity in managing the experiment, and the conflict generated by differing viewpoints or goals. These barriers to understanding and interpreting the impact of the experiment reveal that the policymaker is caught in the middle between unraveling the complexities of the evaluation and presenting the findings to the public. Similarly, the evaluator or research designer is also often trapped between his concept of an unbiased experimental plan and the pressure for supportive results from the policymaker. Often programs are administered by professional staffs that are opposed to any form of rigorous evaluation or are hesitant to use random processes to determine those to be assisted. In this they are frequently aided by organized community groups suspicious of scientific research. How can these problems be resolved?

One fundamental political and managerial issue that must be decided concerns the proper placement of the program within an administrative context. There are two possible approaches: (a) the program can operate in conjunction with ongoing institutions, that is, as a new unit within an existing organization, or (b) somewhat independent of it as a new, separate organization, or a new division or branch of a larger organization. Thus, for example, the voucher demonstration has been managed by the existing public school apparatus instead of as a separately funded, administered, and newly established program. This resulted in the serious erosion of the voucher concept. Although the entire $800 basic voucher was, in theory, to be used at the discretion of the consumer to pay for a specific school, deductions were made to support a central staff and school personnel leaving only an average of $8.50 per student for such "discretionary spending."[22] From an evaluative standpoint, programs placed in a separate organization are obviously more desirable in that their effects are more easily isolated and disentangled from those of the larger institution. Moreover, a new program embedded within an existing organization with multiple goals and functions will have to compete for resources with departments or components of the organization. The process of competition, as well as the outcome, may result in limiting the policy relevance of the program through a reduction in effort, a change in procedure, and lower morale for program personnel. It is in just such contexts as indicated by the voucher experience that one is most likely to encounter entrenched professional staffs already convinced of a program's utility or disutility and openly resistant to its assessment or proper implementation. All of these factors will, of course, seriously hamper the chances of the program achieving its desired goals.

This does not mean that programs should always be separate entities unto themselves. Once a program has been allowed to develop and has proven effective during a period of incubation and evaluation, it should be placed within a larger organization or budgetary context. This will encourage competition for scarce resources and provide a continuing incentive for evaluation and flexibility in meeting social needs. Competition should also prevent organizational complacency from developing and insure staff responsiveness to real needs other than organizational survival.

While the placement of the experimental program within an organizational context is a critical political and managerial issue, it is highly likely that other programs with similar goals will be already available in the immediate environment. This implies that most innovative, social-action programs operate in parallel with other programs not being evaluated. Thus, for example, an experimental program of medical care will more than likely be competing with numerous other programs with similar objectives. For service-oriented policy assessment, this parallelism among operating programs poses serious threats to the internal validity of evaluation in that clients availing themselves of the innovative program may also be using various other services as well, and that such use may differ with variations in the treatment programs. In fact, in these situations it is possible that control group members who are being observed as a comparison may attempt to gain access to the treatment. For example, in one hospital study nurses with patients in a control condition were surreptitiously placing them in the treatment condition (a socialization therapy) that seemed superior.

There are other ramifications of social experimentation within the larger societal or organizational framework that also must be considered. Just as the conduct, analysis, and policy implications of an evaluation form their own system, the policy experiment itself represents a new element in the larger social system. There are some important considerations to be derived from this perspective that help illuminate additional problems in experimental inference. For example, the evaluative process ultimately results in a single, discrete decision—namely, did the program work? This poses a threat to the temporal validity of the findings for larger and more slowly developing factors such as the public's reaction to a new policy, changing economic conditions, and the like that usually cannot be assessed within a single evaluation. This would imply either replications of the policy study as is occurring with the income maintenance program or more extended long-term studies with numerous measures at many points in time such as are provided by a time-series design. Furthermore, the observations should not only be tailored to the social innovation or experiment, but also to the organization or community within which it would eventually operate. The relativistic nature of social science phenomena require such additional observations. This information also has obvious benefits in detecting secondary effects—both positive and negative.

A System for Assessing Social Policy

A number of points that are essential for a meaningful assessment of social policy have been implicit in the above discussion and need further explication. Of utmost importance is the tacit assumption that social program evaluations will be policy relevant. The New Jersey example is again unfortunately atypical of most evaluations. There are a number of reasons for this: (a) the statistical jargon of the evaluation research methodologist is often incomprehensible to the policymaker, (b) the distance between high-level governmental policy and local program administration leads to communication breakdowns, (c) the policy may be too broad to infer specific program goals, or (d) there is local pressure or evaluation apprehension by program personnel to deflect, alter, or subvert the evaluation of a new policy. There are, no doubt, other causes for the occurrence of policy irrelevant program evaluations, but these are some of the most common ones found in final reports. All of this further supports the need for prior planning and coordination between policymakers, program personnel, social scientists, and other evaluation methodologists. It takes time to design and implement a useful evaluation. Attempts to do this ex post facto, after the program is in place, have yielded faulty and misleading results.[23] To correct this requires a mutual sharing of control in all phases of the policy assessment process. Only in this manner will valid evaluations that are neither sabotaged nor irrelevant be conducted. Otherwise, competition and conflict will develop among the various parties that will ultimately be harmful to the viability of the program.

It is at the point of prior planning that social scientists—political scientists, economists, psychologists, and others—can and must play an important role in the formation and evaluation of policy. The crucial question that must be asked of the differing and competing constituencies involved in (and also by) the policy is: What evidence (i.e., amount of benefit, magnitude of program effect, and level of statistical significance) will these groups need to act—either favorably and implement the program or unfavorably and not implement it? Lawyers, political scientists, and sociologists can identify competing policies and their constituencies; economists can devise income-oriented approaches and make cost estimates of these and other programs derived from particular policies; psychologists can measure attitudes and values and can obtain quantified estimates of the level of persuasion the program outcomes must achieve to affect a decision; and statisticians can create the techniques for prescribing the design of the social experiment and the analysis of the data derived from it. These are all new areas that have yet to be thoroughly explored. Given the ascendance of evaluation research and social experimentation, it is imperative that the necessary research be undertaken to allow policy-relevant results to be obtained. The alternative is social disillusionment, economic waste, and the abandonment of a useful approach before it has been properly implemented.

In addition to the immediate need for multidisciplinary basic research on these essential problems, it is also imperative that a new approach to conducting evaluations be established. It is by now obvious that the proper assessment of social reforms requires the talents of many different social scientists. A research plan for a social experiment has as an implicit assumption that not only shall this expertise be relevant to particular components or aspects of the social experiment, but, more importantly, that those viewpoints be coordinated at the onset of the project. That is, a research plan or design is a blueprint for action requiring the combined efforts of this disciplinary expertise before the program is implemented. Thus an interdisciplinary team must be assembled at the very onset of a social policy experiment to design, conduct, analyze, and present the results of the experiment. The team will have to answer the research questions posed above before it can proceed to the experiment proper. For the results to be meaningful in a policy sense, they must provide enough information to allow an informed choice for or against program implementation on a wide scale—they must be policy relevant! To achieve this, the team must determine the criteria of relevance of those involved in the decision-making process. And this requires preliminary research to ascertain the level of persuasion of these constituencies as noted above. Thus evaluation research is a three-stage multidisciplinary process that first involves basic research on various aspects of the policy process, then the application of these findings in the specific political context to determine the objectives and design of the social experiment prior to its implementation, and finally, the conduct of the program including the collection and assessment of systematic information measuring the impact of the program.

Notes

1. *New York Times,* Sunday, October 27, 1974. Pp. 1ff.

2. D. T. Campbell and J. C. Stanley, *Experimental and Quasi-Experimental Designs for Research* (Chicago: Rand McNally, 1966).

3. E. A. Suchman, *Evaluative Research* (New York: Russell Sage Foundation, 1967).

4. D. T. Campbell and A. Erlebacher, "How Regression Artifacts in *Quasi-Experimental* Evaluations Can Mistakenly Make Compensatory Education Look Harmful." in J. Hellmuch (ed.), *Compensatory Education: A National Debate, The Disadvantaged Child,* Vol. III (New York: Bruner/Mazel, 1970), 185-210.

5. D. N. Kershaw, "A Negative Income-Tax Experiment," *Scientific American* 227 (1972): 19-25.

6. See, for example, D. Weiler, *A Public School Voucher Demonstration: The First Year at Alum Rock,* Report R-1495-NIE (Santa Monica, Calif.: Rand Corp, 1974).

7. P. M. Wortman, "Evaluation Research: A Psychological Perspective," *American Psychologist* (1975): 562-575.

8. M. Rokeach, "A Theory of Organization and Change Within Value-Attitude Systems," *Journal of Social Issues* (1968):13-35.

9. D. P. Moynihan, *The Politics of a Guaranteed Income* (New York: Random House, 1973).

10. D. N. Kershaw and S. Skidmore, *The New Jersey Graduated Work Incentive Experiment,* Policy Analysis Series, No. 1 (Princeton, New Jersey: Mathematica, 1974).

11. M. Rokeach, "Long-Range Experimental Modification of Values, Attitudes and Behavior," *American Psychologist* 26 (1971): 453-459.

12. B. Kutchinsky, "The Effect of Easy Availability of Pornography on the Incidence of Sex Crimes: The Danish Experience," *Journal of Social Issues* 29 (1973) 163-181.

13. Moynihan, *Politics of a Guaranteed Income.*

14. I. Illich, *Deschooling Society* (New York: Harper & Row, 1970).

15. D. P. Moynihan, "Annals of Politics (Family Assistance Plan—I), *The New Yorker* (January 13, 1973): 34-57.

16. C. S. Jencks et al., *Inequality: A Reassessment of the Effect of Family and Schooling in America* (New York: Basic Books, 1972).

17. H. W. Riecken and R. F. Boruch, *Social Experimentation: A Method for Planning and Evaluating Social Intervention* (New York: Academic Press, 1974), pp. 87-116.

18. H. L. Ross and D. T. Campbell "The Connecticut Speed Crackdown: A Study of the Effects of Legal Change," In H. L. Ross (ed.), *Perspectives on the Social Order: Readings in Sociology* (New York: McGraw Hill, 1968).

19. D. T. Campbell, "Reforms as Experiments," *American Psychologist* 24 (1969): 409-429.

20. R. E. Klitgaard, "Preliminary Analysis of Achievement Test Scores in Alum Rock Voucher and Nonvoucher Schools, 1972-73," In Weiler (ed.). *Public School Voucher Demonstration,* pp. 105-119.

21. T. K. Glennan, "Institutional and Political Factors in Social Experimentation," In Riecken and Boruch (eds.), *Social Experimentation,* pp. 203-244.

22. Weiler, *Public School Voucher Demonstration,* pp. 53-54.

23. Campbell and Erlebacher, "Regression Artifacts."

Part II
Sociology and Social Work

5 Sociology in Public Policy Analysis

Duncan MacRae, Jr.

The study of public policy may be conducted with two different aims: either
to contribute to choice between better and worse policies (which I shall call
"policy analysis"), or simply to study causal relations objectively. These
two approaches coexist within sociology as within political science. But in
a number of sub-fields of sociology they seem to merge, because of the
particular dependent variables studied. In these sub-fields, one may study
causal relations between policies as means, and valuative dependent variables as ends or outcomes.

Policy-Relevant Dependent Variables

This merging of the two approaches is especially characteristic of sociology, because many sociological concepts (or their opposites) may plausibly
be taken as ends: social integration, social mobility, intergroup communication, morale; or the reduction of social disorganization, prejudice, aliena-
tion, or crime. Thus sociologists have often claimed to seek objective
knowledge both for its own sake, and at the same time to provide means to
"given" ends whose valuative aspect is exogenous to the discipline.[1] Such
ends may be defined by the judgment that a "social problem" exists,[2] or by
clients' support for research. And even though radical critics within sociology have criticized their discipline's cooperation with powerful clients, the
critics themselves often feel they can combine objective study with the
service of "given" values through the study of power.

Insofar as these values are generally agreed on, and do not appear to be
mere preferences of the sociologist, he can engage in objective study of
means to given ends. But these plausible values or disvalues are open to
valuative criticism; for example, social integration is not an ultimate or
unconditional value, nor crime an ultimate disvalue, in most ethical systems. This problem of valuative criticism also arises for other variables
studied by sociologists, such as job satisfaction, marital satisfaction, organizational effectiveness, the frequency of use of services,[3] and equality
of educational opportunity.[4] A list of such variables suggests their relation
to the conceptual schemes of sociology; because of this relation, sociology
is more easily applied to particular practical tasks than is political science.
But this connection with the concepts of the discipline also has the disad-

vantage that these valuative variables are less often related to those of other disciplines, such as preference satisfaction in economics or personality development in psychotherapy. The problem is a general one, shared by various disciplines, and a broader philosophical view is required to connect the separate systems of values of the disciplines.

A comprehensive approach to policy analysis also leads us toward systematic ethics. Only by interrelating the particular values and disvalues sought by means of particular policies can we choose rationally among allocations of resources in disparate fields. By such a broader perspective we can also select valuative "unanticipated consequences" of policies and programs, to balance against the given goals of the organizations we study.

Political Sociology and Political Science

This close relationship between scientific study and policy relevance, which exists for the sub-fields of sociology mentioned above, is less clear for the sub-field of political sociology. The reasons for this separateness in political sociology are somewhat akin to those for political science.

In political science the approaches of policy choice and objective study are more distinct than in sociology, since the variables of political science are less often results of policy that may be taken as ends. They do, of course, include important aspects of decision *processes*, such as democracy. The variables studied may be *causes* of policies; but if they are, we cannot then consider the policies themselves (e.g., laws enacted) as ends without assuming we know their valued or disvalued results. Moreover, the causal variables in political scientists' objective study of policy are often beyond the range of voluntary choice (e.g., socioeconomic characteristics of political systems); or they may be manipulable only through choices such as those of constitution-making, municipal reform, or the reform of legislative or electoral procedures. Thus when political scientists study party competition, participation, and degree of representation as antecedents of policy, they may face the problem as to how these variables can be changed. The variables they study may also be the results of policies; but in this case political scientists are likely either to study results that are less clearly valuable or harmful than those studied by sociology, such as regime stability or support for the authorities; or to be driven outside the realm of political science, to study economic outcomes such as welfare expenditures.

This separation between scientific research and relevance to policy choice also exists for a branch of sociology that might appear especially relevant: political sociology. The focus of this field is largely on the "social bases of politics"—a phrase used by Lipset as the subtitle to *Political Man*.[5] "Politics," the dependent variable, has included voting behavior, political attitudes and ideologies, the development of political movements and organizations, structures of power, regimes, and occasionally particular policies themselves.[6]

But political sociology is difficult to relate to policy choice for several reasons. Concentration on *social* bases of politics can lead us to an incomplete model that largely ignores the *economic* sources of intervention in politics by firms and industries.[7] Social sources of politics also tend to be non-manipulable variables; although these relations can provide an enlightening perspective on policy choices, they are less directly relevant than studies in applied sociology. The analysis of social sources of ideology also conduces to what Mannheim called the "unmasking" perspective, at the expense of reasoned debate with our fellow citizens on the merits of policies. This approach to rightist ideologies has been criticized by Dorn and Long.[8]

A final problem which political sociology shares with other branches of sociology is the lack of generality of its implicit values. Lipset once wrote that "[D]emocracy is not . . . a means through which different groups can attain their ends or seek the good society; it is the good society itself in operation."[9] The value of democracy is important; but without further specification and relation to other values, it cannot guide us in a wide variety of specific policy choices. Other analyses have often taken power as a central disvalue or problem.[10] But power can be used for various purposes, and the diagnosis of power alone can neglect the distinctions among these purposes.

Types of Applied Sociology

Sociology is applied to a wide variety of policy problems through diverse channels. In classifying these applications, we must first ask whether general sociological theories can make useful contributions. A simplistic view of functionalism would lead to the conclusion that it could not, since it appears to look only for features that contribute to the maintenance of a social system. Nevertheless, Parsons' policy recommendations for treatment of Germany after World War II show clearly that the notion of interdependent structures in society need not paralyze policy recommendations but can lead to a particular style of intervention, concerned with minimizing unanticipated consequences.[11]

The aspects of sociology that can be applied to policy choice are somewhat parallel to divisions within the university. Like some other disciplines and like the university itself, sociology contains both basic and applied specialties. Some of the applications of sociology to policy choice may be classified according to basic specialties, including social stratification, ethnic relations, urban and rural sociology, organization theory, the study of occupations, social psychology, population, and human ecology. Parallel with these substantive specialties are methods which sociology has developed, together with other disciplines: survey studies (which have long been applied to the measurement of social conditions), and causal models.

Certain methods have been developed with particular relation to policy choices: evaluation research[12] and social indicators.[13] Although the techniques used in these approaches are not completely distinct from those of basic research, they tend to be used in more specific situations (evaluation of particular projects) or with the assumption that many uncontrolled variables are present. The use of social indicators may parallel that of economic indicators—first used for generating behavioral models of business cycles, then adapted to control of such cycles by intervention.

In addition, a number of applied fields are more closely linked to particular applications and to professions that apply this knowledge. Criminology, industrial sociology, and mass communications studies are among the routinized branches of applied sociology. Some of these study the attitudes and reactions of individuals as they are altered by "people-changing organizations";[14] others study individuals' mobility through role-sequences as they may be affected by policy, and still others the changes in structure that may be produced by policy choices.

Sociology is also applied in conjunction with professions that are not simply parts of sociology: social work and counseling, medicine, law, education, psychotherapy. In such cases, a sociological specialty emerges whose graduates must prepare to work in collaborative research and treatment teams—or as consultants, or in some cases subordinates to the profession in question. If the profession is a strongly established one such as law or medicine, sociologists will have to work in a subordinate capacity to it or as teachers to members of the profession who wish to acquire the skills and carry out the relevant work or research themselves.

In addition to the routinized and structured sub-fields that train sociologists for established careers, other fields and tendencies deal with less established policy applications. The extensive recent interest in radical sociology involves efforts to critize the existing social order as well as prevailing research methods.[15] Voluntary associations as clients sometimes support studies of prejudice and race relations. Policy institutes, establishmentarian or otherwise, develop interdisciplinary combinations of specialties to cope with newly arising problems.[16] And sociologists writing for the public may provide reinterpretations of social structures and trends that are themselves influential in policy formation.

Sociology as an Ingredient of Policy Analysis

Sociology and political science are thus potentially complementary with respect to policy analysis. Political science explicitly includes the discussion of ethical questions (normative political theory), while sociology does not. Political science studies governmental processes of decision, while sociology tends more to study informal decision processes and their outcomes. Political science is best fitted to advise national or local constitution-makers, while sociology advises clients concerned with more specific policy choices.[17] Thus if policy study is concerned with choosing or recommending better policies, it requires cooperation between disciplines that reflect systematically on the goals of policy (including political science) and those that measure the attainment of such goals (including sociology).

In comparison with political science, sociology provides more skills and knowledge that are directly useful to policymakers, but its perspective is less self-conscious and analytic about the goals and legitimate conditions for use of this knowledge. This may relate to the fact that the sources of policy choice for sociology tend more to be found outside the discipline itself. Thus there may be a lack of sophistication (or perhaps simply a lack of success) in many applications of sociology to issues of national policy. Major efforts have been abandoned because of political resistance, or have failed to fulfill their goals.[18] (This is not to say, necessarily, that political science has done better.) In addition, some successes have been obtained by questionable means. Tactics similar to those implied by Coleman's model of community conflict[19] were used by the supporters of flouridation in a referendum campaign, and outsiders were excluded from speaking on the topic; but one wonders whether such a one-sided organization of opinion creates a desirable precedent. Similarly, the use of socioeconomic characteristics by defense lawyers to screen jurors in the Berrigan trial[20] seems an extremely questionable precedent, possibly more so than electronic eavesdropping on juries for research purposes.[21]

The sociological policy analyst (or the policy-oriented social scientist generally) thus needs to know more than the scientific predictions of consequences of alternative policies. He must have some concern with the values or disvalues that correspond to these consequences, and some capacity for proposing new or modified policies. He must learn something about the conditions affecting the political feasibility of one or another policy—not in the determinate form of "power structure" or "elite behavior" but in terms of possibilities affected by his own intervention.[22] And especially relevant to sociology is awareness of the possible changes in norms that might result from the means used to affect policy in particular cases.

What is needed, therefore, is a general view of the political processes in which social science intervenes; perhaps political science can provide this, although it will not come from behavioral studies alone. In addition, a structural perspective on the conditions for social scientists' supplying accurate policy-related advice is desirable. This includes the motivation of scientists to contribute such advice and to engage in reasoned criticism of it; the distinction between societal and organizational feedback; and the enlightenment of the public and their representatives.[23] This general perspective on the application of social science, in which sociology can complement political science and other disciplines, may find expression in the developing field of policy analysis.[24]

Notes

1. James S. Coleman, in *Policy Research in the Social Sciences* (Morristown, N.J.: General Learning Press, 1972), stresses the origin of research problems "in the world of action."

2. See the journal *Social Problems,* published by the Society for the Study of Social Problems.

3. See Paul F. Lazarsfeld, William H. Sewell, and Harold L. Wilensky, *The Uses of Sociology* (New York: Basic Books, 1967).

4. For a review of a major applied study, see Frederick Mosteller and Daniel P. Moynihan, *On Equality of Educational Opportunity* (New York: Vintage Books, 1972).

5. Seymour Martin Lipset, *Political Man: The Social Bases of Politics* (Garden City, N.Y.: Doubleday, 1960). Lipset has subsequently pointed out that the field includes study of the reciprocal effects of politics on society; see his "Political Sociology," in Neil J. Smelser (ed.), *Sociology* (New York: Wiley, 1973), pp. 401-402.

6. A major study of regime development is Barrington Moore, Jr., *Social Origins of Dictatorship and Democracy* (Boston: Beacon Press, 1966). A study comparing policy outcomes is Gaston V. Rimlinger, *Welfare Policy and Industrialization in Europe, America, and Russia* (New York: Wiley, 1971).

7. See John Kenneth Galbraith, *The Modern Industrial State* (Boston: Houghton Mifflin, 1967).

8. See Karl Mannheim, *Ideology and Utopia* (New York: Harcourt, Brace, 1949), pp. 34-37; Dean S. Dorn and Gary L. Long "Sociology and the Radical Right," *American Sociologist,* (May 1972): 8-9.

9. Lipset, *Political Man,* p. 403.

10. These include criticisms not only of the power of classes, but also of the power of organizations; see James S. Coleman, *Power and the Structure of Society* (New York: Norton, 1974).

11. Talcott Parsons, "The Problem of Controlled Institutional Change," *Psychiatry* 8 (1945): 79-101. Reprinted in his *Essays in Sociological Theory* (New York: Free Press, 1954).

12. See Peter H. Rossi and Walter Williams (eds.), *Evaluating Social Programs* (New York: Seminar Press, 1972).

13. Social indicators, or time-series measures of social conditions, may be based on either valuative variables or the variables of basic science. Kenneth C. Land has referred to the corresponding models as "social policy" and "social indicator" models respectively, in his "Social Indicator Models: An Overview," in K.C. Land and Seymour Spilerman (eds.), *Social Indicator Models* (New York: Russell Sage Foundation, 1974). See also Land, "On the Definition of Social Indicators," *American Sociologist* 6 (November 1971): 322-325. An extensive bibliography is Leslie D. Wilcox et al. (eds.), *Social Indicators and Societal Monitoring* (San Francisco: Jossey-Bass, 1972).

14. A recent reference is Yeheskel Hasenfeld, "People Processing Organizations: An Exchange Approach," *American Sociological Review* 37 (June 1972): 256-263.

15. For example Alvin W. Gouldner, *The Coming Crisis of Western Sociology* (New York: Basic Books, 1970); Robert W. Friedrichs, *A Sociology of Sociology* (New York: Free Press, 1970).

16. Institutional frameworks for the application of sociology include those of the Bureau of Applied Social Research at Columbia University and of Etzioni's Center for Policy Research.

17. On the degrees of generality that distinguish the sociologist's "policy research" from the narrower "applied research," see Amitai Etzioni, "Policy Research," *American Sociologist* 6 (Supplementary issue, June 1971): 8. This entire issue is devoted to "Sociological Research and Public Policy." The distinct role of political science is pointed out in David Robertson (Univs. of Wisconsin and Essex), "Political Science as Policy Science: Some Philosophical Worries," presented at the Midwest Political Science Association, Spring 1973.

18. See Gideon Sjoberg (ed.), *Ethics, Politics, and Social Research* (Cambridge, Mass.: Schenkman, 1967); Irving L. Horowitz (ed.), *The Rise and Fall of Project Camelot* (Cambridge, Mass.: MIT Press, 1967); Lee Rainwater and William L. Yancey, *The Moynihan Report and the Politics of Controversy* (Cambridge, Mass.: MIT Press, 1967); Daniel P. Moynihan, *Maximum Feasible Misunderstanding* (New York: Free Press, 1969).

19. James S. Coleman, *Community Conflict* (New York: Free Press, 1957).

20. "Scientists Helped Pick Favorable Jury for Berrigan," *News and Observer* (Raleigh, N.C.), May 6, 1973 (UPI).

21. See Ted R. Vaughan, "Governmental Intervention in Social Research: Political and Ethical Dimensions in the Wichita Jury Recordings," in Sjoberg, *Ethics, Politics.*

22. Here the developing field of interorganizational relations may be especially relevant. A recent reference is Howard Aldrich, Cornell University, "An Organization-Environment Perspective on Cooperation and Conflict Between Organizations in the Manpower Training System," presented at conference on Conflict and Power in Complex Organizations, Kent State University, May 1972. See also Richard H. Hall (ed.), *The Formal Organization* (New York: Basic Books, 1972); and Arnold J. Meltsner, "Political Feasibility and Policy Analysis," *Public Administration Review* 32 (Nov.-Dec. 1972): 859-867.

23. See Morris Janowitz, "Sociological Models and Social Policy," in his *Political Conflict* (Chicago: Quadrangle Books, 1970); Albert J. Biderman, "Information ≠ Intelligence ≠ Enlightened Public Policy: Function and Organization of Social Feedback," *Policy Sciences* 1 (Summer 1970): 217-230; and MacRae, *The Social Function of Social Science* (New Haven, Conn.: Yale University Press, forthcoming).

24. See Duncan MacRae, Jr., "Policy Analysis as an Applied Social Science Discipline," *Administration and Society* 6 (February 1975): 363-388.

6

Social Work and Policy Studies

Alfred J. Kahn

Most social workers are prepared in the course of their professional education for what are described as "direct service" roles (in such fields as family and child welfare, school social work, medical social service, grassroots organizing for mutual aid, etc.). Others concentrate in an alternate career line which prepares for administration, program development, policy formulation and planning. It has always been this way. Although the leaders and officials who founded what became the National Conference on Charities and Corrections about 100 years ago were initially administrators and members of advisory boards, social work has been dominated by casework and group work, not by administration or planning. It has been largely preoccupied in its scholarship with the knowledge base upon which direct service roles rest. Psychiatry, individual and social psychology, and cultural anthropology therefore have had major attention. Many of the researchers, analysts and managers in social welfare have come from other professions and disciplines.

When serious social science borrowing began after World War II, as social work broadened its intervention strategies and was challenged on the issue of effectiveness with reference to large-scale social problems, those fields of sociology related to stratification, social change, organization theory and deviance moved to center stage. Economics and political science, while always of major interest to a social work minority involved in income maintenance questions or public administration, have come into their own only in the past decade—in the context, first of social work's major role in community action and welfare rights and, subsequently, as a larger component of social work attention has turned to social planning, policy analysis and program development.

Efforts systematically to formulate a specific social work concept of social planning and program development are relatively recent, and can be traced to the 1960s. Indeed, the bibliography is as yet still quite modest. The research is fragmentary. And because social work has tended to be eclectic, it has been able to relate to other developments which come from social psychology, political science, economics, and sociology. There are some social workers who draw upon each, and a number who are closely connected with several of these disciplines and their scientific developments.

A good number of the some seventy-five graduate schools of social work have now launched "concentrations" or "tracks" in program development, social administration and policy analysis—both at the M.S. and doctoral levels. There are identifiable programs of research at the University of Chicago, Brandeis University, Columbia and a number of other universities. Social work scholars from these and related institutions participate generally in interdisciplinary and inter-institutional activity in this field. A number of social scientists, particularly economists, sociologists and political scientists, trained in academic departments, have identified themselves with social work education and policy research.

A Concept of Social Planning

Social workers tend to identify their interest in policy studies as involving (a) *planning and administration of "social sector" programs*. A smaller group also is concerned with what might be described as (b) *a "social perspective on domains and activities which are not traditionally within social welfare"*.

With reference to the first, the social sector programs, there is a tendency to define social welfare or the social sector as being preoccupied with those programs implementing access to benefits, entitlements and services by other than market criteria. Market devices nonetheless may be employed in service delivery. A typical list would include: income maintenance; medical care and mental health; corrections; leisure time and recreation; general or personal social services, including family and child welfare and services to the aging; education; housing, renewal and relocation; manpower programs; rural welfare; and migrant programs.

It will be recognized, of course, that social work is the primary service delivery profession only in a number of these fields. A variety of occupations and professions are involved in several of the above domains. Especially important for present discussion is the fact that there are a variety of conceptions of these programs and their meaning to society. For example, there are some people who do not identify corrections with social welfare, and some who do. A number of the above programs are so well established in western society that they have been separately institutionalized, and are not conceived of as part of "social welfare," even though most industrialized countries list them among the "social services." A frequently made distinction defines as "social welfare services" those social services available by means test, whereas the others are considered as universal, and often become separately institutionalized as they gain general acceptance. These distinctions have major consequences with reference to stigma, concept of client-user, preference with reference to financing, administrative arrangements, staff-user relationships, points of view about the availability of alternatives and options, quality—and a number of other factors.

Social planners from the social sector (among them planners from social work), then, relate to the above systems and are concerned with policy development, programming, implementation and administration, evaluation and feedback. The general feeling is that serious planning and evaluation is an interdisciplinary effort, requiring both subject matter specialists from the relevant professions and experts in administration, planning, systems analysis, operations research. Sometimes social workers master these technical skills and can become the generalists in such planning operations, but the number of social workers so trained is thus far quite limited. More often, social workers tend to be field specialists, particularly with regard to the general or personal social services, community mental health, corrections, some aspects of migrant programs, some aspects of leisure time programs.

A limited number of social welfare scholars and social planners have defined an even more ambitious domain in which they would function. The author of this paper identifies with this aspiration, while recognizing that thus far accomplishments are modest, as is sanction so to function.

Generally, the perspective is this: the welfare state seeks demand management of the economy and to provide a "social minimum" and more. Its points of departure are concepts of social justice, a viewpoint of what individuals must be assured if they are to be loyal and effective citizens in a complex society, an assessment of what is needed for families to conform to societal objectives and ideals, and a perspective on how the society can avoid further violence to the environment. Social planning finds its goals and constraints shaped out of such variables. Perhaps some scholars will argue that the most basic of these criteria for welfare state programs is the latent objective of preparation and motivation of a labor force suitable for its era. I would hold that there are mixed objectives in any pluralistic society. Certainly the creation and maintenance of a labor force is a major component in determining social policy. In any case, it would seem reasonable to argue that what now occurs in the United States suggests that the American welfare state is hardly dominated in every policy and every action by market considerations alone. Programs are enacted, policies implemented, on the basis of criteria which are derived along the following lines: concepts of social justice; concepts of requirements for adequate citizenship; concepts of environmental protection; and concepts of family policy.

Concepts such as these may enter into social planning, policy development, and administration. They may be found to contribute, in fact, or have a potential contribution, in the future, in such realms as: tax policy, housing, road building, tariff, environmental policy. The social welfare policy analyst brings to these realms alertness to the social justice, citizenship, environment, and family policy dimensions to the extent that he enters into planning and policy-making as researcher or as citizen-participant. While his more typical contribution is towards income maintenance and general social services, he is increasingly trained to raise questions about family consequences of tax policy, socialization consequences of housing design, community consequences of tariff policy or road building, family structural consequences of wage policy or education policy.

Social workers who are trained in this field, then, undertake a relevant social science concentration and then seek a degree of expertise in general social services, housing, education, health or mental health, or manpower. Occasionally, and the writer would hope increasingly, some of them may work with groups concerned with tax policy (Is it not time that somebody looked seriously at the consequences of sales taxes?) and less familiar fields as they seek to make their contributions as participants in planning and policy development in the broader field.

In effect, if the society increasingly chooses its goals by other than market criteria, there will be need for a contribution from professions and disciplines which focus on new variables, particularly those variables related to "person-in-situation" and "man-in-society." The enterprise will require professionals with access to community and individual preferences, with intimate knowledge of consequences of policies and programs for individual life and with a potential contribution to program and institutional invention. Such professionals in turn, will need sophistication about the micro and macro politics of social policy formulation and implementation. In short political science will become increasingly important to them. Well-trained social welfare professionals aspire in these domains, although one must confess that the record of accomplishment in this entire field is as yet quite modest.

References

Encyclopedia of Social Work. Sixteenth Issue, 2 vol. Washington, D.C.: National Association of Social Workers, 1971, pp. 1324-1434.

Journal of Social Policy. New York and London: Cambridge University Press.

Kahn, Alfred J. *Social Policy and Social Services*. New York: Random House, 1973.

Kahn, Alfred J. *Studies in Social Policy and Planning*. New York: Russell Sage, 1969.

Kahn, Alfred J. *Theory and Practice of Social Planning*. New York: Russell Sage, 1969.

Kamerman, Sheila B., et al. "Knowledge for Practice: Social Science in Social Work." In Alfred J. Kahn (ed.), *Shaping the New Social Work*. New York: Columbia University Press, 1973, pp. 56-84.

Perlman, Robert and Arnold Gurin. *Community Organization and Social Planning*. New York: John Wiley, 1972.

Rein, Martin. *Social Policy*. New York: Random House, 1970.

Robinson, William A. and Bernard Crick (eds.). *The Future of the Social Services*. Baltimore: Penguin Books, 1970.

Schorr, Alvin L. *Explorations in Social Policy*. New York: Basic Books, 1968.

Schorr, Alvin L. *Poor Kids*. New York: Basic Books, 1966.

Titmuss, Richard M. *Commitment to Welfare*. New York: Pantheon Books, 1968.

Titmuss, Richard M. *Essays on 'The Welfare State'*. New Haven: Yale University Press, 1959.

**Part III
Economics**

7

Approaches to Legal-Economic Policy and Related Problems of Research

Warren J. Samuels

It is not too much to argue that the interrelations between legal-political and economic processes comprise the most fundamental and critical area of policy and policy analysis. Although both ideologists and analysts frequently postulate their separability, albeit for different purposes, the economy is an object of legal control and government is an instrument for the realization of economic goals, the two processes being not only inseparable but complexly intertwined in the real world.

The purpose of this chapter is to identify and differentiate, first, the two primary approaches to the study of legal-economic policy that are pursued by economists and, second, the major problems of legal-economic research.

Approaches to Legal-Economic Analysis

Orthodox Neoclassical Microeconomics and Welfare Economics

Microeconomics is primarily concerned with the theory of the allocation of resources through the market. It is formal, static, partial equilibrium analysis. It is formal in that it does not directly encompass specific content of economic decision-making but presents functional tendencies which abstract from the radical indeterminacy of the real world, specifically from the forces governing the preferences and social values given effect through the market and the institutions which weight alternative preferences and values. It is static in that it typically abstracts from changes in technology, resources, population, and institutional arrangements; and it is partial equilibrium in that it typically is used in analyzing sub-sectors (e.g., particular industries or the markets for particular goods) while abstracting from the operation of other sub-sectors. Dynamic and general equilibrium models do exist but are even more formal than the static, partial equilibrium models.

Aside from the methodological character of the inquiry, the preoccupation of microeconomics is with the allocation of resources through the market. Some models introduce important variations, but most tend to assume competition, knowledge, and rationality (profit and utility maximization). Considered somewhat differently, economic choice is postulated as that of constrained maximization, ergo of incrementalist decision-making in pursuit of some given objective function, generally that of welfare maximization in the allocation of private or social resources, and as such has been applied to the analysis of government, as indicated below.

Microeconomics takes for granted, however, the development, operation, and change of the legal and moral rules governing the terms of access to and participation in the economy by various potential economic actors. That is to say, microeconomic theory abstracts from such phenomena as property and other rights which govern whose preferences will be given effect through the market. Legal rights, and other bases of economic position and participation, are antecedent to economic theory. Nevertheless, additional premises introducing particular antecedent rights and other bases of economic position are often introduced in the conduct and application of microeconomic theory.

Normative applications of microeconomics presume either explicitly or implicitly the antecedent specification of the propriety of both the market system and/or some particular structure or distribution of rights. Thus normative welfare economics explicates the nuances and implications of Pareto optimality, but because the substance of particular optimality solutions are a function of the antecedent specification of rights there is no unique Pareto optimal solution but a family of such solutions, each of which is correlated with a particular structure of rights, or power. There is, then, considerable opportunity for implicit ethicizing as particular applications of the Pareto rule give effect to some selectively perceived or chosen rights and not to others. Conclusions as to optimality thus tend to depend upon the factors given normative status *ab initio,* so that policy conclusions generally are tautological with the premises assumed. Normative welfare economics, more specifically the so-called new welfare economics, is also highly consonant with libertarianism and laissez-faire conservatism.

One application of microeconomics has been to the state itself. Here government is seen as an economic variable, as an economic alternative, and its actions examined in terms of a maximizing model in which the behavior of particular individuals or groups both in and out of government office is understood to seek to maximize their private (as distinct from public) welfare. Government is contemplated not as a neutral mechanism or black box but as a sphere, indeed, a market, of activity analogous to general market activity, and therefore one dominated by calculations of advantage in the development of legal-political institutions and rules. Some analyses examine only politics as a maximizing process; other examine the economics (i.e., rational choice) of constitution making (seen in part as a matter of collective choice); and still others examine the use of government to establish positions of privilege or, more generally, of power in regard to market activity.

Heterodox Institutional Economics

Some of the applications of orthodox microeconomic theory come close to the inquiries of institutional economists. But whereas neoclassical micro-economics is primarily concerned with the allocation of resources through a market economy, the institutionalist movement, representing a major part of a diffuse second tradition within economics, is concerned with the organization and control and evolution of the economic system, whether it be market or non-market. Although there has emerged no corpus of theory as highly developed as the neoclassical, the institutionalist orientation is fairly clear and detailed studies have been produced.

With regard to the study of legal-economic policy, the institutionalists have been concerned with such phenomena and subjects as: (a) the forces operating through the market governing resource allocation nominally attributed by neoclassical theory to market forces (demand and supply), when in fact the operative forces are themselves dependent upon the power structure, legal action, and institutions, making themselves felt through the market in a system of truly general equilibrium; (b) the historical development of institutions—the state, property, corporation, and economic institutions constituting the market—which operate through market forces in part by structuring and channeling nominally private choice; and, *inter alia,* (c) the factors and forces governing the distribution of economic welfare going beyond the formal conditions of neoclassical equilibrium and presumptive-optimality reasoning. Accordingly, institutional economists have produced (i) analyses of capitalism as an economic system (with the market being only one facet thereof); (ii) theories of the economic system as a system of organization and control; (iii) theories of political economy, that is to say, of the interrelation of legal-political and market processes, with the state as both a dependent and independent variable; and, all things considered (which includes the typical institutionalist preoccupation with cultural and technological factors), (iv) an understanding of the deep and profound participation of government in the economic system, even when nominally capitalist, with regard to the institutions determining the economic system per se, the structure of rights (private power), and the structure, conduct, and performance of the private sector.

Institutional economists have been as normative as the libertarian new welfare economists and their policy conclusions are more or less equally as tautological with their normative premises. Whereas the libertarians have been generally pro established rights and pro capitalist, at least superficially, the institutionalists have been generally critical of capitalism (and therefore the orthodox economics which they perceive as its emanation and rationalization) and in favor of a greater diffusion of power and a greater responsiveness of both economy and state to the interests of hitherto neglected interests, generally the working class and the poor. Accordingly institutionalists have been leaders in the development of the welfare state (property-right equivalents in the interests of the nonpropertied but for the most part available to all) and the interpretation of trade unions. Traditional Marxism and the newer radical political economy have much in common with these and related aspects of institutional economics.

Problems of Legal-Economic Research

All research and especially all paradigm-level analyses have limits which are manifest in controversies over their respective problems. Legal-economic research, and the neoclassical and institutional paradigms, are no exception. Indeed, there are a number of particularly acute problems in the field, even quite aside from the ubiquitous problem of implicit ethicizing or the introduction of normative premises into ostensibly positive analysis, and they augur to become even more abrasive.

One of the most profound methodological problems of policy studies is the tension between two desiderata. On the one hand, policy analysts want to, indeed must, retain the policy or decision-making character of their subject matter; on the other, they want to utilize deterministic models developed in the social and policy sciences. The use of the latter tends to obscure and obviate the thrust of the former; and emphasis upon the former tends to weaken the ostensible power of the latter.

A parallel tension arises between the competing procedures of inductive and deductive analyses, particularly in an age of operational (and especially quantitative) meaningfulness. The tension perhaps is greatest in regard to the work of those interested in constructing interpretive but nonoperational paradigms and in introducing deep philosophical problems (whatever their particular positions) not amenable to operational procedures.

The distinction between positive and normative analysis is another fundamental problem. Both positive and normative may be specified in varying and conflicting ways. There are often if not typically implicit normative elements in positive analysis and, moreover, the positive study of normative subjects—such as the interrelation of legal and economic processes—tends to have normative implications, although they often differ between readers. Also relevant is the casuistic manipulation of substantive assumptions and methodological procedures to enable the retention of analytical systems with desired policy nuances and inferences. More generally, it is difficult to escape the tautological relations which exist between definitions, paradigms, and assumptions, on the one hand, and conclusions, nuances, and inferences, on the other.

A further set of intractable problems arises because of the joint-determination character of legal-economic processes. That is to say, there is in fact the joint determination (a) of ends and of means; (b) of optimal (efficient) solutions and of the rights with respect to which the solutions are optimal (efficient); (c) of rights, of loss, and of compensation; and, *inter alia,* (d) of resource allocation and of income and wealth distributions. This means that most if not all relevant variables are both dependent and independent variables; that preferences and social values are endogenous; that economic and legal meaning and significance are each a function of both private and public sector phenomena and not necessarily of their nominally corresponding sectors alone; and so on.

A tension therefore arises from the juxtaposition of the general inter-dependence (or equilibrium) character of perhaps all subjects of policy studies to the almost inevitable necessity to rely upon incomplete partial-equilibrium models as part of the process of abstraction required in coming to grips with the enormous complexities involved.

Substantively, there are many ways in which questions about the relationships between economic and legal-political systems can and do differ. As developed by the late Henry Oliver, the sources of difference include: (a) variations in the direction of the flow of causation; (b) flexibility of the concepts of economic and of political (and legal) system; (c) variations in concrete versus abstract environments; (d) variations in the routes of the flow of causation; (e) problematic distinctions between past and future; and (f) distinctions between necessary, sufficient, and contributory causes; as well as (g) differences in the methods of reasoning employed in analyses of the relationships. Legal-economic models and theories are all subject to such differentiations and accordingly are not readily collated, integrated, reconciled or compared.

Related problems arise because of the deep involvement of legal-economic processes and policy with the problem of order, by which is meant the continuing resolution of the subsidiary conflicts of freedom and control, including hierarchy and equality, and continuity and change. Looked at somewhat differently, problems of analysis and policy arise because legal-economic choice may be interpreted as a function of three sets of variables: power, knowledge, and psychology. Each of these sets of variables is important and not only may be variously formulated but may be more or less substitutable; moreover, their interactions are extremely important as well as very complex and intractable for both research and policy purposes.

The distribution problem, viz., of power, income, wealth, opportunity, exposure, and sacrifice, is critical to legal-economic research and policy—although many models fail to acknowledge and provide for the causes and consequences of asymmetry and inequality of position. The recent study by Bartlett is a welcome exception.

Further intractable research problems arise because of the dual nature of rights, that is, because the possession of a right by Alpha signifies the denial of a right to Beta; and because of the contingent character of rights in a kaleidoscopic economy, such that the significance of a right depends upon the total matrices of power and social change in the future, each right comprising as it were a bundle of possibilities. Because of these conditions, it is technically impossible to fully define the legal-economic status quo: both the structure of the status quo, in terms of rights, is too complex, and the prospective future significance and therefore discounted present status of the respective rights is too uncertain. In all cases the status of the status quo is a problem also because (a) positive models tend to build in the status quo, (b) policy analysis tends to give effect to the status quo answer to the question of whose interests are to count, and (c) alternative specifications of the status quo are possible.

One of the most intriguing problems of legal-economic research is that of the selective perception and identification of such variables or phenomena as government, coercion, freedom, injury, rights, control, regulation, and so on. For example, certain actions of government are perceived as such and others are not. In a somewhat similar fashion, distinctions between private and public are heterogeneous, variable, and ultimately ambiguous and equivocal. So also is the distinction between change through legal and change through non-legal processes, ultimately because of the complex interactions between legal and non-legal processes and therefore because of the inextricable legal element in what is nominally private and the inevitable private elements in the nominally legal or governmental.

Such problems occasion further difficulties for research, specifically those of the identification, definition, and measurement of such phenomena as public sector output and, in all respects, power. With regard to public sector output, for example, the definition may be in terms of specific activity or particular outcomes; the outcomes may be specified in terms of varying and also multiple goals which may be addible or substitutable vis-à-vis each other; and the outcomes further can be specified in terms of a variety of complex behavioral and performance consequences. There are also substantive problems in differentiating between more intensive performance by government in areas historically governmental and the extension of government into new areas; between the force and impact of changes in belief systems, power play, technological imperatives, and population growth; and so on. As another example, there are problems in articulating and differentiating the consequences of the interaction of different types of rules—such as rules governing the scope of decision-making, the scope and structure of decision participation (including representation), decision-making procedures (including voting, bargaining, and decision choice or strategy), and access to and use of property or property equivalents—all of which are extremely important in comprehending the play of power and of legal-economic interrelations.

As the Oliver analysis suggests, alternative approaches to the economic role of government convey varying analytical as well as policy (normative) consequences, in part depending upon who is interpreting or using them. Not only may the economy be contemplated as a function of law *and* the legal-political system as a function of economy, but there are radically different theories of such phenomena as politics, collective action, public choice, bureaucracy, power, ideology, voting, democracy, bargaining, imperialism, federalism, judicial review, political competition, political parties, and the state, each with profound but distinctive implications for understanding legal-economic interrelations. In addition, there are the different normative theories of the economic role of government, and also harmony versus conflict theories, system analytic versus incremental decision-making models, and authoritative versus composite (or pluralist) choice models. Furthermore, it is true both that functionally equivalent performance may be the result of significantly varying legal arrangements and institutional patterns, each a different mode of giving effect to the same power structure (Seidman); and that functionally dissimilar performance may result from substantially similar legal arrangements, say, because of varying power structures. Both market and government are each dependent and independent variables and both tend to give effect to the power structure operating through them. For legal-economic research, the general problem arises of having to differentiate the *theory of* the economic role of government from the *determination of* the economic role of government.

Finally there are a number of what may be called technical factors, although interpretive and practical problems exist with regard to the relevance of decisional discretion to their development and operation. Included among these technical factors are excludability, joint supply, appropriability, information costs, organizability, transaction costs, indivisibilities, scale economies, capital-labor substitutability, large versus small numbers, preference revelation, and, *inter alia,* free rider vis-à-vis forced rider problems. Somewhat closely related are variations in public sector agenda: the causes and consequences of governments (especially local units) serving as markets for public goods.

Conclusion

What policy scientists, particularly political scientists, can contribute to legal-economic analysis of greatest value are, first, models of legal-political and economic interaction; second, objective, positive, empirical studies of government as both a dependent and independent variable, and of economic activity as both an input and an output of political-legal processes; and third, endeavors to wed both theoretical and empirical analyses toward a self-consciously objective, positive comprehension of law and economics. This would provide not only a more powerful understanding of legal and economic processes both separately and in their interrelations, but perhaps also a more realistic and knowledgeable basis on which to predict the probable performance consequences of both political and economic change or reform as well as a basis on which to interpret the probative meaning or policy significance of particular normative systems and ideologies. Major advances in these directions would be no mean feat!

Bibliography

The items listed below by Warren Samuels contain elaborations of the points made in this article. A bibliography on the problem of organization and control from the perspective of legal-economic policy, and an essay on government in the history of economics are also available upon request from the author.

Bartlett, Randall. *Economic Foundations of Political Power*. New York: Free Press, 1973.

Buchanan, James M. and Warren J. Samuels. "On Some Fundamental Issues in Political Economy: An Exchange of Correspondence." *Journal of Economic Issues* 9 (1975).

Oliver, Henry. "Study of Relationships Between Economic and Political Systems." *Journal of Economic Issues* 7 (1973).

Samuels, Warren J. "Interrelations Between Legal and Economic Processes." *Journal of Law & Economics* 14 (1971).

_____. "In Defense of a Positive Approach to Government as an Economic Variable," *Journal of Law & Economics,* vol. 15 (1972).

_____. "Welfare Economics, Power, and Property." In G. Wunderlich and W. L. Gibson, Jr. (eds.), *Perspectives of Property*. University Park: Institute for Research on Land & Water Resources, Pennsylvania State University, 1972.

———. "Law and Economics: A Bibliographical Survey, 1965-1972." *Law Library Journal* 66 (1973).

———. "Legal-Economic Policy: A Bibliographical Survey." *Law Library Journal* 58 (1965).

———. "The Scope of Economics Historically Considered." *Land Economics* 48 (1972).

———. "Ecosystem Policy and the Problem of Power." *Environmental Affairs* 2 (1972).

———. "The Economy as a System of Power and Its Legal Bases: The Legal Economics of Robert Lee Hale." *University of Miami Law Review* 27 (1973).

———. "The Coase Theorem and the Study of Law and Economics." *Natural Resources Journal* 14 (1974).

Seidman, Robert B. "Contract Law, the Free Market, and State Intervention." *Journal of Economic Issues* 7 (1973).

8

The Public Choice Approach to Policy Analysis

Larry L. Wade

The Public Choice Orientation

Following a period of search for an appropriate appellation, economic approaches to politics and public policy are now commonly grouped under the rubric of "public choice." Because of space limitations, the following discussion provides only a cursory orientation to public choice analysis and to the types of policy issues where such analysis may be helpful. The public choice approach is based upon the presumption that individuals in both private and public forums make rational (i.e., transitive, consistent, and instrumental) decisions aimed at improving (maximizing) their personal well-being and other values and that, consequently, political and economic man may be understood within the same logic of choice. What distinguishes public from private choice is not, then, the nature of individual decision-making itself, but rather the structure within which it occurs and the objects toward which it is directed (Mitchell 1971). Fundamental to public choice analysis is the notion, drawn from economic theory, of exchange (Curry and Wade 1968). Political actors are held to enter into exchanges with other political actors for reasons of mutual advantage: politicians make exchanges with voters (Downs 1957); interest group leaders with members and potential members (Olson 1965); interest groups with interest groups (Riker 1962); bureaucrats with clients (Niskanen 1971); and so forth. The modalities, terms, and content of these exchanges must be discovered empirically. In most formulations it is presumed that political action will be entered into by individuals (if at all) until the marginal costs of so doing equal the marginal benefits derived from so doing. Individuals who do not enter the political arena bear costs and receive benefits ("externalities") from decisions taken by others. The incidence of externalities must also be discovered empirically. Public policy arises from the exchanges entered into by individuals. The extent to which these exchanges can in principle be efficient is a matter of continuing discussion, although it is clear that even the most democratic polity must impose restrictions on citizen/voter/taxpayer sovereignty which an idealized private-choice system need not (Musgrave 1959; Baumol 1965).

The costs which the polity does or may impose on its members in one

Section I and part of Section V of this chapter were published earlier in "Economics Applied to Policy Studies," *Policy Studies Journal* 2 (Autumn 1973): 15-19.

form or another (e.g., costs of negotiating agreement; external costs imposed on those not privy to a binding decision; costs imposed upon those who, because of the decision rule in effect, are on the losing side) should be considered in evaluating the manner, public or private, in which an activity should be organized. The manner in which such costs may be minimized at the constitutional level is developed in Buchanan and Tullock's seminal work (1962). The structures within which public choices are made are unique socially in that their outcomes are authoritative for whole societies. Consequently, an individual who participates in making public choices is in a radically different position than he is when making private choices; in the former case he chooses for everyone else, while in the latter he chooses only for himself. His normative and strategic problems are correspondingly different under these alternative situations. The normative problem is compounded when he understands that his choice, if determinate, will be binding upon others and, hence, involves the "public interest." His strategic problem is compounded by the inducements to other political actors to conceal their preferences (in the hope that others will incur the costs of creating goods and services available to all) and the primitive (therefore ambiguous) quality of the terms of trade arrived at with others.

Public choice occurs, then, under conditions of greater uncertainty than does choice in most other circumstances. This fact presents the public policy analyst with positive and normative problems as well. The analyst's normative problem is in part one of prescribing remedies for a society whose individual members may well refuse for reasons of strategic bargaining to reveal their true wants. (The Wicksellian criterion, which requires unanimity upon the allocation of both costs and benefits on any matter, solves this problem conceptually but not practically.) The positive problem is that predictive theories of public policy are apt to be unreliable to the extent that they are based upon the uncertainty inherent (if only for reasons of strategic bargaining) in the public process. In the face of such obstacles, perhaps the first lesson to be learned from applying the radical individualism of economics to policy studies is to remain both humble and non-dogmatic.

Structurally, public choice in democratic society differs from private choice in two significant ways: (1) it is authoritative for a community, and (2) it requires that the diverse preferences of contending individuals be reconciled, or aggregated, into a single choice which we come to recognize as public policy. The rules by which this reconciliation takes place are, because of their importance in shaping outcomes, among the central foci of public choice analysis (Niskanen 1971). In its targets, public choice differs from private choice in several ways: (1) it involves goods and services that must be provided collectively or not at all or in reduced degree; (2) it involves efforts to stabilize the entire system at some level of performance, efforts that cannot be given effective meaning through private-choice behavior. The structural uniqueness of the polity is familiar to political scientists while the matter of policy targets as classified by political economists is less so. Although it is not a necessary element of the public choice approach, writers in the field have tended normatively to place a high value on policy adjustments which injure no one (and will be adopted unanimously) and which maximize private or voluntary action as against coercive public action when the costs of public action are equal to, or greater than, the costs of private or voluntary action. It has been charged that such policy orientations contain contradictions: ". . . a policy to eliminate a restriction on the free market will meet the second criterion, but will not meet the first if the elimination entails some groups foregoing some special privileges" (Goldberg 1973). It is not clear that such criticisms are particularly telling, however, inasmuch as few if any public choice theorists are prepared to defend special privilege. On the contrary, their orientation leads them to search for inequities and inefficiencies produced by the structure of choice in both public and private sectors. For example, once an activity is to be organized and managed publicly, public choice theory suggests that the activity be structured in a decentralized manner, either by establishing competing agencies at the same level of government as Niskanen (1971) has suggested and/or by political jurisdiction as Bish (1971) has proposed. Monopoly in both sectors is regarded as inefficient.

The public treatment of problems often becomes "reasonable" when, either because of the nature of things or conceptual primitiveness, property rights bearing on a problem are ambiguous or lacking altogether. Land held in common may be subjected to overuse as each individual exploits his neighbors by using land which could have been used by them. If voluntary compromise is not possible, a reconciliation can occur only if individual property rights become defined precisely or if the government intervenes to coerce a behavioral adjustment of some sort. This kind of problem is familar to some aspects of the contemporary environmental debates with one exception: in many instances involving rights to clean air, aesthetically-pleasing surroundings or large bodies of water it may be difficult, impossible or undesirable to assign individual property rights. Government action is often indicated in such cases if the negative externalities associated with the overuse of the public domain are to be internalized.

Government action is also often, but not always, indicated in connection with public goods, or goods which, if provided, are simultaneously available to everyone. Because. of their characteristics (the impracticality/impossibility of rationing them selectively) such goods typically must be provided by government or not at all. In some peculiar cases private action may create and distribute such goods, which serves to remind one that the public character of a good is not by itself sufficient justification for its provision by government. By the same token, public goods need not be produced at all in the absence of a felt need: expenditures on national defense would be absurd if no external enemies existed.

Public choice analysis is useful, then, in enhancing understanding in matters involving the political process, rule-making, political organization, and the identification of goods concerning which public action may be indicated. Since public choice analysis seeks to locate the structures of incentives and constraints which condition individual choice, it can also be used to investigate and improve the administration of virtually any public policy.

Collective Choice Norms

However, public choice analysis cannot always or even often be helpful in identifying the *precise* content of desirable public policy, if only because what is "desirable" is not a matter to be settled analytically from the "outside" but, more appropriately, from the "inside" on the basis of the preferences of individual members of the polity. (Of course, the same logic leads to an inevitable suspicion of approaches to policy analysis which may be less hesitant in this regard.) If the "right" policies are impossible to specify, it is nonetheless possible to state certain criteria which, ideally, the policy process "should" not violate to the extent that such violations inhibit mutually advantageous exchanges (Curry and Wade 1968). What public choice analysis can do is identify the rules and institutions which are apt to facilitate policy choices which are related authentically and, in a manner acceptable to individualistic democratic theory, to the structure of individual preferences in the community. It is well known that such rules and institutions cannot always be devised. Voting even under optimal democratic conditions may yield paradoxical or "inauthentic" outcomes (Arrow 1951; Zeckhauser 1973). Vote trading, which can occur most effectively in reasonably small parliamentary bodies, has been recommended as a procedure for giving due weight to intensity of preferences (Tullock 1970) and for eliminating voting paradoxes (Coleman 1966). Others, however, while conceding that decisions may be "improved" through vote trading, have suggested that voting paradoxes are not necessarily eliminated as a consequence (Mueller 1967). Riker and Broms (1973) have sought to show that, while the positions of the active participants may indeed be improved through vote-trading, the welfare of inactive but impacted citizens may suffer. Moreover, when it is recognized that a seemingly obvious rule of democratic practice—such as simple majority rule, or $N/2+1$—has no particular validity apart from the preferences of individuals and the issue being decided, the analyst is faced with the intractable problem of asserting which rule is appropriate to which circumstance. Such determinations are possible only at the stage of constitution-building, since, in any existential case, the rules in effect are in effect. Considerations such as these alert the policy analyst both to the limitations and opportunities which adjustments in the policy process may have for human welfare. It is clear that no fully satisfactory collective-choice system can be devised, although improved systems are altogether possible.

Non-heroic or practical systems, based on the presumption that the democratic policy analyst is under no obligation to prove that the world is other than it is, have been presented by, for example, Braybrooke (1968), who poses such rules for collective choice as simple and representative majority rule, the availability of serious and genuine choices, and the reassortment of minorities and majorities across issues so as to prevent the development of either chronic majorities or minorities. Somehow, and however imperfectly or indirectly, citizen preferences must rule on public policy. Public choice analysis seeks to make the connection between preferences and policies as efficient as possible by the establishment or advocacy of appropriate rules for achieving such a connection.

To this end also, it is consistent to offer strategic and tactical advice to citizens who may be interested in enhancing their influence as policymakers and improving their welfare as policy-takers. Citizens might be encouraged, depending upon their objectives, to ascertain the likely costs as well as benefits associated with any proposal; consciously to separate, relate, and rank their goals in at least an ordinal fashion; to examine their existing and potential resources and the manner in which resources might be distributed most advantageously in pursuit of their goals. Such calculations must necessarily be grounded in a social theory because one's own tactics will provoke others into supportive or opposi-tional activity and the efficacious activist must make judgments as to how the opposition might be reduced or neutralized and support, if not max-imized, built to whatever point is necessary to "win." This prescriptive rule is consistent with Riker's analytic/empirical proposition that minimum winning coalitions are all that rational actors, if informed, will pursue (Riker 1962). Corollary advice to both reformers and radicals, has been advanced by Mitchell and Mitchell (1969: 483-674). Reformers will be more successful if the problems they seek to remedy are presented as solvable as well as urgent and if they reassure the apprehensive, seek reciprocal benefits and appear sincere in their motives. Radicals are encouraged to dramatize injustice, identify with the highest values of the culture, keep up the pressure and embarrass and isolate the opposition. The uses of these tactics are available for exploitation by conservatives, of course.

Inasmuch as voting for a person or party produces a bundle of policies, or what Breton (1974) calls a "full-line supply," a more specialized and differentiated strategy which demands particular decisions from particular decisionmakers may yield "better" results than complete reliance on the full-line suppliers. Specialization is often the key to success in a refracted polity and with respect to highly technical and complex policy issues.

Individual political efficacy is also related to the manner in which activity is organized in the polity. "Community control" is a slogan of both mystical communitarians and those who argue, as does Dahl (1970), that a policy matter should be discharged democratically "by the smallest association that can deal with it satisfactorily" because individual preferences can be more influential in smaller jurisdictions. The question has been raised (Price 1974) as to whether this suggestion is consistent with Dahl's earlier (1956) argument on behalf of "minorities rule" which stressed the problems associated with the fact that intensities are not reconciled with a majority's selection of a full-line of policies through periodic elections. The much-needed theoretical task of reconciling the gains to be had from minorities' rule with those to be had from creating more majorities through decentralization has not yet been undertaken.

The interplay of "democratic" decision-rules and the choices of citizens with all of their preferences and given resources result in public policy. Whether policy so derived will bear any resemblance to what might be advised abstractly in terms of the logic of public choice is not entirely clear. In one sense the logic holds no answers to such questions as "what public goods shall be produced, financed or distributed by government and to what degree?" "To what extent should income and wealth be redistributed?" "How should taxes be apportioned?" "How should the costs of economic regulation be allocated?" In the first place, we do not know what answers will be given to these questions in the future, although we know rather precisely what answers have been given in the past. *Some* past answers seem altogether consistent with rational-choice analysis. For example, the task of redistribution has been, by common agreement, assigned largely to the federal government because of the worldly recognition that decentralization of redistribution would allow many citizens to avoid contributions to such noble initiatives by moving to the next jurisdiction. Many public goods—national security, a common currency, civil rights and civil liberties—are lodged in the central authority for compelling reasons as well. On the other hand, public activity gets organized by jurisdictions and institutions as often as not for historical reasons that have lost their logical but not political force. Whether medical education should continue to be a state function—thereby permitting California to benefit from the spill-in of physicians educated at the expense of Indiana taxpayers—is not altogether clear except, perhaps, to those whose career and other interests are served by the existing system. The coordination of fiscal policy is made similarly difficult by the federal system which not only permits but often encourages state legislatures to pursue policies at odds with national stabilization policies. As previously limited-range decisions ripple-out to effect, often negatively, larger numbers of people, the old jurisdictions lose their viability if only because those affected will demand accommodation. A reduction in interest rates in Washington designed to stimulate production may exacerbate inflation in Europe. An oil cartel may form, administer prices, and bring a halt to a decade of international economic growth.

In some cases, such externalities can be democratically and cooperatively managed by adjustments in the old jurisdictions or the creation of new ones. In other cases, internalization is impossible and the attendant costs either borne with a certain stoicism or, not infrequently in human history, disputed with armed force. If, then, public choice analysis cannot guarantee a peaceful resolution of policy disputes, can it at least be helpful in answering the broad question, what policies, at least economic policies, should be undertaken by government? Here the answer is a qualified "yes."

Although we have no way of comparing very precisely the social benefits of various public goods, say of education relative to health relative to security, or of comparing the social welfare produced by resources allocated either publicly or privately, merely *thinking* about the comparisons may improve the quality of public choices. Ideally, of course, marginal returns between private and public uses should be equal, just as marginal returns from all public uses should be equal. Certain analytic aids may assist in these adjustments (various rational/comprehensive decision schemes seek to do just that) as may improvements in the political process (efforts to make the process more open, competitive, and de-centralized have more efficient decision-making as a central objective). Nonetheless, the use of marginal analysis in public sector decision-making, however intellectually attractive, will unavoidably confront dilemmas, paradoxes, and ironies at many points. Avoiding efforts to apply the marginal principle, however, may entail even more damaging consequences.

Public Goods and Services

Certain economic principles can serve as reasonable guides to public policy. Most obviously, meritorious public goods and services ought at least be distributed by government. The determination of merit, of course, is one to be made, ideally, through a political process that, to whatever extent is possible/feasible, meets such tests of democracy as discussed above. Merit, in other words, should be established by the active consent of the governed. When the production and distribution of such goods entail a high social risk, the argument for governmental production and financing as well as distribution is strong if, again, the consent of the governed has been secured. If the private provision of goods and services generates real or potential widespread positive externalities, there is an argument for public subsidy to the private provider or for governmental production and distribution of the benefits in question. Negative externalities generated by private decisions should be internalized and such costs minimized either through tax incentives (or in effect, "tax expenditures"), governmental regulations (requiring costs to support the surveillance machinery *and* higher prices) or governmental production of the goods in question (requiring higher taxes). In the case of natural monopolies, either governmental control over price and output should be maintained or the good involved should be produced and distributed by government directly. The technical justification for these and similar policy decisions cannot be made here but is widely available in the standard economics literature.

Redistribution

Standards governing redistribution objectives are far more difficult to develop. Criteria governing public goods decisions are, while normatively-based, apt to be found broadly, if often abstractly, convincing by general opinion. In the case of redistributive criteria such congenial outcomes are, to say the least, problematical.

One may begin, in this regard, by noting the "social dilemma" involved (Tullock 1974). It is in everyone's interest to secure a redistribution in one's own favor. The social outcome may produce either more or less inequality or, if transfers are made within income groups, none at all. The dilemma arises when it is recognized that all interests will rationally invest resources in the struggle for redistribution but that the *net* consequence, regardless of the outcome, is a social loss. Beyond recognizing the problem, Tullock indicates that there seems to be no way of avoiding these losses. Dramatic examples of such costs are those incurred in war, national defense, robbery or, more prosaically, conventional pressure politics such as lobbying. The institutions created to minimize these costs are themselves costly. Public financing of political campaigns shifts but does not eliminate the costs of campaigns. Police agencies may reduce certain illegal transfers but are themselves expensive to maintain. As long as individuals, groups, classes, and nations are intent on redistributing resources, the costs of getting and defending them will be considerable on all sides. Of course, a social loss may create opportunities for individuals: an amusing illustration of these possibilities occurred recently in California.

One of the lawyers, Daniel Lowenstein, who *wrote* the 20,000 word initiative proposal adopted by the voters as law in June 1974 establishing the Fair Political Practices Commission for purposes of regulating lobbying activity, campaign finance and conflicts of interest, was appointed the first chairman of the Commission. Lowenstein's salary as chairman of $39,072 was bolstered, under the terms of the initiative legislation, by a guaranteed four-year term and an annual Commission budget of $1 million plus cost-of-living adjustments. Governor Brown's justification was that the legislation was so complex that only the authors could understand and hence administer it!

Of course, certain moral communities will find certain redistributive criteria convincing (Mitchell 1971: 330-334). A transfer that advantages the affluent at the expense of the poor is apt to be unattractive both to the poor and to some other "concerned" citizens as well. (One may put aside the observation that many affluent citizens who are sympathetic to the poor apparently believe that someone still more affluent than themselves should bear the cost of redistribution.) A transfer to populations injured by an act of God, profound social change over which they have no control, an historic pattern of state legitimized discrimination, traumatic illness, a decline in income accompanying old age, may all justify the granting of transfers. So may many more unfortunate circumstances. As incomes are restored or problems solved, subsidies should normally be ended or reduced, if only because, by definition, not all segments of society can be subsidized. Subsidies for various organizational undertakings—mass transit, the merchant fleet, railroads, agriculture—may or may not be legitimate but, in all cases, as Mitchell notes, the "burden of proving" their legitimacy "should rest upon the advocate." Domestic transfer payments by the federal government totaled some $120.7 billion in 1975. Of that, for example, retirement and disability payments (including black lung and supplemental security income benefits) amounted to $83 billion; hospital and supplementary medical insurance, $13.3 billion; food stamps, $3.8 billion; veterans benefits and insurance, $10.3 billion; unemployment benefits, $6.5 billion (and rising). So-called tax loopholes are popular forms of subsidy as well. For example, deductions from federal taxes of interest and property taxes on owner-occupied homes exceeded $5.1 billion in 1972, which compares with the $1.5 billion appropriated for low-rent public housing loan insurance and debt service payments. In the same year, a $.6 billion subsidy in tax exemptions for students (some of whom may not have been among the deserving poor) was allocated, as was $5.6 billion for individual capital gains tax; $.4 billion for corporation capital gains tax credit; $1.1 billion in tax exclusions of interest on life insurance; $3.2 for tax deductibility of charitable contributions; $2.6 for tax exemptions on state and local bonds; and $3.7 billion for tax exclusions of pension contributions for employees. Other sorts of subsidies were granted that year, including $2.7 billion for agriculture; $1 billion for urban renewal and neighborhood development; and $1.8 billion to the U.S. Postal Service. The reader will have his or her own preferences concerning these subsidies, but a cursory glance will reveal that not all subsidies reach the more disadvantaged sectors of society. In truth, all should not be expected to if other socially ratified objectives are served by them, such as gratitude to returning veterans, private philanthropy, home-ownership, or economic growth. Objectives such as these are contentiously debated in democratic society and cannot be resolved by any policy scheme purporting to show that one objective is superior to another. Policy analysis can, however, clarify the terms of debate: it may be possible to show for example, that a long-term growth strategy will yield more equity, and at a higher level, than a short-term welfare strategy (Kuznets 1973).

For every benefit—public good or transfer—that the polity distributes, an equivalent cost must be imposed. The coincidence between costs and benefits organized by the political process is often, and sometimes appropriately, remote. The level and incidence of costs, which largely but not exclusively take the form of taxes, are established politically, of course, although there are normative justifications for one pattern of distribution rather than another. Two main principles, which often clash in specific decision situations, are (1) the benefit principle (those who receive benefits should pay for them), and (2) the "ability to pay" or equity principle. An economic argument for ability to pay or progressive taxation does exist (individuals should be taxed to whatever extent is possible as long as their propensity to work and produce is not diminished). The normative basis of the principle is derived from tenuous empirical grounds (the presumed diminishing marginal utility of income) but a solid and altogether sensible political strategy.

The cost-effectiveness of alternative taxing authorities is itself dependent to an important extent on the type of taxation that must be administered. A tax which satisfies normative objectives but which cannot be collected or collected only at relatively great cost (to both the authority and the taxpayer) has little to commend it beyond its moral elegance. Hidden taxation (e.g., inflation, receipts from the public domain) inhibit assessment of one's true tax burden and hence the quality of one's political decisions (Buchanan 1960). Self-deception may result in welfare losses if individuals become convinced, erroneously, that certain taxes, (e.g., corporation taxes) are progressive when in fact they are not. The manner in which corporation taxes are shifted backward to employees or stockholders or forward to consumers is almost impossible to determine (Zrzyzaniak and Musgrave 1963). When tax incidence is unknown, there is a good reason for employing some other tax.

Rules and Behavior

An empirical literature is emerging which seeks to establish the relationship between formal rules governing the political process and political behavior. This is an important and much needed reaction to the reductionism which characterized some behavioral research during the 1960s. Increased sensitivity to the fact that different behavior and policies will often accompany changes in the rules is conveyed in a number of recent studies.

Crime control, for example, is one substantive area in which public choice analysis is being fruitfully applied. Tullock's treatment (1971) of the subject presumes that individuals make self-interested cost/benefit calculations when considering any potential violation of the law and that the law is or is not broken depending on what the optimal course turns out to be. Among other possibilities for controlling crime is the inculcation of ethical systems, which make it psychologically painful to commit a crime, increase the cost of crime, and reduce its incidence. Banfield (1968: 160), too, has an important place for morality in maintaining the peace but, in an explicit adoption of the rationalistic approach, deems narrow calculation of advantage to be more important: "The juvenile who steals 'to punish his father' almost always steals something he wants and almost always takes some account of his being caught." Space permits mentioning only two corollaries of this view: (1) punishment for criminal acts should take into account the costs in pain and suffering to the convicted criminal and should not be set to deter whatever level of crime is deemed by democratic process to be socially "tolerable." (2) Normally, anti-crime policy should aim at making the probable costs of crime exceed its probable benefits. However, even when probable benefits outweigh probable costs, crime will not be entered into if an *even more profitable* legal opportunity exists. Anti-crime policy might well go beyond creation of a strengthened deterrence system and the inculcation of ethical norms to improvements in society's legal opportunity structure.

Rohde and Shepsle's study (1973) of the strategic choices of members of the House of Representatives in seeking committee assignments, the rules which govern their success (those with seniority and from highly competitive districts outside the South have been more successful) and the consequences (still conjectural) of these choices and rules for policy is another case in point. Another effort (Browne and Franklin 1973) analyzes the payoffs that occur in the governing coalitions of European parliaments and reasons backward from payoffs to the discovery of rules; viz., with certain qualifications, payoffs are received in proportion to a group's contribution of resources to the coalition. A particularly clever study of presidential campaigns shows that the winner take all rule of the Electoral College (the popular vote winner in a state gets all the state's electoral votes) ". . .

induces candidates to allocate campaign resources roughly in proportion to the 3/2's power of the electoral votes of each state'' (Brams and Davis 1974: 113). The authors show (1) rational candidates should, to get elected, allocate their resources according to the 3/2's rule and (2) that they in fact do so. This is remarkable, because the 3/2's rule is non-obvious and does *not* refer simply to the electoral votes of each state but to their proportions and consequent campaign strategy, e.g., ''if one state has 4 electoral votes, and another has 16 electoral votes, even though they differ in size only by a factor of four, the candidates should allocate eight times as much in resources to the larger state . . .'' (Brams and Davis 1974: 121-22). Saalfeld's study (1972) of voting and educational finance is another impressive empirical effort at policy-relevant theory-building based on the public choice orientation.

References

Arrow, Kenneth. *Social Choice and Individual Values*. New York: Wiley, 1951.

Baumol, William J. *Welfare Economics and The Theory of The State*. Rev. ed. Cambridge: Harvard University Press, 1965.

Bish, Robert L. *The Political Economy of Metropolitan Areas*. Chicago: Markham, 1971.

Brams, Steven J. and Morton D. Davis. ''The 3/2's Rule in Presidential Campaigning,'' *APSR* 68 (March 1974): 113-134.

Braybrooke, David. *Three Tests for Democracy: Personal Rights, Human Welfare, Collective Preference*. New York: Random House, 1968.

Breton, Albert. *The Economic Theory of Representative Government*. Chicago: Aldine, 1974.

Browne, Eric C. and Mark N. Franklin. ''Aspects of Coalition Payoffs in European Parliamentary Democracies.'' *APSR* 67 (June 1973): 453-469.

Buchanan, James M. *The Public Finances*. Homewood, Ill.: Irwin, 1960.

Buchanan, James M. and Gordon Tullock. *The Calculus of Consent*. Ann Arbor: University of Michigan Press, 1962.

Coleman, James. ''The Possibility of a Social Welfare Function.'' *American Economic Review* 56 (December 1966): 1105-1122.

Curry, R. L. and L. L. Wade. *A Theory of Political Exchange*. Englewood Cliffs, N.J.: Prentice-Hall, 1968.

Dahl, Robert A. *After the Revolution? Authority in a Good Society*. New Haven: Yale University Press, 1970.

Dahl, Robert A. *Preface to Democratic Theory*. Chicago: University of Chicago Press, 1956.

Downs, Anthony. *An Economic Theory of Democracy*. New York: Harper and Row, 1957.

Goldberg, Victor P. "The Peculiar Normative Economics of The Public Choice—Property Rights Nexus." Research Report No. 25, Institute of Governmental Affairs, University of California, Davis, June 1973.

Kuznets, Simon. *Population, Capital and Growth*. New York: Norton, 1973.

Mitchell, Joyce M. and William C. Mitchell. *Political Analysis and Public Policy*. Chicago: Rand McNally, 1969.

Mitchell, William C. *Public Choice in America*. Chicago: Markham, 1971.

Mueller, Dennis E. "The Possibility of a Social Welfare Function Comment." *AER* 57 (December 1967): 1304-1311.

Musgrave, Richard A. *The Theory of Public Finance*. New York: McGraw-Hill, 1959.

Niskanen, William A. *Bureaucracy and Representative Government*. Chicago: Aldine, 1971.

Olson, Mancur. *The Logic of Collective Action*. Cambridge: Harvard University Press, 1965.

Price, David E. "Community and Control: Critical Democratic Theory in The Progressive Period." *APSR* 68 (December 1974): 1663-1678.

Riker, William H. and Steven J. Brams. "The Paradox of Vote Trading." *APSR* 67 (December 1973): 1235-1247.

Riker, William. *The Theory of Political Coalitions*. New Haven: Yale University Press, 1962.

Rohde, David W. and Kenneth A. Shepsle. "Democratic Committee Assignments in the House of Representatives: Strategic Aspects of a Social Choice Process." *APSR* 67 (September 1973): 889-905.

Saalfeld, Bernard F. "Taxpayers and Voters: Collective Choice in Public Education." Ph.D. dissertation, University of Oregon, 1972.

Tullock, Gordon. "A Simple Algebraic Logrolling Model." *AER* 60 (June 1970): 419-26.

Tullock, Gordon. *The Logic of The Law*. New York: Basic Books, 1971.

Tullock, Gordon. *The Social Dilemma: The Economics of War and Revolution*. Blacksburg, Va.: University Publications, 1974.

Wade, L. L. and R. L. Curry. *A Logic of Public Policy*. Wadsworth, 1970.

Zeckhauser, Richard. "Voting Systems, Honest Preferences and Pareto Optimality." *APSR* 67 (September 1973): 934-946.

Zrzyzaniak, M. and Richard A. Musgrave. *The Shifting of The Corporation Income Tax*. Baltimore: Johns Hopkins University Press, 1963.

9

The Limits of Rational Choice in Evaluating Criminal Justice Policy

James Levine,
Michael Musheno, and
Dennis Palumbo

Introduction

Rational choice theory is being used increasingly as a means of understanding and prescribing public policy. But it has very severe limitations. Some of these limitations have been pointed out by organizational theorists such as Herbert Simon, James March, Richard Cyert, and Charles Lindblom. Economists, nevertheless, insist that rational choice theory is superior to other social science theories. Curry and Wade, for example, write: "The economy, lucidity, and force of economic reasoning should make possible an equally adequate (as compared to systems theory) and, we suspect, superior understanding of the same (public policy) issues" (Curry and Wade 1968: 116). Robert Bish agrees: "I do feel that the deductive approach (of economics) has one advantage that has contributed greatly to the higher level of sophistication and prediction achieved by economics as a social science. It is the opportunity for continuity in method that enables new scholars to take up where their seniors have left off" (Bish 1971: 13).

But even these economists admit that the formal model of rationality has glaring weaknesses when it is applied to public policy. Attempts have been made to correct some of these difficulties. We shall consider the more important revisions and show that they have not always been successful. Our purpose is to explore the limits of rational choice by demonstrating some of the problems it fails to resolve when applied to criminal justice policy.

Classical Rational Choice

Even though rational choice theory is used extensively, the definition of rationality is very unclear. Some scholars believe it means achievement of

To the extent to which it is ever possible, this chapter is a joint product of the three of us. We have listed our names alphabetically to emphasize this. We would like to acknowledge the financial support of the "Study of Alternatives to Conventional Adjudication" done under the auspices of the Institute for Studies in Justice and Social Behavior of the American University Washington College of Law. The latter project was supported by Grant Nos. 73-NI-99-0023-G and 75-NI-99-0050 by the L.E.A.A., U.S. Department of Justice, under the Omnibus Crime Control and Safe Streets Act of 1968, as amended.

goals (Dahl and Lindbloom 1953), some associate it with individuals maximizing satisfaction (Bish 1971), other conceive of it as a decision-making
process without regard to how successful a person is in achieving goals
(Downs 1957), and still others consider rationality to be broadly synony-
mous with intelligent and purposeful behavior (Mitchell and Mitchell 1969).
Then there are the distinctions between classical rationality and intended
rationality (Simon 1945), between individual and social rationality (Arrow
1951, 1974), and between rationality and consistency (Lindblom 1965,
1968). In spite of this ambiguity, there is broad agreement on major aspects
of the formal model of rational choice. It is this formal model that is the
subject of this paper.

Charles Lindbloom describes the classical model of rational choice as
follows: A rational person is one who (1) clarifies his goals, values, or
objectives, and then ranks or otherwise organizes them in his mind. (2) He
then lists all important possible ways of achieving his goals. (3) He investi-
gates all the important consequences that would follow from each of the
alternative policies. (4) Then, the person is in a position to compare consequences of each policy with goals. (5) Finally, he chooses the policy with
consequences most closely matching his goals.

This describes rational choice at the micro-level where the individual is
the unit of analysis and his motive is to advance his own self-interest. When
the theory is applied at the macro-level, the level of organizational behavior, two additional axioms are needed. These are: (6) The organization
has a single goal it is trying to maximize, and (7) Members of the organization are to be treated as a team who all agree on the desirability of the single
goal (Downs 1957).

Criticisms of Rational Choice

Criticisms of this model of rational choice have taken many forms. We will
focus only upon the following. Criticisms of the assumptions that
(1) individuals can measure their satisfactions; (2) it is possible to maximize; (3) organizations have single goals; and (4) there is complete agreement among members of organizations about goals.

Before turning to these criticisms we must say a word about whether the
assumptions of a theory must be empirically accurate. Theories can be
useful even if their underlying assumptions are not empirically accurate,
since assumptions are conceptual simplifications which enable us to organize out thinking about reality. The only requirement for good theory is
that its assumptions and theorems enable us to make hypotheses about the
empirical world that are predictively accurate and prescriptively useful.
But these hypotheses will not be accurate or useful if estimates of the
parameters in the hypotheses are widely at variance with empirical reality.

A good example is plea bargaining (Nagel and Neef, 1975). We can set up a rational choice model in which the objective of the district attorney is to reach an optimum solution. The mathematical solution arrived at by axiomatic reasoning can be applied in the real world only if the probability estimates the analyst uses are empirically accurate. If these are wrong, the solution we impute is not likely to be very accurate, and thus, it will not be optimum in the sense that it maximizes goals. Thus, when Nagel and Neef (1974) prescribe rules for determining advisable bail procedures, whether these can be successfully implemented hinges upon the empirical accuracy of the values put in the payoff matrix. Nevertheless, purely deductive analysis may be useful when it clarifies relationships and helps us understand what may occur under various hypothetical circumstances. Our critique of rational choice is directed at the question of how empirically useful these deductions are.

The most frequent criticism of rational choice theory is that it is not possible to quantify goals, particularly in public policy. Individuals, it is contended, are unable to add and subtract units of satisfaction as if they were so many pounds of soap since they are only vaguely aware of their wants and needs. But this attack rests on a misunderstanding since rational choice theory does not require that individuals be able to quantify their desires or that they should always be certain of the likely outcomes of their choices. It is perfectly possible to be rational even if the most we can do is rank preferences and measure, subjectively, the probabilities of various consequences.

The criticism that individuals cannot quantify their satisfaction has been adequately answered by the development of indifference analysis. Indifference analysis does not assume that utility can be measured or that maximizing implies achieving the largest sum total of satisfaction. Rather, maximizing merely involves reaching a more preferred position (Curry and Wade 1968: 9); it is argued that individuals can differentiate between the combinations that yield the same satisfactions to them (and towards which he is indifferent) and those that yield greater or lesser satisfaction, and it is unnecessary that they be able to measure this exact difference. The rational individual maximizes when he reaches his more preferred position, and he does not have to find an "objectively" optimum position.

Indifference analysis is somewhat like the satisficing principle in organization theory. The satisficing principle says that organizations cannot search for all possible alternatives or even for all the important ones, because they have limited information processing capabilities. They search only until they find a satisfactory alternative that is somewhat better than present needs, and then stop. Such behavior is rational because it follows rational procedures, even though only a limited kind of rationality is involved.

But there are other limitations which cast doubt on the possibility of even limited rationality. The major one is that rational choice theory focuses only upon means and not ends. There is little in rational choice theory that tells us what criteria to use when we have to select one of several different and competing goals and where trade-offs among goals are necessary. Rational choice tells us how to act efficiently, not how to select goals. In classical rational choice, goals are given. In response to the question: "What goals should we prefer in criminal justice?" rational choice theory simply directs us to consult our values or ideology without giving us any guidelines.

Rational choice theorists have not yet coped with this last criticism. In fact, one of the most significant theoretical discoveries of the past half-century is that social rationality may not be possible since it may ultimately hinge upon power considerations rather than rational choice. One form of this argument is the Arrow paradox which states that social rationality cannot be achieved by aggregating individual choices through democratic rules (Arrow 1951; Luce and Raiffa 1957). Arrow concludes that because aggregating individual preferences always poses the possibility of producing socially irrational choices, ". . . there cannot be a completely consistent meaning to collective rationality" (Arrow 1972, p. 25).

Of course, the Arrow paradox refers only to decision systems where social choice is made by democratic means. It is possible to achieve social rationality, if we mean by this clear, transitive, and consistent policy choices, by different decision rules. For example, social rationality may be achieved through synoptic systems in which coordination is attained through central management. Or social rationality may be attained through a single dominant purpose (Lindblom 1965, 1968). There is a problem however, with these solutions: both are non-democratic. A democratic society cannot accept central control, nor can it base all decisions on a single, overriding principle. What, then, are the prospects for rational choice in a democratic society? Is it *never* achievable? Our position is that there are times when rationality is not possible but there are times when it is. We will use the classical analytic game called "Prisoner's Dilemma" to illustrate the case where rationality is *not* possible.

In Prisoner's Dilemma, each prisoner, pursuing his own self-interest is forced into an undesirable position, a position that is harmful to all the prisoners as long as they act competitively. The illustration is as follows: Two individuals are taken into custody and separated. The district attorney is certain they committed the crime but does not have enough evidence to get a conviction. The D.A. tells each prisoner that if he does not confess, he will book them both on some trumped up charge which will get them a year each. If they both confess, they will be prosecuted but he will recommend leniency and get them five years each. Buf if one confesses and the other does not, the confessor will get off scot-free while the other will get ten

Prisoner 2

		b_1 does not confess	b_2 confesses
a_1	does not confess	1,1	10,0
a_2	confesses	0,10	5,5

(Prisoner 1 labels rows)

Figure 9-1. Prisoner's Dilemma

years. This is represented in figure 9-1, where a_1 and a_2 are the strategies of Prisoner 1; b_1 and b_2 are the strategies of Prisoner 2; the first entry in each cell represents the time Prisoner 1 receives; and the second entry represents the time Prisoner 2 receives. For example, if Prisoner 1 selects strategy a_1 (does not confess) and Prisoner 2 takes as his strategy b_2 (he confesses), Prisoner 1 gets ten years and Prisoner 2 gets off free.

What should each prisoner do? If they are rational, they will each confess because strategies a_2 and b_2 each dominate the other. This means that for Prisoner 1, a_2 is better than a_1 for each choice that Prisoner 2 can make: 0 is better than 1 year, and 5 is better than 10 years. The same is true for b_2. However, suppose the two prisoners agree to cooperate. They would prefer $a_1,$ b_1 because they each get a year. But this is not a stable solution because each has good reason to defect. If Prisoner 1 defects but Prisoner 2 does not, he gets off scot-free, and if he fails to, but Prisoner 2 does defect, he gets ten years. Thus each prisoner must defect, which produces a worse situation than if they cooperate. The dilemma consists of the fact that the rational solution is worse than the non-rational one.

There are many decisions where such socially non-rational outcomes result. For example, if all wheat farmers restrict their output, the price of wheat will be higher and they will all benefit. But each farmer will assume that his output cannot affect the total price level so he is better off with full production. But if each farmer follows the same reasoning, as they must, then full production occurs and they all fare badly (Luce and Raiffa 1957).

How often is such a socially undesirable situation likely to occur in criminal justice policy? If the answer is that it occurs frequently, then we must conclude that rationality is not a frequent possibility in criminal justice. Unfortunately, it seems that socially undesirable outcomes are frequent because cooperative action seldom is possible in the criminal justice system. The criminal justice system has a number of different actors and clientele, each of which has its own set of goals, and these often are in conflict. Maximizing one goal detracts from achievement of another. The problem in this situation is to find some accommodation or balance among these sub-units and goals. This is hard, however, because the authority structure in criminal justice is complex and fragmented. Rational choice is possible only in a limited number of cases under these circumstances.

A Theory of Limited Rational Choice

We assume that the principal purpose of various actors in the criminal justice system (i.e., police, courts, lawyer, correction institutions) is to achieve certain public interest goals such as reducing crime or achieving due process. But there are a number of factors that inhibit achievement of these goals. They prevent policymakers from identifying all relevant alternatives and from selecting and implementing the alternative that will maximize the public interest. The result is that an alternative may have an impact quite different from the one intended by its adoption. The reasons for this are the fragmented authority structure and the conflict of goals and interest in the system.

Fragmented Authority Structure

The creation and implementation of criminal justice policy alternatives rest with an authority structure consisting of at least three subdivisions: (1) the local criminal justice bureaucracy (the police, courts, and correctional agencies and personnel); (2) the local political-administrative structure that periodically influences criminal justice policies (e.g., local elected officials, locally based interest groups—local ACLU chapter, citywide administrators—city manager, press, universities); and (3) state and federal actors and institutions that regularly and periodically are affiliated with criminal justice policy-making and implementation (e.g., governors, crime commissions, appeals courts, state bar associations, LEAA). Thus, while most criminal justice policy alternatives are locally administrated, they are dependent on a wide range of actors and processes that must be viewed in an intergovernmental context.

Due to this complex and fragmented authority structure, the various actors in the criminal justice system operate in an environment of incomplete and uncoordinated information. For example, in many municipalities, the local courts keep their record of individuals processed on a calendar basis while police departments' files are maintained on a fiscal basis. Moreover, each of the major components of the local criminal justice bureaucracy makes policy decisions without consulting the other respective units. By this we mean that most of the time actors do not have to rely on other groups in order to maximize their own interests. Each group can usually define for itself what goals it wants to achieve and how it will try to go about doing this.

Judges, for example, pursue their goals in a manner that is determined largely by judges and lawyers rather than police or other members of the system. There are, of course, limits to the autonomy of each group. The police are not completely free to determine how they shall behave when they must make an arrest. They must modify their behavior as a result of pressure from other groups in the system (especially activist judges at the municipal level, and state courts of appeal). They will compromise at times, which is to say that they must behave in a manner they consider to be less than optimal. But, in general, most groups are independent of other groups in the system. As a result, cooperation and coordination aimed at achieving the public interest requires bargains, trade-offs, and compromises.

Additional fragmentation associated with the local criminal justice bureaucracy is caused by the discretionary power exercised by personnel within police, court, and correctional institutions. While much has been written on patrol officers' on-the-beat decision-making powers (Bittner 1967; H. Goldstein 1967; Skolnick 1967), a few studies have also traced the range of discretion exercised by assistant district attorneys in performing their daily tasks (Cole 1970; Eisenstein 1968). Thus, more than elite coordination and communication is required in the formulation and implementation of criminal justice policies. The behavior of "line" personnel must be supervised and constrained.

Many policy decisions are significantly influenced by actors outside the local political-administrative arena that have only limited contact with the municipal criminal justice bureaucracy. Policy alternatives to the criminal processing of whole categories of individuals (e.g., public inebriates, vagrants, drug addicts) have grown out of state and federal appeals court decisions (Kittrie 1971). Also, while the federal government has used its fiscal capacity to improve information flow and coordination in this policy area, grant-in-aid mechanisms have often stimulated "spillover effects" among agencies and municipalities (Emmer 1973).

Thus, the criminal justice authority structure, with its intergovernmental fragmentation and its semi-autonomous local decisionsmakers, greatly impedes the quality of information and the focus of control available to actors. Such an "uncertain" environment reduces the applicability of rational choice models to this policy area.

Conflicts of Goals and Interests

We said above that two of the major assumptions of the rational choice model of decision-making are that there is a single goal to be maximized by the organization, and all members of the organization agree about this goal. Performance of individuals, organization of work, definitions of responsibilities, use of incentives, and lines of authority all are assumed to be directed toward the end of promoting achievement of the single goal. This model, in its pure form, is not appropriate for the criminal justice system because there are multiple and sometimes competing goals in the system which require bargaining and compromises.

Indeed, a great deal of confusion in the evaluation of criminal justice policy has developed because of a failure to recognize that various programs being compared are often directed at achieving different goals. To determine which policies are better, it is necessary to sort out means and ends. In other words, there must be clarification of the specific purposes to be served by alternative courses of action before we can in any way figure out the most effective measures.

The famous dialogue between Alice and the Cheshire Cat in *Alice in Wonderland* makes the point well. Alice asks the Cat which way she ought to go, and the Cat says that depends on where she wants to get.

"I don't much care where—" said Alice. "Then it doesn't much matter which way you go," said the Cat (Carroll 1960: 88).

The point is that assessing which direction is wisest requires us to specify our destination—in both the fantasy world of children's literature as well as the field of public policy analysis.

Furthermore, we shall frequently come across situations where several clearly defined goals all seem meritorious but it is impossible to simultaneously optimize all of them. Under such conditions, choices of priorities must inevitably be made, and these decisions cannot be made rationally. The ranking of goals requires value judgments which are subjective in nature and which vary among individuals, groups, and societies. Subjective values depend upon emotional rather than rational factors. Packer has persuasively argued (1968), that the aims of crime control and due process may be incompatible: while the former emphasizes social interests the latter puts the individual accused of crime ahead of society's self-protection. Likewise, in the formulation of corrections policy, the goal of equal justice is surely irreconcilable with the achievement of humanization in the care of prisoners since the latter requires divergent methods of handling like offenders (who have different problems to be cured) while the former militates in favor of identical treatment. Rational choice cannot resolve which of these goals is best.

A persistent police quandary illustrates the fact that the means and ends are inseparable. Police departments are continuously questioning their method of deploying manpower: what is the best way to allocate a given number of police to the various kinds of units in the force? Is it better policy

Table 9-1
Estimated Relative Utility of Alternative Police Deployment Methods[a]

| | Goals | | | |
Methods	Prevent Street Crime	Improve Police-Community Relations	Reduce Public Fears of Crime	Control Commercialized Vice
Cruising squad cars	3	2	1	4
Foot patrolmen	4	1	2	3
Anti-crime units	1	3	4	2
Tactical forces	2	4	3	1

[a]The utilities are all estimated on the basis of a general knowledge of how the various units function; other rank-orderings of the contribution of different methods to the various goals could also be defended. The correctness of the rank ordering is not crucial to our point.

to put more men in cruising squad cars, on foot patrol, in anti-crime (decoy) units, or in tactical forces (large roving units which saturate particular trouble spots)?

The answer, as table 9-1 suggests, is complicated by the fact that multiple goals are at stake, and all of the above methods of using police have varying utility depending on how these goals are ordered. Different approaches are necessary to prevent street crime and control commercial vice. Each of the methods listed in table 9-1 is quite use*ful* in accomplishing one or two of the enumerated goals and virtually use*less* in achieving others. For example, foot patrolmen may well foster better relations between the police and the community by increasing personal communication and reducing anonymity; but because of their low mobility and minimal surveillance capabilities, they may have a negligible impact on deterring street crime. Therefore, before the correct means can be rationally selected, we must first decide which goals are to be preferred.

Indeed, we contend that the only legitimate way to arrive at these value-based decisions is through the political process where the preferences of various sectors of the public are articulated and aggregated in an essentially non-rational fashion. However, both logical dilemmas (Arrow 1951) and biases in the political system (Schattschneider 1960) make the problem of reaching a collective choice which satisfies all (or even a majority) quite formidable. There is absolutely no assurance that socially satisfactory outcomes can be obtained democratically. Nevertheless, inadequate as this approach appears, the only alternative seems to be unilateral imposition of ultimate values by some autocratic force—an arbitrary procedure which a democracy must find indefensible.

Does this model, then, preclude practitioners of rational analysis from playing a constructive role in deciding ultimate goals? The answer is, unequivocally, no; there is a great need for well-reasoned advocacy of overriding normative principles which should be considered along with political inputs. One example of such an exposition is that the highest consideration in criminal justice policy should be equalization of the burdens of crime (Levine, Musheno, and Palumbo 1975); another is that primacy should be given to protection of individual rights (Packer 1968); still others have proposed that judicial efficiency is of greatest importance (Botein 1972: 19-33). The policy process will be considerably improved if it is informed by a dialogue about the relative merits of various criteria for aggregating individual choices into public policy by participants who have no direct stake in these outcomes.

Of course, abstract principles cannot be put to the test of empirical validation, but they can be grounded (as all sound ethical principles should be) in a reasoned understanding of human needs, social imperatives, and system constraints (Russell 1952). And the ultimate measure of their acceptability in contributing to the making of public policy will no doubt be whether a significant part of the body politic finds such ethical statements compatible with and expressive of their own unarticulated and inchaote sense of public morality.

There are times when policy choices are even more complex. Frequently it may not be possible to evaluate objectively the possible impact of a given alternative even when there is consensus on the importance of the goal being sought. This may occur whenever the system faces an "uncertain" environment as opposed to the condition decision theorists call "risk." Uncertainty is defined as a situation where it is not possible to assign objective probabilities to the various levels of outcomes for a given alternative. This may be because there has not been enough previous experience with the alternative or because it cannot be repeated a number of times under controlled conditions.

The only solution in this case is to develop subjective measures of the probable outcomes for the alternative. The judgment of policemen, lawyers, and judges may be used as a way of developing a probability distribution for given outcomes in these cases. We will illustrate this problem with a simplified example based on alternatives to prosecution. Assume that the alternatives available to be evaluated include diversion programs based on employment and/or counseling, formal settlement procedures, informal diversion based on discretionary powers of prosecutors or judges, and traditional criminal prosecution. The important outcomes to be achieved contingent upon selection of each of these alternatives are percentages by which recidivism rates may be cut. If it were possible to assign objective probabilities to various levels of recidivism rates for each alternative, and if we could measure the costs associated with each alternative, then it would be possible to select the alternative that optimizes an expected outcome function. This is to say that it would be possible to make a rational choice about which alternative is to be preferred.

However, some of the alternatives mentioned above are new. We may not have sufficient past experience with them to assign objective probabilities to the effects each alternative may have on recidivism rates, nor can we determine what the probability distribution might look like. In this case, it is necessary to use the judgment of various people in the system to assign probabilities to the effects. We can use the subjective judgment of prosecutors, program directors, and judges about the probable impact of each alternative. But since we have no way of knowing how accurate these subjective estimates are, we have a case of decision-making under conditions of uncertainty. Even if we could try a few experiments with the alternatives, we still would not have sufficiently good data to compute objective probabilities. It therefore will not be possible to optimize. However, even though we cannot be objectively rational, we can be subjectively rational, and this may be sufficient for evaluating policy impact in this case.

Another complexity pertains to the assumption that organizational behavior is primarily concerned with goal achievement. Some theorists have begun to question whether it is fruitful to conceive of organizational choice as behavior directed at goals (Etzioni 1964; Simon 1964; Palumbo 1975). Individuals in organizations are not primarily concerned with achieving goals; they are concerned with maximizing their own self-interests. Their own self-interest may only be incidently related to the goals of the organization. It is entirely possible that manifest goals serve only a minor function in motivating people in organizations. For example, it is possible that deterrence, rehabilitation, and punishment are primarily symbolic goals that are used to garner political support for budgets, but are relatively unimportant if we want to understand what motivates individuals. University of California law professor Caleb Foote emphasizes this point: ''The alleged rehabilitation goal in a prison setting is to some extent a smoke screen to satisfy an ambivalent public which sometimes feels guilty at merely punishing, and is primarily a management device to make it easier to manipulate prisoners in ways that minimize administrative problems.''

Certainly there is nothing in the theory of rational choice that tells us why members of organizations should try to achieve organizational goals. It is rational for them to pursue their own interest, but their own self interest does not necessarily correspond with the public interest in the criminal justice system.

A Policy Impact Model

We will now describe a theoretical model that we believe is useful for analyzing criminal justice policy. The model assumes that alternatives in criminal justice will be supported by members of the criminal justice system only if the alternatives help these individuals achieve their own self-interest. We do not assume that the interests of various groups in the system such as police, judges, and prosecutors, are necessarily related to goals of the entire system (i.e., the public interest). It is only under very special circumstances that the personal goals of individuals, the goals of groups (e.g., police), and the goals of the entire criminal justice system will be congruent.

The framework of our policy analysis model is depicted in figure 9-2. The model portrays the authority structure as the independent variables (i.e., the variables that explain degrees of achievement of goals), self-interests of actors in the authority structure as the intervening variables (i.e., they modify or change the intentions of members of the authority structure), and the public interest goals as the dependent variables (i.e., the goals that are achieved in the criminal justice system).

Conceptually, the model may be characterized as a "limited rational choice model." Stated simply, this means that perfect rationality and efficiency is not always possible in selecting and evaluating a program in criminal justice. What can be accomplished is clarification of conflicting goals and analyses of how personal self-interest either facilitates or hinders goal achievement.

All public policy choices, including those in criminal justice, must be viewed in the context of the authority structure of a community. A community's authority structure determines what new programs and alternatives are possible. It does this not only by regulating information about new programs and by allowing some programs to be tried, but also by giving or withdrawing support from programs introduced by agencies outside the community (i.e., by the federal government).

No matter how worthwhile a program may seem on the surface, it has no chance of being adopted unless it is sufficiently attractive to the authority structure to compel acceptance. In other words, a new program has to be politically, administratively, and economically sound as well as aimed at desirable, public interest goals. We are not saying that opposition in the authority structure precludes the taking of new initiatives, only that it is a crucial variable in determining goal achievement.

It is one thing to say that achieving public interest goals is desirable, and quite another to get people to adopt behavior that will in fact do so. In organizational affairs, it is not sufficient to issue commands to be virtuous or to extol the values of public interest objectives. Individuals who are asked to work for these things have their own interests to worry about. Elected officials must win votes, administrators want to increase their budgets, workers want better working conditions and higher salaries, and

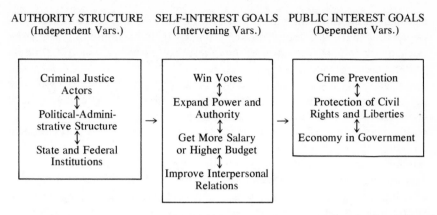

AUTHORITY STRUCTURE   SELF-INTEREST GOALS   PUBLIC INTEREST GOALS
(Independent Vars.)   (Intervening Vars.)   (Dependent Vars.)

Figure 9-2. A Model for Policy Analysis in Criminal Justice[a]

[a]Not all variables that could be listed or all that are discussed in this chapter are included in this model.

the community wants protection. It is frequently the case that in pursuing their own interests, people may have to put aside considerations of working for the general public interest. By this we mean that the self-interests of individuals and groups and those of the general public are not always coterminous.[a] We conclude, therefore, that even though an alternative or program in criminal justice is an effective and efficient way of achieving public interest goals, it is not likely to be implemented unless it also contributes to the attainment of the self-interests of those who are asked to implement it.

Political, administrative, and economic feasibility involves a number of complicated factors. We mentioned above the potential incompatibilities among public interest goals; there also is the potential conflicts among self-interest goals. The authority structure in a community is not homogeneous and unified. There often are competing interests in a community so that, at times, the cooperation that may be required between two or more groups to achieve a public interest goal will be difficult to attain. Cooperation, of course, will be especially difficult if a program results in a potential loss of power, authority, or money on the part of one of the cooperating groups. Bargaining and trading usually is required before such a program will be accepted. This does not necessarily mean that only incremental changes are possible. The fact that the authority structure is not homogeneous also facilitates the opportunity to get change, and change

[a]From one theoretical perspective, the public interest can be conceived of as nothing more than the sum of individual self-interests. In this perspective, it is desirable and necessary that individuals pursue their own interests. However, we assume in this chapter that the public interest, at times, may be more than the aggregate of individual and group interests.

that may sometimes be significant and important. For there is always a possibility that a particular mix of interests in the community will form, perhaps through the leverage of the federal government, that allows large-scale change to take place.

An individual also may change his mind about goals. Any individual in the authority structure has a number of goals he wants to achieve. These goals are often conflicting such that gain in one requires some sacrifice of another. Because each person has a number of interests, it is possible to convince him to alter his preference for a particular program. There are any number of reasons why he might do so. For example, economic incentives may compensate for a loss in one goal, or an individual's relative weighting of different goals may itself change so that personal consequences of supporting a program no longer appear negative to him. For example, a policeman who previously viewed empathizing with gang members as "pussyfooting" may learn to understand the importance of communicating with them.

Although we hesitate to conclude that these difficulties mean that rational achievement of goals in criminal justice is not possible, we do conclude that there are limits to rationality. This does not mean that the system is irrational; only that it is necessary to understand the limits of rationality before adequate evaluation of criminal justice policy is possible. When there are multiple and competing goals that cannot be compromised or coordinated, one or more will have to be sacrificed according to some set of subjective priorities. Moreover, if self-interests of critical personnel conflict with achievement of these goals which are preferred, attempting to attain them will be a utopian quest which will only lead to frustration.

At other times it is possible to be rational. When one goal is clearly more important than all others and its achievement is in the self-interest of most affected groups, there will be fewer obstacles to rationality. Recognizing and working within the confines of these limits is likely to produce better criminal justice policy.

References

Arrow, Kenneth. *The Limits of Organization*. New York: W.W. Norton, 1974.

Arrow, Kenneth. *Social Choice and Individual Values*. New York: Wiley, 1951.

Bachrach, Peter and Morton Baratz. *Power and Poverty: Theory and Practice*. New York: Oxford University Press, 1970.

Bish, Robert. *The Public Economy of Metropolitan Areas*. Chicago: Markham, 1971.

Bittner, Egon. "The Police on Skid-Row." *American Sociological Review* (October 1967): 699-715.

Botein, Bernard. *Our Cities Burn While We Play Cops and Robbers.* New York: Simon & Shuster, 1972.

Carroll, Lewis. *The Annotated Alice.* New York: Bramhill House, 1960.

Cole, George. "The Decision to Prosecute." *Law and Society Review* (February 1970): 313-343.

Curry, R.L. and L.L. Wade. *A Theory of Political Exchange.* Englewood Cliffs, Prentice-Hall, 1968.

Dahl, Robert and Charles Lindbloom. *Politics, Economics, and Welfare.* New York: Harper & Brothers, 1953.

Downs, Anthony. *An Economic Theory of Democracy.* New York: Harper & Row, 1957.

Eisenstein, James. "The Federal Prosecutor and His Environment." American Political Science Association's Convention (1968).

Emmer, Gerald. "The Management of Change in LEAA's Impact Program." From LEAA Symposium, *The Change Process in Criminal Justice,* June 1973.

Goldstein, Herman. "Administrative Problems in Controlling the Exercise of Police Authority." *Journal of Criminal Law, Criminology, and Police Science* (1967): 160-172.

Kittrie, Nicholas. *The Right To Be Different.* Baltimore: The Johns Hopkins University Press, 1971.

Levine, James; Michael Musheno; and Dennis Palumbo. "Evaluating Alternatives in Criminal Justice: A Policy Impact Model." Unpublished manuscript, 1975.

Lindblom, Charles. *The Policy-Making Process.* Englewood Cliffs: Prentice-Hall, 1968.

Lindblom, Charles. *The Intelligence of Democracy: Decision Making Through Mutual Adjustment.* New York: Free Press, 1965.

Luce, R.D. and H. Raiffa. *Games and Decisions.* New York: Wiley, 1957.

Mitchell, Joyce and William Mitchell. *Political Analysis and Public Policy.* Chicago: Rand McNally, 1969.

Nagel, Stuart and Marian Neef. "Decision Theory, Equilibrium Models, and Plea Bargaining." Unpublished manuscript, 1975.

Nagel, Stuart and Marian Neef. "Policy Optimizing Models and the Legal Process." Paper delivered before the 1974 APSA meetings.

Packer, Herbert. *The Limits of the Criminal Sanction.* Stanford, Calif.: Stanford University Press, 1968.

Palumbo, Dennis. "Organization Theory and Political Science." In Fred

Greenstein and Melson Polsby, *Handbook of Political Science*. Reading, Mass.: Addison-Wesley, 1975.

Russell, Bertrand. *Human Society in Ethics and Politics*. London: Allen & Unwin, 1959.

Schattschneider, E.E. *The Semi-Sovereign People*. New York: Holt Rinehart & Winston, 1960.

Simon, Herbert. *Administrative Behavior*. New York: Macmillan, 1945.

Skolnick, Jerome. *Justice Without Trial: Law Enforcement in Democratic Society*. New York: John Wiley & Sons, 1967.

Part IV
Psychology and Education

10 Psychology and Public Policy

Serena Stier

Introduction

Psychology, both as a scientific discipline and as a profession, has affirmed its concern with the relevance to social issues and public policy in the last half decade.[1] The relative novelty of looking at psychology and public policy in tandem is indicated by the fact that *Psychological Abstracts* did not index policy as a heading until 1973.

This chapter focuses on the role of the psychologist in the public policy process in terms of the "is-ought" distinction. This distinction is used here to signify both the epistemological problem of the meaning of the "is" of psychology—principally scientific data and theories—and the methodological or procedural problem of moving from "is" to "ought" in the formulation of a policy. It is hoped that such a discussion will lead to a better understanding of the potential conflict between the roles of psychologist as objective investigator, on the one hand, and policy consultant on the other.

Interaction of Psychology and Public Policy

Psychology's impact on policy involves what may be distinguished as either process-oriented skills or outcome-oriented skills. Process-oriented skills contribute to methods of evaluating the policy-making process itself, hoepfully leading to the improvement of that process. For example, the work of Irving Janis illustrates how psychological research on communication can be utilized to permit policymakers to study how they arrive at decisions and enhance the rationality and effectiveness of the process of decision-making (see Chapter 11 in this volume). In a similar fashion, psychology can enhance the policy process by contributing to interdisciplinary efforts, as in the development of health policy[2] or approaches to environmental issues.[3]

Evaluation research, which was pioneered by Suchman[4] and contributed to by Campbell,[5] Guttentag et al.,[6] and Riecken et al.,[7] illustrates what I would call an outcome-oriented skill. By developing methods for determining the effectiveness of various strategies utilized by policymakers to solve social problems, psychology may permit the policymaker to better maximize his or her allocation of resources. At a more preliminary point, psychological research can produce information to allow the policymaker to devise programs which may have a higher probability of producing a more successful outcome. For example, research on the effects of early intervention in the development of cognitive skills in children has contributed to the development of programs in the home and efforts to promote early education.[8]

Policy, in turn, affects psychology. The horror of the atomic scientists, whose work produced Hiroshima and Nagasaki, precipitated American science into a wrenching exploration of individual scientific accountability. Today, when research subjects can be misled into believing they are giving another subject life threatening shocks,[9] when the work of a learning theorist can be degraded and abused for the purpose of demeaning a group of prisoners,[10] and when the theoretical research on sensory deprivation (through its application to interrogation techniques) can be utilized for the purpose of destroying political dissidents,[11] psychologists find themselves in a crisis of identity requiring some careful analyses of their roles.

In an attempt to be more responsible and as a result of increasing sanctions for "ivory tower" undimensionsal vision, psychology has begun to be more aware of the need to balance its scientific and professional interests against ethical considerations of the rights of research subjects and patients.[12] Moreover, the profligate days of ample research and therapy budgets have vanished along with other American perquisites, forcing psychologists to set priorities related to the perceived needs of society. In positing manpower needs and research strategies, psychology has consequently become much more sophisticated about appreciating various limitations on the availability of material resources and the influence of competing interest groups. Efforts to organize in increasingly systematic and assessible ways the results of psychological research and to bring this material to the attention of executive, legislative, and judicial authorities are also partly a result of an increased awareness of psychology's relevance to policy matters.

Campbell's "Experimenting Society"

One of psychology's major impacts on public policy has been through the work of Donald T. Campbell, who has been described by the journal *Evaluation* as the person their readers most wished to interview.[13] Campbell's work illustrates both the best of what psychology has to offer to the field of policy studies, as well as some of the major problems inherent in any partnership between psychology and policy.

In 1969, Campbell recommended "an experimental approach to social reform, an approach in which we try out new programs designed to cure specific social problems, in which we learn whether or not these programs are effective and in which we retain, imitate, modify or discard them on the basis of apparent effectiveness on the multiple imperfect criteria available."[14]

Like another famous psychologist, B. F. Skinner,[15] Campbell is not merely interested in supporting a facile truism that "we ought to know what we're doing when we do something" but is in fact positing the creation of a particular kind of society—the "Experimenting Society." Such a society would be *active*; it would be committed to action research in the Lewinian tradition.[16] It would be *honest*, *non-dogmatic*, and *scientific*—in the sense of showing a willingness to change once-advocated theories in the face of conflicting evidence from empirical, though not exclusively experimental, sources. This would not be a society run by scientists, however, but a society which is *accountable* and *challengeable*. *Due-process* considerations would prevail so that there would be public access to the records upon which social decisions were based and there would be competitive criticisms of social experimentation in the atmosphere of an *open society* like that envisioned by Popper.[17] The "Experimenting Society" would be decentralized and committed to *means-idealism* as well as *ends-idealism*. It would be popularly responsive, voluntaristic, and equalitarian.[18] This is probably not the kind of society which would be envisioned by an artist, a philosopher or a housewife. However, social scientists, too, should be able to construct their dreams—at least in print.

Let us focus on what Campbell envisages the role of the social scientist to be in the "Experimenting Society." In such a society, the social scientist would be a methodological servant. He or she would offer the methods of science, of experimentation, and of quasi-experimentation.[19] "This technology, rather than our disciplinary knowledge is what we social scientists have to offer to the social policy process"[20] (see Chapter 3 in this volume).

However, Campbell is aware of a complex problem involved in the social scientist's interaction with the policy process:

I believe that much of the methodology of program evaluation will be independent of the content of the program, and politically neutral in this sense. This stance is augmented by emphasizing the social scientist's role in helping society keep track of the effects of changes that its political process has initiated and by playing down the role of the social scientist in the design of program innovations. Whether this independence of ideology is possible, and even if it is, how it is to be integrated with the social scientist's duty to participate in the development of more authentic human consciousness and more humane forms of social life are questions I have not adequately faced, to say nothing of resolved.[21]

The next section of this chapter will explore the feasibility of a value free methodology in the service of public policy.

The Is-Ought Distinction

While psychology has only recently begun to grapple with the problem of values infusing science in its application to public policy, the legal profession has long been concerned with an analogous problem. A judicial decision, such as the enunciation or interpretation of a rule of law, may have identifiable public policy consequences. Traditionally, legal theorists have sought to understand the judicial decision-making process as a pure logical exercise independent of the social values at stake. Social and policy concerns were considered to be the exclusive province of the legislature, which is elected and presumably responsive to democratic processes. More recently, however, some legal theorists have challenged the traditional view on the grounds that such pure legal decisions are not possible or desirable, and have urged that full awareness of the normative implications of a judicial decision is necessary to avoid arbitrariness.[22,a]

The lawyer's problem is often characterized in terms of a distinction between what the law is and what the law ought to be. Similarly, in the interaction between psychology and public policy, the "is-ought" distinction becomes critical both as an epistemological issue (defining the "is" of scientific fact or theory) and as a methodological or procedural issue (moving from "is" to "ought" in the formulation of a policy).

Our objective should be the delineation of the meaning of a statement without falling into the positivistic fallacy of interpreting language as if its meaning were writ in concrete, or, conversely, taking the position of the extreme realist and treating a statement as if it were writ on water. Just as skepticism about the sanctity of rules often leads the inexperienced law student into the realm of realism *ad absurdum*, where the law is simply seen as whatever the judge says it is, the current increasing attack on the sanctity of science can lead to an extreme skepticism. For example, Levine writes:

Science is basically a social enterprise. Science is what scientists feel comfortable in recommending to others as principles through which the world may be manipulated, predicted, or understood. Science is what scientists say it is at any given point in time. Science is what scientists feel comfortable in writing about in articles in textbooks . . .

. . . Science, then, at any given point in time, is that which one scientist is able to convince at least one other member of his community, and hopefully some small group, to accept as the best approximation to the truth.[23]

Seesawing between the failings of a concretist sureness and a vapid pessimism in order to achieve a sense of balance in evaluating the "is" of psychology is no easy task. When psychology "gives away" its findings to

---

[a]I hope I will be forgiven for simplifying complex philosophical and legal issues for pedagogical purposes.

society,[24] it is not always sufficiently cautious about affirming the limitations of its findings. As Paul Meehl has demonstrated, disagreements among psychologists and failings of methodology are often obscured for the benefit of public consumption.[25] Psychologists may portray themselves as having achieved a level of consensus about the "is" of human behavior, which has not been achieved in fact. One result is an expectation of a capacity for "wizardry"[26] which simply does not exist. An even more serious consequence is fearfulness about psychology's impact on society, which may also seriously threaten the integrity of both the science and the profession.[27]

Psychology produces a descriptive statement about some human beings or group of human beings—a statement with probabilistic boundaries. That is, the statement is not intended to be true in any absolute sense, but only true with some less than perfect degree of precision within the given context. Such a statement may have to do with an individual's problem-solving capacity or level of self-control or the statement may seek to characterize a more generalizable quality of human behavior as reflected on some psychological test. Unfortunately, the decision-maker or policymaker often takes this descriptive, probabilistic information and treats it as a fact without regard to the tentative and contextual nature of this "is" statement.

Without falling into the premature cynicism of total operationism (a thing is that which measures it),[28] in dealing with the relativity of a scientific finding, especially in the realm of public policy, it is still essential to emphasize how fragile the "is" statements of psychology are. Working hypotheses and heuristic strategies must not be permitted to be translated into absolute truths. Campbell has expressed a reasoned, centrist position in emphasizing that "our current standards of experimental design represent a *scientific* achievement, an *empirical* product, not a logical dispensation. They represent generally verified hypothetical laws—in the philosophers' terms, contingent, descriptive, synthetic, and therefore corrigible "truths," rather than logical or analytic truths."[29]

There is no way of turning the "is" into a Platonic "truth" since the "is" always operates within some complex context. It is particularly essential for psychologists to understand and express this observation when cooperating with policymakers. This may not be a popular stance to take since decision-makers, restricted by the demands of the political arena, prefer to hear guarantees from their consultants.

Nevertheless, such guarantees cannot and should not be forthcoming from psychology. Distortions of the value of psychology's tentative "is" hypotheses can have disastrous social consequences, such as condemning a culturally distinctive child to the bottom of the educational system as a "retardate"[30] or placing a young offender in what amounts to a prison for an indeterminate period of time for being "dangerous."[31]

Moving from "Is" to "Ought"[b]

Once we have established the vulnerability of the "is" statement, we are faced with the even more difficult task of recognizing and acknowledging the difficulty of translating tentative "is" statements into "ought" decisions, of turning descriptive fact into prescriptive action. Campbell's "Experimenting Society" is quite sensitive to the ambiguities of the "is" statement. A major aspect of his contribution to the methodology of evaluation involves attempts to focus on the limits of the "is" statement and to devise means of enhancing the generalizability of such statements.[32] However, I am concerned that in opting for the position of methodological servant to the "Experimenting Society," Campbell underestimates the impact of the social scientists' own political priorities upon the policymakers' use of social science. Consider the recent comment, upon receiving a major grant for evaluation research, of another eminent evaluation specialist: "Evaluation is a function performed within a system which is largely political. Hence, an evaluation is to be judged by its effect on the working of the system, not by its internal scientific rationale alone."[33]

In his book *Maximum Feasible Misunderstanding*, Moynihan posits an explanation for the failure of the war on poverty. His hypothesis is that one of the major faults of the poverty program approach to juvenile delinquency was reliance on a limited and inappropriate theory. Moynihan's essential question is: "Why then, it will be asked, did the social scientists involved in these events not insist on the limits of their knowledge and methodology?"

Moynihan's reply to this question is that "the answer would seem to lie in part in the essentially dual nature of the American social scientist. He is an objective 'seeker after truth'. But he is also very likely to be a passionate partisan of social justice and social change to bring it about."[34] This pinpoints one of the major problems in moving from "is" to "ought." Social science, particularly in its application—in its translation of fact into program—is necessarily permeated with the humanness, the perspective, the Weltanshauung, of its practitioners. This necessarily influences the psychologist toward overemphasizing the relevance of his or her findings to the social problem at hand and toward minimizing the ambiguities.

In their critique of Campbell's "Experimenting Society," Shaver and Staines echo Moynihan to some extent by worrying that "if social scientists become increasingly influential in the policy-making process, it is possible that they will sell administrators and the public incorrect theories which then act as norms for behavior. An example might be 'Social Darwinism.' . . ."[35]

---

[b]In this section the broader designation of social science, which includes psychology, will be used since the issues are relevant to many of the social sciences and the illustrative material is not exclusively from psychology.

I do not feel that the issue is whether or not social science is going to sell administrators incorrect theories so much as whether or not they are going to portray themselves as unbiased consultants who have nothing to sell. It is in the very nature of theory that at some time in the future it may well be disproven. Social scientists cannot be held any more responsible for the failure of Social Darwinism than can Newton be held responsible for the birth of Einstein. It is, however, the responsibility of the social scientist to acknowledge his or her impact on the decision-making process and the presence in social science decision-making of value determinants.

That social scientists have values and that these not only influence their choice of research interests, their interpretation of results, and their application of these results to social problem solving is not in itself unique or alarming. The problem is the promotion of the mystique of a value free science and the consequent failure to take into account the personal influence of the scientist. The American political system is based on the recognition that data presented by various groups reflect the interests sought to be vindicated by the group. The only requirement is that these interests be explicated so that they may be known and so that the resulting advice of the interested parties can be interpreted in the light of this knowledge.

Once having acknowledged the responsibility of the social scientist to enunciate his or her value orientation, one is then faced with evaluating the extent to which the social sciences can be held responsible for the impact of their contributions on policy-making institutions, for example, in analyzing the impact of extra legal facts.

In his history of Supreme Court decisions, Paul Rosen shows how support for the nineteenth and early twentieth century court decisions, which maintained the de facto slavery of blacks and resisted attempts to ameliorate the destructive effects of "rugged individualism" with social support programs, was provided by social science theory through the impact of Social Darwinism.[36]

In this early example of the impact of a social science theory on a major policy institution, the application of this questionable theory does not appear to have been a deliberate contribution from social science itself. However, with the first use by Louis Brandeis (then a practicing attorney) of what came to be called the "Brandeis Brief" in the case of *Muller* v. *Oregon* in 1908, the use of extra-legal social science facts was officially inaugurated. Brandeis' presentation utilized what we would call psychological, medical, and biological information and opinion for a very limited purpose. His intention was merely to demonstrate that a statute might not be viewed as unreasonable or arbitrary since the legislature had some social facts on which to base it decision.[37]

Since the 1954 *Brown* v. *Board of Education* decision, which declared "separate but equal" schools to be unconstitutional racial discrimination, the use of extra-legal social science facts by the court has become a fairly accepted practice. Rosen feels "the Brandeis brief was first used in a period of constitutional crisis, when the court stood behind the Constitution to block urgent social and economic reforms. Brandeis thus resorted to nascent social science for the ultimate purpose of facilitating social change." The civil rights movement, in a comparable way, represented a second constitutional crisis to which the court more deliberately applied social science information. The opinion by Chief Justice Earl Warren in *Brown* clearly demonstrates the major impact of social science studies on the thinking of the court.[38]

Although one might achieve fairly general consensus among social scientists that social policies backed up by Social Darwinism are "bad" while the social policy reflected in the *Brown* decision is "good," both kinds of theories have been used by the Court. Clearly, both "good" and "bad" results are possible in any case in which social science is relied upon, and the consequences can be of fundamental importance to the nation.

What is required of social scientists is a humility that is rarely present or acknowledged, at least if sound decisions using social science are to be maximized. The prophets of old have been replaced by the social scientist with a modernized reading of the signs, ostensibly objective, which in fact can represent levels of prejudice that may range from a blindness to alternative explanations for observed phenomena to the formulation of grandiose plans for the salvation of humanity without knowing if the recipients want to be saved in quite the way the scientist might have designed. These kinds of policy decisions must ultimately be left in the hands of social institutions, such as the legislatures and the courts, which have evolved appropriate mechanisms for weighing a broader range of interests—with that of social science representing only a part of the measure, albeit a significant part. I do not mean to suggest by emphasizing these problems that social science and psychology, in particular, do not have much to offer, as I believe the *Brown* decision illustrates.

Thus, Rosen notes that while social science can provide the Court with

empirical explanations of society, [it] cannot be used to answer the ultimate questions a policy-making Court must ponder. The Court is an arbiter of facts. But, more important, it is also an arbiter of values. . . . Social science cannot tell the Court what value should be preferred. . . . The Court should not use social science findings that are statements *about* values as if they were actually statements *of* values . . . The Court will always have to cope with the underlying tension that is bound to exist between a discipline that prescribes what society ought to be (the Court) and one that explains what society is (psychology and social science). Whatever else the Court does, it still must reconcile the legal 'ought' with the social 'is.'[39]

The Supreme Court can utilize the process of judicial interpretation and the flow of cases over time to work out the problems of translating from "is" facts to "ought" decisions. In the same way, lower courts can utilize the jury system and the adversary process to translate information from "experts" into conclusions, when the expert witness does not usurp the traditional role of the jury and make conclusory judgments.[40] Legislatures and administrative agencies use the hearing process to elucidate competing views. One may then inquire what comparable procedures exist for psychology and social science in general? How can the "is" statements of these disciplines acquire appropriate credibility in the policy process?

The Golstein, Freud, and Solnit book *Beyond the Best Interests of the Child* reviews, from a psychoanalytic point of view, child-parent relationships and child development and then proposes some new ways of viewing and arranging custody decisions for children. This book not only concentrates on psychological "is" statements, but also makes a number of policy recommendations as well. The authors' main contribution is to shift from a preference for biological parents to a choice of psychological parents in custody proceedings.[41] In their critique of this work, Katkin, Bullington, and Levine attempt to focus on responsibilities of those who would influence social policy with knowledge derived from the social sciences.[42]

Katkin et al. castigate the authors first for failing to include a single reference to any empirical study and then, more significantly, for showing in their narrow review of the relevant literature an "insensitivity to the limitations of the evidence cited in support of the book's major psychological premises." In this criticism, Katkin et al. support our earlier point that psychologists and social scientists have a responsibility for acknowledging the fragility of their findings and theories. "Responsible policy formulation requires that competing explanations of a phenomenon be pitted against one another and that the evidence for each position be carefully evaluated." One part of the answer, then, to the question as to what comparable procedures exist for psychology and social science when operating in the policy area would be to create some mechanism for psychological findings to be exposed to an adversary procedure wherein their limitations are most likely to be exposed.[43]

Second, in making recommendations to policy administrators and institutions, psychologists and social scientists must not only be sensitive to their own value orientation but must share this value orientation. Katkin et al. are most critical of Goldstein et al. for their failure to appreciate and properly acknowledge the operation of their own biases, their psychoanalytically determined value system. The third responsibility of social science and psychology is pinpointed by Katkin et al. when they note that "in pursuit of social change every solution brings with it a set of new problems. Thus proposals for change must be evaluated not only on the basis of their responsiveness to existing problems but also on the basis of their own problem-generating capacity." They are concerned that the Goldstein et al. book fails to explicate the consequences of giving judges increased discretion in making custody decisions.[44]

Psychology should not evade its responsibility for enunciating the dimensions of its "is" statements and "ought" proposals by expecting or arranging to be rescued by surrogate value determiners such as the courts, nor should the value of social science be lost to the policy process by denying its relevance. In the final section of this chapter we shall explore the complexities of attempting to articulate ways in which psychology can take responsibility not only for its "is" statements but also for the process of moving from "is" to "ought."

Proposed Method for Dealing with the Is-Ought Distinction

Psychology might borrow from law in attempting to resolve the dilemma of dealing with value laden science. One such suggestion has been made by Levine in his proposal that research programs incorporate the adversary process in the design and evaluation of their research.[45] While there is a danger in the wholesale substitution of legal procedures for psychological dilemmas,[46] I should like to explore some of the ways in which rule, role and self—a concept proposed[47] to comprehend the judicial decision-making process—can be utilized by psychology.

The meaning of these three concepts—rule, role and self—emerge from the opinion in *Rochin* v. *California* by Mr. Justice Frankfurter. The facts of the case are that Mr. Rochin's stomach was pumped, forcing him to expel two capsules found to contain morphine and resulting in conviction and a prison term. The conviction was overturned by the Supreme Court on constitutional grounds. The issue is framed by Frankfurter as whether regard for the requirements of the Due Process Clause of the Constitution "inescapably imposed upon this Court an exercise of judgment upon the whole course of the proceedings (resulting in a conviction) in order to ascertain whether they offend those canons of decency and fairness which express the notions of justice of English-speaking peoples even toward those charged with the most heinous offenses."[48]

Frankfurter goes on to assert that there is a *rule* (the Due Process Clause) to guide the decision-making process even if the meaning of the rule is not fixed.

In dealing not with the machinery of government but with human rights, the absence of formal exactitude, or want of fixity of meaning, is not an unusual or even regrettable attribute of Constitutional provisions. Words being symbols do not speak without a gloss. On the one hand the gloss may be the deposit of history, whereby a term gains technical content . . . on the other hand, the gloss of some of the verbal symbols of the Constitution does not give them a fixed technical content. It exacts a continuing process of application.[49]

However, Frankfurter asserts that "the vague contours of the Due Process Clause do not leave judges at large. We may not draw on our merely personal and private notions and disregard the limits that bind judges in their judicial function." This leads Frankfurter to the function of *role*. "The Due Process Clause places upon this court the duty of exercising a judgment within the narrow confines of judicial power in reviewing state convictions, upon interests of society pushing in opposite directions."[50]

Finally, Frankfurter acknowledges the impact of *self* on the judicial decision-making process. "To practice the requisite detachment and to achieve sufficient objectivity no doubt demands of judges the habit of self-discipline and self-criticism, incertitude that one's own views are incontestable and alert tolerance toward views not shared."[51]

Although these concepts of rule, role, and self are not a widely accepted paradigm of the judicial decision-making process, they are very helpful in distinguishing and balancing the various factors that go into the determination of a judgment. Frankfurter implicitly calls upon the concepts of rule, role and self to establish the authority of a judge on the basis of the constraints these factors impose on his or her judgment. Similarly, parallels to these concepts can be drawn with respect to psychology in that analogous restraints do operate to encourage responsible psychological judgments.

The statement of a *rule* in law is epistemologically comparable to statements involving the data, the fact, and the evolving theory—the "is" of psychology. Here too, the gloss of history, including past research, experimental method studies and the possible impact of experimental artifacts, makes it necessary to interpret carefully each piece of datum. The adequacy of the experimental design permits one to have a base level of confidence in interpreting the data just as the *rule* in law has a base level meaning when it is taken in light of its history and context.

Psychotherapists have a long tradition of attending to the impact of *self*. A shorthand word for this from the language of psychoanalysis is countertransference—the distortion of the therapist's perception of the patient as a function of some unresolved problem in the therapist being triggered by some action (verbal or behavioral) of the patient. In the professional training of clinical psychologists primary emphasis is placed on the development of the self—including self-awareness, self-respect, and self-determination. The expectation has been that given this kind of an "authentic" person, the appropriate value decisions, would be achieved almost automatically. Only a few years ago, Abraham Maslow wrote that "the best way for a person to discover what he ought to do is to find out who and what he is, because the path to ethical and value decisions, to wiser choices, to oughtness, is via "'isness': via the discovery of facts, truth, reality, the nature of the particular person."[52]

For the scientist-psychologist the concept of self has not been articulated in such an interpersonal way. Instead the notion of self is firmly tied to interpretations of the scientific endeavor. This involves examining the nature of "truth," learning to maintain objectivity, and being receptive to other points of view.

Traditionally, *role* for psychology has represented the capacity for living with sustained uncertainty, for viewing with the eye of empiricism, which is the professionalism of the trained psychologist. Increasingly, role is being perceived as including a sense of responsibility for one's research contributions. The role of the psychologist creates a unique perspective on public policy of value to the decision-making process while inducing responsible professional behavior. Those who choose psychology as a profession, undertake years of training, and spend additional years as professionals, are not unaffected by their experiences. A psychologist is a psychologist because of the unique way in which he or she frames an issue, the unique range of data he or she will take into account in formulating judgments, and the selection of the objective of his or her pursuit. At the same time, these factors implicitly limit the alternative judgments a psychologist is likely to make. The professional standards of the peer group further influence a psychologist's judgment away from biased or unsupportable findings, and toward responsible behavior.

Although instances of judicial impropriety are not unknown, the role of judge has been much better enunciated through the centuries old accretions of practice and evolving tradition than has that of psychologist. The role of psychologist is an identity that has existed for less than a century. Consequently, the dimensions of appropriate behavior and the borders of responsibility are still permeable for most psychologists. An understanding of the tentative nature of psychological statements, of the problems of moving from "is" statements to "ought" policies, and the ways in which rule, role, and self operate to encourage responsible judgments would seem to be helpful if psychology is to participate effectively in the policy-making process. As organized psychology and the universities proceed with the continuous process of evolving concepts of professionalism, this would assist in creating teaching materials, professional standards, and ethical standards that consciously seek to encourage responsible, credible, and authoritative inputs.

The major responsibility for making these analyses, for proposing standards of responsibility, and for enforcing such standards should come from the psychology profession itself. Organized psychology (the American Psychological Association) has recognized this responsibility through participation as *amicus curiae* in law suits designed to obtain rights for mental patients and improve the standards of institutional treatment (*Wyatt*, *Morales*).[53] In creating groups such as the Commission on Behavior Modification and a Task Force on Privacy, organized psychology has shown an appreciation of the issues in the forefront of social concern with psychological practice. However, these efforts have too often been reactive, have too often been stimulated by a fear of government intervention rather than representing a searching examination of appropriate areas of responsibility in advance of public alarm.

Wikler, a philosopher, has suggested that "the skills needed for solution of many kinds of policy questions are different from those imparted to students for solving problems of practice. They are often philosophical in nature." He goes on to suggest that the curriculum of various professional schools, which would include psychology, should include the kind of course in ethics provided by philosophy.[54] Psychology, in its anxiety to attain scientific status, has studiously tried to ignore its roots in philosophy and to align itself with the natural sciences. It would certainly seem time to put aside some of the belligerence generated by the confrontation of quantitative and qualitative approaches to human behavior[55] and to focus on the potential understanding provided by philosophy. This should not be an externalized process, with the bringing in of consultants on ethics from a different discipline, but psychology itself should infuse its educational, training, and continuing professional development programs with a new sensitivity to the primacy of values in science. Psychology should treat the value dimension as inherent in the psychological role and seek to maximize the contributions of psychology to public policy on this assumption.

Notes

1. F. F. Korten, S. W. Cook, and J. I. Lacey (eds.), *Psychology and the Problems of Society* (Washington, D.C.: American Psychology Association, 1970).

2. *Health Politics* 4, 3 (May 1974):12-16.

3. Joachim Wohlwill and Daniel H. Carson (eds.), *Environment and the Social Sciences: Perspectives and Applications* (Washington, D.C.: American Psychological Association, 1972).

4. E. Suchman, *Evaluation Research* (New York: Russell Sage, 1967).

5. Donald T. Campbell, "Reforms as Experiments," *American*

Psychologist 24 (April 1969):409-28; "Prospective: Artifact and Control," in R. Rosenthal and R. L. Rosnow (eds.), *Artifact in Behavioral Research* (Academic Press, 1969), pp. 35-82; "Quasi-Experimental Designs," in H. W. Riecken and R. F. Boruch (eds.), *Social Experimentation: A Method for Planning and Evaluating Social Intervention* (New York: Academic Press, 1974), pp. 87-115; See also Chapter 3 in this volume.

6. Marsha Guttentag and Kurt Snapper, "Plans, Evaluations and Decisions," *Evaluation* 2, 1 (1974):58-64; 73-74; Marcia Guttentag, Ward Edwards, and Kurt Snapper, "A Decision-Theoretic Approach to Evaluation Research," in Elmer Struening and Marcia Guttentag (eds.), *Handbook of Evaluation Research* (Beverly Hills: Sage Publications, 1975); Marcia Guttentag and Ward Edwards, "Experiments and Evaluations: A Reconsideration," in *Experiments and Evaluations* (New York: Academic Press, 1975).

7. H. W. Riecken et al., *Experimentation as a Method for Planning and Evaluating Social Innovations* (New York: Seminar Press, 1975).

8. J. McV. Hunt, "Psychological Assessment, Developmental Plasticity, and Heredity, with Implications for Early Education," in Gertrude J. Williams and Sol Gordon, *Clinical Child Psychology* (New York: Behavioral Publications, 1974), Ch. 11.

9. Stanley Milgram, *Obedience to Authority* (New York: Harper-Row, 1974).

10. Edward M. Opton, Jr., "Psychiatric Violence Against Prisoners: When Therapy Is Punishment," *Mississippi Law Journal* 45 (1974):605-44.

11. Rona M. Fields, *A Society on the Run* (London: Penguin, 1973); T. Shallice, "The Ulster Depth Interrogation Techniques and Their Relation to Sensory Deprivation Research," *Cognition: International Journal of Cognitive Psychology* 1,4 (1972):385-405.

12. Ethical Standards of Psychologists, *American Psychologist* (January 1963); *Ethical Principles in the Conduct of Research with Human Participants*, American Psychological Association, 1973; "Guidelines for Psychologists Conducting Growth Groups", *American Psychologist* (October 1973):933; *Standards for Educational and Psychological Tests*, American Psychological Association, 1974.

13. Susan Salasin, "Experimentation Revisited: A Conversation with Donald T. Campbell," *Evaluation* 1, 3 (1973):7-13.

14. Donald T. Campbell, "Methods for the Experimenting Society," paper delivered to the American Psychological Association Convention, Washington, D.C., 1971.

15. B. F. Skinner, *Beyond Freedom and Dignity* (New York: Knopf, 1971).

16. Donald T. Campbell, "Qualitative Knowing in Action Research," Kurt Lewin Award Address, Society for the Psychological Study of Social Issues, Meeting with the American Psychological Association, New Orleans, September 1, 1974; K. Lewin, "Action Research and Minority Problems," *Journal of Social Issues* (1946):34-46. Reprinted in K. Lewin, *Resolving Social Conflicts* (New York: Harper, 1948).

17. K. R. Popper, *The Open Society and Its Enemies* (London: Routledge, 1945, Harper Torch Books, 1973).

18. D. T. Campbell, "Methods for the Experimenting Society."

19. D. T. Campbell, "Quasi-Experimental Designs."

20. D. T. Campbell, "The Social Scientist as Methodological Servant of the Experimenting Society," *Policy Studies Journal* 2 (1973):72-75.

21. D. T. Campbell, "Assessing the Impact of Planned Social Change," in Lyons (ed.), *Social Research and Public Policies* (Dartmouth: New England Universities Press, in press).

22. William Bishin and Christopher Stone, *Law, Language and Ethics: An Introduction to Law and Legal Method* (Mineola, New York: The Foundation Press, 1972); Steven Burton, "The Psychodynamics of Judicial Discretion and the Concept of Law," unpublished manuscript; Albert A. Ehrenzweig, *Psychoanalytic Jurisprudence* (Dobbs Ferry, New York: Oceana Publications, Inc., 1971); John Rawls, *A Theory of Justice* (Cambridge, Mass.: Harvard University Press, 1971).

23. Murray Levine, "Scientific Method and the Adversary Model," *American Psychologist* (September 1974):661-77.

24. George A. Miller, "Psychology as a Means of Promoting Human Welfare," Presidential Address to the American Psychological Association Convention, Washington, D.C., September 1, 1969, pp. 5-21, in F. F. Korten et al. (eds.), *Psychology and the Problems of Society* (Washington, D.C.: American Psychological Association, 1970).

25. Paul E. Meehl, "Law and the Fireside Inductions: Some Reflections of a Clinical Psychologist," *Journal of Social Issues* 27, 4(1971):65-100.

26. David L. Bazelon, "The Perils of Wizardry," *American Journal of Psychiatry* 131, 12 (December 1974):1317-22.

27. "Individual Rights and the Federal Role in Behavior Modification," a study prepared by the Subcommittee on Constitutional Rights of the Committee on the Judiciary ,U.S. Senate, 93rd Congress, 2nd Session, November 1974. "The common element of all the programs investigated by the subcommittee is that each employs methods that depend upon the direct and systematic manipulation by one individual of the personality of

another through the use of consciously applied psychological, medical, and other technological methods. Because it is not based upon the reasoned exchange of information, behavior modification is not a traditional learning process. Analogous to a surgeon operating to remove a tumor, the behavior therapist attempts to remove an undesirable aspect of an individual's behavior through direct intervention into the latter individual's basic thought processes." (pg. 1.)

28. Paul E. Meehl, "Second-Order Relevance," *American Psychologist* (October 1972):932-940.

29. D. T. Campbell, "Prospective: Artifact and Control," p. 357.

30. Nicholas Hobbs, *The Futures of Children* (San Francisco, Calif.: Jossey-Bass, 1974).

31. Jessica Mitford, *Kind and Usual Punishment: The Prison Business* (New York: Alfred A. Knopf, 1973).

32. Campbell (see note # 5).

33. *Behavior Today* 6 (February 10, 1975):6.

34. Daniel Patrick Moynihan, *Maximum Feasible Misunderstanding* (New York: The Free Press, 1969), p. 177. "A Recipe for Violence: Promise a lot; deliver a little. Lead people to believe they will be much better off, but let there be no dramatic improvement. Try a variety of small programs, each interesting but marginal in impact and severely under-financed. Avoid any attempted solution remotely comparable in size to the dimensions of the problem you are trying to solve. Have middle-class civil servants hire upper-class student radicals to use lower-class Negroes as a battering ram against the existing local political system; then complain that people are going around disrupting things and chastise local politicians for not cooperating with those out to do them in. Get some poor people involved in local decision-making, only to discover there is not enough at stake to be worth bothering about. Feel guilty about what has happened to black people; tell them you are surprised they have not revolted before; express shock and dismay when they follow your advice. Go in for a little force, just enough to anger, not enough to discourage. Feel guilty again; say you are surprised that worse has not happened. Alternate with a little supression. Mix well, apply a match, and run. . . ." (Frontpiece).

35. Phillip Shaver and Graham Staines, "Problems Facing Campbell's 'Experimenting Society'," *Urban Affairs Quarterly* 7 (1971):173-86.

36. Paul L. Rosen, *The Supreme Court and Social Science* (Chicago: University of Illinois Press, 1972).

37. Ibid, p. 82.

38. Ibid, pp. 178-79.

39. Ibid, pp. 225-28. "The court should use social science to determine

whether there are situations in which law arbitrarily grants privileges to some categories of persons or imposes disabilities on others . . . This reconciliation (of is and ought) is achieved as the dialectical fruit of the process of judicial interpretation, wherein, the precise meaning of the Constitution is hammered out in the context of specific fact situations.''

40. Saleem A. Shah, ''Some Interactions of Law and Mental Health in the Handling of Social Deviants,'' *Catholic University Law Review* 23 (1974):674-719.

41. Joseph Goldstein, Anna Freud, Albert J. Solnit, *Beyond the Best Interests of the Child* (New York: The Free Press, 1973).

42. D. Katkin, B. Bullington, and M. Levine, ''Above and Beyond the Best Interests of the Child: An Inquiry into the Relationship Between Social Science and Social Action,'' *Law and Society Review* (Summer 1974):669-87.

43. Ibid, p. 675.

44. Ibid, p. 678.

45. Levine, ''Scientific Method and the Adversary Model.''

46. Serena Stier, ''Psychology Working in the Legal Process,'' paper delivered to the American Association for the Advancement of Science Convention, New York City, January 26-31, 1975.

47. Bishin and Stone, *Law, Language, and Ethics*.

48. Ibid, p. 542.

49. Ibid, p. 543.

50. Ibid, pp. 543-544.

51. Ibid, p. 544.

52. Abraham H. Maslow, *The Farther Reaches of Human Nature* (New York: Viking Press, 1971), p. 111.

53. *Legal Rights of the Mentally Handicapped* (New York: Practicing Law Institute, 1974).

54. Daniel Wikler, ''Philosophy as Problem-Solving,'' *The American Behavioral Scientist* (in press), p. 1.

55. D. T. Campbell, Editorial, *APA Monitor* (February 1975).

11 What Group Dynamics Can Contribute to the Study of Policy Decisions

Irving L. Janis

Risky Group Decisions

Year after year newscasts and newspapers inform us of gross miscalculations by groups of policymakers in local, state, and federal governments. Most people, when they hear about these fiascoes, simply remind themselves that, after all, "organizations are run by human beings," "to err is human," and "nobody is perfect." But platitudinous thoughts about human nature do not help us to understand how and why avoidable miscalculations are made.

Fiasco watchers who are unwilling to set the problem aside in this easy fashion will find that contemporary psychology has something to say (unfortunately not very much) about excessive risk taking and other sources of human error. The deficiencies about which we know the most pertain to disturbances in the behavior of each individual in a decision-making group—temporary states of elation, fear, or anger that reduce a person's mental efficiency; chronic blind spots arising from a person's social prejudices; shortcomings in information-processing that prevent a person from comprehending the complex consequences of a seemingly simple policy decision. One psychologist has suggested that because the information-processing capabilities of every individual are limited, no responsible leader of a large organization ought to make a policy decision without using a computer that is programmed to spell out all the probable benefits and costs of each alternative under consideration. The usual way of trying to counteract the limitations of individuals' mental functioning, however, is to relegate important decisions to groups.

Groups, like individuals, have shortcomings. Groups can bring out the worst as well as the best in man. For example, subtle constraints, which the leader may reinforce inadvertently, may prevent a member from fully exercising his critical powers and from openly expressing doubts about a risky course of action when most others in the group appear to have reached a consensus. In order to take account of what is known about the causes and consequences of such constraints we must draw upon some of the main findings of research on group dynamics.[1]

This chapter is adapted from the author's recent book, *Victims of Groupthink: A Psychological Study of Foreign-Policy Decisions and Fiascos* (Boston: Houghton-Mifflin, 1972). It is an extended version of "Groupthink and Group Dynamics. A Social Psychological Analysis of Defective Policy Decisions," which was published in *Policy Studies Journal* 2, 1 (1973).

The use of theory and research on group dynamics is intended to supplement, not to replace, the standard approaches to the study of political decision-making. Group dynamics is still in the early stages of scientific development, and much remains to be learned. At present there are only a few concepts and generalizations in which we can have confidence when we are trying to understand the behavior of policy-making groups. Social scientists concerned with policy-making in the government—most notably, Karl Deutsch, Alexander George, and Joseph de Rivera—have started to use group dynamics concepts that hold the promise of enriching political science.[2] The rapprochement between the two fields, however, is still mainly a perspective for the future rather than a current reality. In the sections that follow, I shall summarize the conclusions from my intensive case studies of major fiascoes resulting from excessively risky decisions made by policy-making groups, which may help to concretize and give added impetus to this new development within the social sciences.

Groupthink

Over and beyond all the familiar sources of human error is a powerful source of defective judgment that arises in cohesive groups of decisionmakers—the *concurrence-seeking* tendency, which fosters over-optimism, lack of vigilance, and sloganistic thinking about the weakness and immorality of out-groups. This tendency can take its toll even when the policymakers are conscientious statesmen trying to make the best possible decisions for their country. I use the term "groupthink" as a quick and easy way to refer to the mode of thinking that group members engage in when they are dominated by the concurrence-seeking tendency, when their strivings for unanimity override their motivation to appraise the consequences of their actions.

The groupthink hypothesis occurred to me while reading Arthur M. Schlesinger's chapters on the Bay of Pigs in *A Thousand Days*.[3] At first, I was puzzled: How could bright, shrewd men like John F. Kennedy and his advisers be taken in by the CIA's stupid, patchwork plan? I began to wonder whether some kind of psychological contagion, similar to social conformity phenomena observed in psychological studies of small groups, had interfered with their mental alertness. When I re-read Schlesinger and examined other accounts, I was struck by many further observations that fit into exactly the pattern of concurrence-seeking that has impressed me in my research on other face-to-face groups when a "we" feeling of solidarity is running high. I concluded that a group process was subtly at work in Kennedy's team which prevented the members from debating the real issues posed by the CIA's plan and from carefully appraising its serious risks.[4] Then I started to look into similar historic fiascoes that occurred during the administrations of three other American presidents: Franklin D. Roosevelt (failure to be prepared for Pearl Harbor), Harry S. Truman (the invasion of North Korea), and Lyndon B. Johnson (escalation of the Vietnam war).[5] Each decision was a group product, issuing from a series of meetings held by a small and cohesive group of government officials and advisers. In each case I found the same kind of detrimental group process that was at work in the Bay of Pigs decision.

I was surprised by the extent to which the groups involved in these fiascoes adhered to group norms and pressures toward uniformity, even when their policy was working badly and had unintended consequences that disturbed the conscience of the members. Members consider loyalty to the group the highest form of morality. That loyalty requires each member to avoid raising controversial issues, questioning weak arguments or calling a halt to soft-headed thinking.

Paradoxically, soft-headed groups are likely to be extremely hard-hearted toward out-groups and enemies. In dealing with rivals, policymakers constituting an amiable group find it relatively easy to authorize dehumanizing solutions. An affable group of government officials is unlikely to raise ethical issues that imply that this "fine group of ours, with its humanitarianism and its high-minded principles, could adopt a course that is inhumane and immoral."

Eight main symptoms run through the case studies of historic fiascoes. Each symptom can be identified by a variety of indicators, derived from historical records, observer's accounts of conversations, and participants' memoirs. The eight symptoms of groupthink are:

1. an illusion of invulnerability, shared by most or all the members, which creates excessive optimism and encourages taking extreme risks;
2. collective efforts to rationalize in order to discount warnings which might lead the members to reconsider their assumptions before they recommit themselves to their past policy decisions;
3. an unquestioned belief in the group's inherent morality, inclining the members to ignore the ethical or moral consequences of their decisions;
4. stereotyped views of rivals and enemies as too evil to warrant genuine attempts to negotiate, or as too weak and stupid to counter whatever risky attempts are made to defeat their purposes;
5. direct pressure on any member who expresses strong arguments against any of the group's stereotypes, illusions, or commitments, making clear that this type of dissent is contrary to what is expected of all loyal members;
6. self-censorship of deviations from the apparent group consensus, re-

flecting each member's inclination to minimize to himself the importance of his doubts and counterarguments;

7. a shared illusion of unanimity concerning judgments conforming to the majority view (partly resulting from self-censorship of deviations, augmented by the false assumption that silence means consent);

8. the emergence of self-appointed mindguards—members who protect the group from adverse information that might shatter their shared complacency about the effectiveness and morality of their decisions.

At present we do not know what percentage of all national fiascoes are attributable to groupthink. Some decisions of poor quality that turn out to be fiascoes might be ascribed primarily to mistakes made by just one man, the chief executive. Others arise because of a faulty policy formulated by a group of executives whose decision-making procedures were impaired by errors having little or nothing to do with groupthink. All that can be said from the case studies I have analyzed so far is that groupthink tendencies sometimes play a major role in producing large-scale fiascoes.

Theory

The central theme of my analysis can be summarized in this generalization, which I offer in the spirit of Parkinson's laws: The more amiability and esprit de corps among the members of a policy-making in-group, the greater is the danger that independent critical thinking will be replaced by groupthink, which is likely to result in irrational and dehumanizing actions directed against out-groups.

I do not mean to imply that all cohesive groups suffer from groupthink, though all may display its symptoms from time to time. A group whose members have properly defined roles, with traditions and standard operating procedures that facilitate critical inquiry, is probably capable of making better decisions than any individual in the group who works on the problem alone. And yet the advantages of having decisions made by groups are often lost because of psychological pressures that arise when the members work closely together, share the same values, and above all face a crisis situation in which everyone is subjected to stresses that generate a strong need for affiliation. In these circumstances, as conformity pressures begin to dominate, groupthink and the attendant deterioration of decision-making set in. The greater the threat to the self-esteem of the members of a cohesive group, the greater will be their inclination to resort to concurrence-seeking at the expense of critical thinking. Symptoms of groupthink will therefore be found most often when a decision poses a moral dilemma, especially if the most advantageous course requires the policymakers to violate their own standard of ethical behavior. Each member is likely to become more dependent than ever on the in-group for maintaining his self-image as a decent human being and will therefore be more strongly motivated to maintain group unity by striving for concurrence.

Although it is risky to make huge inferential leaps from theory to practice, we should not be inhibited from drawing tentative inferences. Perhaps the worst mistakes can be prevented if we take steps to avoid the circumstances in which groupthink is most likely to flourish. The prime condition repeatedly encountered in case studies of the fiascoes is *group cohesiveness*. Two additional conditions are suggested by comparing the fiascoes with well worked out decisions (the Marshall Plan and the Cuban missile crisis).[6] One condition is *insulation* of the decision-making group from the judgments of qualified associates who, as outsiders, are not permitted to know about the new policies under discussion until after a final decision has been made. Another condition suggested by comparative case studies is *authoritarian leadership*: The more actively the leader of a cohesive policy-making group promotes his own preferred solution, the greater are the chances of a consensus based on groupthink, even when the leader does not want the members to be yes-men and the individual members try to resist conforming.

Preventing Groupthink

The problem of preventing costly miscalculations and lapses from rational thinking in decision-making bodies is complicated: How can policymakers benefit from the cohesiveness of their group without suffering serious losses from groupthink? This sort of intricate psychological issue has been called a pretzel-shaped question and it may require pretzel-shaped answers.

What is urgently needed is a new type of intervention research, in which experienced executives familiar with the policy-making system from the inside and a variety of specialists familiar with decision-making processes from the outside collaborate to develop viable improvements. If this type of enterprise materializes, one line of intervention research might be devoted to testing plausible recommendations, inferred from tentative generalizations about the conditions under which groupthink flourishes, for improving the quality of executive decision-making.

My answer to the acid-test question "Therefore, what?" is heavily influenced by many prior social psychological experiments and detailed observations bearing on group dynamics, including my own studies of task-oriented groups. In this field of research, we become sensitized to the vagaries of human response to seemingly straightforward treatments for improving the quality of group products—vagaries that often force the investigator to conclude that the remedy is worse than the disease. Furthermore, even if free from undesirable side effects, the new treatments are undoubtedly a long way from providing a complete cure. In most cohesive groups, concurrence-seeking tendencies are probably much too powerful to be subdued by administrative changes of the type to be proposed. At best, those changes might somewhat decrease the strength of concurrence-seeking tendencies, thereby reducing the frequency of error.

From my analysis of the conditions that foster groupthink I have suggested the nine prescriptive hypotheses listed below, all of which must be validated before they can be applied with any confidence. In my opinion, despite potential drawbacks, they warrant the trouble and expense of being tested as potentially useful means for partially counteracting groupthink whenever a small number of executives in my organization meet with their chief executive to work out new policies. Certain of the anti-groupthink procedures might also help to counteract initial biases of the members, prevent pluralistic ignorance, and eliminate other sources of error that can arise independently of groupthink. The nine prescriptive hypotheses are compatible with Alexander George's analysis of the conditions that promote the benefits of "multiple advocacy,"[7] when there is genuine give-and-take participation, with a variety of alternative options being advocated by different members of the policy-making group.

1. The leader of a policy-forming group should assign the role of critical evaluator to each member, encouraging the group to give high priority to airing objections and doubts. This practice needs to be reinforced by the leader's acceptance of criticism of his own judgments in order to discourage the members from soft-pedaling their disagreements.

2. The leaders in an organization's hierarchy, when assigning a policy-planning mission to a group, should be impartial instead of stating preferences and expectations at the outset. This practice requires each leader to limit his briefings to unbiased statements about the scope of the problem and the limitations of available resources, without advocating specific proposals he would like to see adopted. This allows the conferees the opportunity to develop an atmosphere of open inquiry and to explore impartially a wide range of policy alternatives.

3. The organization should routinely follow the administrative practice of setting up several independent policy-planning and evaluation groups to work on the same policy question, each carrying out its deliberations under a different leader.

4. Throughout the period when the feasibility and effectiveness of policy alternatives are being surveyed, the policy-making group should from time to time divide into two or more sub-groups to meet separately,

under different chairmen, and then come together to hammer out their differences.

5. Each member of the policy-making group should discuss periodically the group's deliberations with trusted associates in his own unit of the organization and report back their reactions.

6. One or more outside experts or qualified colleagues within the organization who are not core members of the policy-making group should be invited to each meeting on a staggered basis and should be encouraged to challenge the views of the core members.

7. At every meeting devoted to evaluating policy alternatives, one or more members should be assigned the role of devil's advocate. In order to avoid domesticating and neutralizing the devil's advocates, the group leader will have to give each of them an unambiguous assignment to present his arguments as clearly and convincingly as he can, like a good lawyer, challenging the testimony of those advocating the majority position. The most effective performers in the role are likely to be those who can be truly devilish by raising new issues in a conventional low-key style, asking questions such as, "Haven't we perhaps overlooked . . .?"

8. Whenever the policy issue involves relations with a rival nation or organization, a sizable bloc of time (perhaps an entire session) should be spent surveying all warning signals from the rivals and constructing alternative scenarios of the rivals' intentions.

9. After reaching a preliminary consensus about what seems to be the best policy alternative, the policy-making group should hold a "second chance" meeting at which every member is expected to express as vividly as he can all his residual doubts and to rethink the entire issue before making a definitive choice.

Tooling up for Innovations

Recognizing that each innovation in policy-making procedures can introduce new sources of error that might be as bad as or worse than groupthink, we can see why public administrators and executives in large private organizations might have solid reasons for resisting any change in their standard procedures. Nevertheless, innovative executives who know their way around the organizational maze may be able to figure out how to apply one or another of the prescriptions successfully, without producing harmful side effects. If they were to invite well-qualified behavioral scientists to collaborate with them, they might obtain something more than academic advice from the sidelines. Some behavioral scientists (though, alas, not many) possess that rare set of skills required for developing and making objective assessments of new administrative procedures.

Imaginative workers in the new field of research on policy-making procedures might be able to develop the equivalent of a wind tunnel for a series of trial runs to pretest various anti-groupthink procedures before going to the expense of setting up a field test. Then, a collaborative team made up of practical-minded men from inside the organization working with behavioral scientists who spend enough time tooling up to understand what the insiders tell them ought to be able to find a relatively painless way to carry out field studies to assess the long-run effectiveness of the most promising innovative procedures. The objective evaluations made by a team of administrators and behavioral scientists could weed out ineffective and harmful procedures and provide solid evidence to keep the good ones going. By accumulating systematic evidence, they could contribute to the transformation of rational policy-making from a haphazard art into a cumulative science.

In the absence of sound evaluation studies, improvements in decision-making procedures have a chancy existence and often get lost in the shuffle of changing personnel at the top of the organization. Consider the promising innovations introduced by President Kennedy after the humiliation of the Bay of Pigs fiasco. He made several major changes along the lines of some of the foregoing prescriptions for counteracting group-think and improved the quality of decision-making on subsequent occasions, including the Cuban missile crisis. What happened to those innovations after Kennedy's death? Evidently they were regarded simply as part of Kennedy's personal style of leadership and were promptly dropped by his successor, who had his own way of doing things. If a solid body of evidence had been available to show that those procedures would generally be effective in various policy-making bodies headed by men other than John Kennedy, there might have been strong pressures to retain the innovations. The better the evidence showing that a given innovation is effective in a variety of different organizations and at all levels of management, the more confidence everyone can have that the prescription is a valid generalization and the better the chances are that it will be retained when new top executives replace those who initiated the change.

Conclusion

Awareness of the shared illusions, rationalizations, and other symptoms fostered by the interaction of members of small groups may curtail the influence of groupthink in policy-making groups, including those that meet in the White House. Here is another place where we can apply George Santayana's well-known adage: "Those who cannot remember the past are condemned to repeat it." Perhaps a better understanding of group dynamics among government leaders will help them avoid being condemned to repeat the fiascoes of the recent past.

Notes

1. For a summary of research findings and theory See D. Cartwright and A. Zander (eds.), *Group Dynamics*, 3rd edition (New York: Harper and Row, 1968).

2. For a comprehensive survey indicating how group dynamics can be applied to the study of policymaking see J. de Rivera's *The Psychological Dimension of Foreign Policy* (Columbus, Ohio: Merill, 1968).

3. A. M. Schlesinger, Jr., *A Thousand Days* (Boston: Houghton Mifflin, 1965).

4. A detailed case study of the Bay of Pigs decision is presented in Chapter 2 of I. L. Janis, *Victims of Groupthink* (Boston: Houghton Mifflin, 1972).

5. Detailed case studies of the three historic fiascos are presented in Chapters 3, 4 and 5 of I. L. Janis, *Victims of Groupthink*.

6. Detailed case studies of the Marshall Plan and the Cuban Missile Crisis are presented in Chapters 6 and 7 of I. L. Janis, *Victims of Groupthink*.

7. Alexander George, "The Case for Multiple Advocacy in Making Foreign Policy," *American Political Science Review* 66 (1972): 751-795.

12

Political Science and Education: Points of Contact

Jack Thomas

The use of paradigms and perspectives from political science in the study of education is still a somewhat new and tentative endeavor. Books and articles in this area usually begin somewhat apologetically by explaining why political scientists have a legitimate interest in educational problems and practice. It is customary to challenge the old adage that education and politics do not mix and to mention that the American states spend about half their budgets on education. It is not uncommon for 20 percent of a research article to be devoted to this ritual.

Philosophers, psychologists, and sociologists rarely clutter up their presentations with such justifications; perhaps political scientists will soon gain the confidence to omit them as well. Evidence that educationists do not need to be convinced that political science perspectives are potentially useful may be found in the growing number of doctorates being awarded to the hybrid field usually referred to as "politics of education." Further evidence is the increased frequency with which political science modes of analysis characterize articles in education oriented journals. Four of the six articles in a recent issue of the *Educational Administration Quarterly* made use of such modes.[1]

The purpose of this chapter is to give the reader a brief overview of the scope of activities of political scientists working in the field of education. For convenience the studies mentioned have been organized into five general categories: power configurations, political socialization, organizational theory, educational innovations, and accountability. The categories are obviously not mutually exclusive, but they may prove useful nonetheless.

Community Power Configurations

A political science concept which has attracted attention among educators is that of community power configurations. Since educational matters at the elementary and secondary level are largely under the control of local communities, educators interested in political science as well as political scientists interested in education have attempted to analyze the implications of various community power configurations for educational policy and practice. Doctoral students in educational administration across the nation are taught the basic elements of the Hunter-Dahl controversy (both methodologies and conclusions). The policy implications of this controversy, however, have never been satisfactorily developed. Perhaps the most simple, straightforward implication is that political power influences education.

In 1964, Ralph Kimbrough pulled together most of the extant research and informed opinion in this area in his book *Political Power and Educational Decision Making*.[2] Frederick Wirt has reviewed the state of affairs regarding theory and research needs in the study of American educational policies in an article which contains 134 footnotes and is a gold mine for scholars wishing to enter the literature of the field.[3]

Stephen K. Bailey and his colleagues have used the concept of power configurations in a study of state level educational decision making. His book, *Schoolmen and Politics,* although somewhat dated now, stands with the Kimbrough work as a seminal contribution to our understanding of the politics of education.[4] Bailey advocates increased state aid to education, and he stresses the need for political leadership among schoolmen. On the basis of his study in eight northeastern states he concludes:

It is . . . evident that political leadership is the keystone to the arch of state educational finance. Political leadership establishes the effective climate within which intellectual, private interest group, and bureaucratic leadership operate. It is for this reason that schoolmen cannot ignore the ballot box if they wish to advance their causes.[5]

Pressure groups are an important component of power configurations, but they are often poorly understood. Most Americans have been taught that their government is comprised of three branches which check and balance one another. They have also been taught the mechanics of electing public officials and of making laws. But group interests have rarely been emphasized, and many of us tend to consider pressure groups as an aberration in the political system. Harmon Zeigler and a number of other political scientists have challenged this view; they assert that pressure groups are a natural, important, and healthy part of American democracy.[6] Mancur Olson has made an important contribution to this area by specifying the conditions under which pressure groups are likely to form.[7] The relevance of the work of these scholars for education, so far, has never been explicated in detail. It is clear, however, that elementary and secondary school teachers are far better organized than are parents and that the policy implications of this state of affairs are numerous and substantial. In fact, the organized teaching profession is already a powerful force within the nation's labor establishment. Albert Shanker, president of New York's United Federation of Teachers is also a vice president of the AFL-CIO.

Political Socialization

Another political science concept which bears directly on education is that of political socialization. Scholars in this area have tried to understand the nature of political attitudes (usually in a particular cultural setting). When and how such attitudes are formed, as well as their strength and resistance to change, have been studied by a number of scholars.[8]

Richard Merelman, using a case study approach, has done much to define and organize the sub-field of political socialization in his *Political Socialization and Educational Climates*.[9] He attempts to reconcile data from two California school districts with the psychological theories of Piaget, with the current literature on teacher behavior, and with his own convictions about educational policy-making.

An important criticism of the role of American schools in the socialization process is presented by John Patrick in *Political Socialization of American Youth: Implications for Secondary School Social Studies*.[10] Patrick believes there is sufficient evidence to justify the conclusion that our public schools are a "tyranny of the majority."[11]

Patrick believes the emphasis which schools place upon conformity and acceptance of the established political system may have unplanned consequences. Characteristics such as docility and conformity are often prized in school, but they are unlikely to lead to a healthy interest in, and open minded consideration of, the political process or social issues. Patrick argues that since positive attitudes toward our country and its government are so naturally strong, it is imperative that we encourage independence and critical thinking about government in our public schools.

Robert Hess asserts that the concept of political socialization may be of limited utility during periods of rapid social change.[12] If political socialization, as a formal function of schools, is thought of as the process of teaching children a unified view of their nation's cultural values, the process is of questionable value when no such unity exists. As Hess sees it,

. . . the ethnic and cultural differences within the nation cannot be easily blended into unity. Divergences and inequities which have been ignored, particularly with respect to Negroes in the society, are dramatically apparent. It is evident to many citizens that the picture of unity, equality, and freedom that is so often presented is distorted, over-simplified, and, to a degree, false. Indeed, political socialization in the schools may have created an attitude of complacency, a willingness to accept the image of unity and freedom—as well as the actions of the government—and in so doing, it may have contributed to feelings of disillusionment and the consequent climate of protest.[13]

Hess' provocative remarks suggest that we should think very carefully about the meaning of political socialization. My own view is that the concept is still useful for policy related research, but that it needs to be modified to include more than the teaching of aphorisms about American government.

Organizational Theory

Organizational theory forms the foundation for most training programs for educational administrators. There are hundreds of books and articles in the sub-field that is concerned with the structure of schools and other educational organizations. Theorists such as James March, Chris Argyris, and Warren Bennis—well known to scholars of business management and organizational psychology—have recently turned their attention rather explicitly to problems in the field of education. In spite of these welcome contributions, there is little in the literature of educational organizations which differentiates them sharply from other organizations. In fact, the conventional wisdom of the last decade tends to be the same for practically all kinds of organizations. The elements of this conventional wisdom include (1) systems analysis, (2) interdisciplinary analysis, (3) "Theory Y" managerial assumptions, (4) management by objectives, and (5) program budgeting/accounting.

Mike M. Milstein and James A. Belasco have recently edited a collection of readings entitled *Educational Administration and the Behavioral Sciences: A Systems Perspective*.[14] This work explicates the elements listed above and reveals the state-of-the-art in educational administration. It is an art which differs little from that in other branches of administration.

Educational Innovations

Closely related to the study of organizational structure is the study of innovations in educational contexts. In the early sixties, there arose among various scholars, influential practitioners, and governmental figures a certain optimism about the possibility of changing the nation's schools. Part of the reason for this optimism was the growing belief that the federal government would soon be able to fund a massive effort aimed at school improvement. One very popular notion which has persisted to this day is that innovations could be developed at sites external to schools, introduced into a limited number of schools, and then spread widely with the result that educational practice would be upgraded on a significant scale.

In 1965, David Clark and Egon Guba published a "quasi-sequential" classification schema which introduced or reinforced this particular way of thinking about innovation.[15] It was an especially influential view to officers in the U.S. Office of Education. The Clark-Guba schema is presented as Figure 12-1.

It is not entirely clear whether Clark and Guba intended their classification schema to become a strategy for changing schools through innovation. In fact, they have denied such an intention.[16] Nonetheless, disciples of Clark and Guba have most certainly taken this schema to be a sequential strategy for educational change. For example, Ronald E. Hull has recently published an elaboration of the adoption phase of what he calls the Clark and Guba R&D Model. Other evidence of the potency of the Clark-Guba schema is the existence of university-based R&D centers, regional R&D laboratories, and demonstration centers—institutions which correspond respectively to the first three states of the schema. Eight years ago, when I became administrative officer of the Stanford Center for Research and Development on Teaching, I was taught both by Stanford professors and by officials in the USOE the logic of this sequence.

Now that federal funds for educational R&D have become scarce, this particular conception of educational change has lost much of its momentum. First rate educational products turned out to be extremely difficult to develop, and we have learned that schools are often stubbornly resistant to change. Accordingly, the Clark-Guba conception has been criticized by numerous scholars.[17] The most common criticisms have been the following:

1. It is too rational and positivistic.
2. It imposes a sequential pattern on a phenomenon which appears rarely to occur in a sequential fashion.
3. It assumes a passive consumer of innovation and change.

These criticisms are often combined in the form of an assertion that the schema tends to impose a business or engineering mentality on the schools (which presumably are considered human and organic). The assumption here is that business and engineering solutions are simply inappropriate to schools.

To these criticisms I would add two of my own. First, the Clark-Guba schema has an unfortunate and unintended implication about the status of various participants in the innovation process. That is, the research function which is carried on in the university by professors, seems to me to be a much higher status activity than those of the demonstrators and classroom teachers at the other end of the sequence. Many of my colleagues question my judgment on this matter, but I have worked on both ends of the spectrum and have witnessed considerable condescension on the part of professors toward classroom teachers, and considerable resentment on the part of teachers toward professors—especially when innovations are being discussed. Of course, not all professors are condescending nor teachers,

		Development		Diffusion	
	Research	Invention	Design	Dissemination	Demonstration
Objective	To advance knowledge	To formulate a new solution to an operating problem or to a class of operating problems, i.e., *to innovate*	To order and to systematize the components of the invented solution; to construct an innovation package for institutional use, i.e., *to engineer*	To create widespread awareness of the invention among practitioners, i.e., *to inform*	To afford an opportunity to examine and assess operating qualities of the invention, i.e., *to build conviction*
Criteria	Validity (internal and external)	Face Validity (appropriateness) — Estimated Viability — Impact (relative contribution)	Institutional Feasibility — Generalizability — Performance	Intelligibility — Fidelity — Pervasiveness — Impact (extent to which it affects key targets)	Credibility — Convenience — Evidential Assessment
Relation to Change	Provides basis for invention	Produces the invention	Engineers and packages the invention	Informs about the invention	Builds conviction about the invention

	Adoption		
	Trial	*Installation*	*Institutionalization*
Objective	To build familiarity with the invention and provide a basis for assessing the quality, value, fit, and utility of the invention in a particular institution, i.e., *to test*	To fit the characteristics of the invention to the characteristics of the adopting institution, i.e., *to operationalize*	To assimilate the invention as an integral and accepted component of the system, i.e., *to establish*
Criteria	Adaptability — Feasibility — Action	Effectiveness — Efficiency	Continuity — Valuation — Support
Relation to Change	Tries out the invention in the context of a particular situation	Operationalizes the invention for use in a specific institution	Establishes the invention as a part of an ongoing program; converts it to a "non-innovation"

Source: *Educational Administration Quarterly* (Autumn 1974): 35-36.

Figure 12-1. A Classification Schema of Processes Related to and Necessary for Change in Education

resentful; but the schema does emphasize the status differences that do exist by implying that innovations are not invented in schools.

My second criticism of the Clark-Guba schema is that it does not adequately focus on the *political* aspects of the innovation process. During the past five years, the phrase "politics of innovation" has increased markedly in frequency of use. Both scholars and practitioners have bemoaned the fate of educational innovations. Many innovations are never tried; of those that are tried, few persist beyond the first year. A growing number of scholars attribute this phenomenon to political forces which are, as yet, poorly understood.

Teacher organizations apparently resist some innovations partly because school administrators support them. Such is often the case with educational versions of PPBS. School administrators, on the other hand, promote some innovations partly because they will serve to reduce the solidarity of teacher organizations. Strategies which encourage parental involvement via problem solving groups at individual schools often highlight this feature. When a district's problems are tackled school by school, there is an increased probability that issues will not escalate to a point where they must be handled in the political context of school board versus teacher organization.

The times seem to call for a reconceptualization of the innovation process. In a recent paper, Clark and Guba have challenged several assumptions inherent in their earlier work in particular and in the systems view of educational change in general.[18] I hope additional alternative views will emerge. The result could shed some light on a number of policy issues in the area of educational innovation.

Harmon Zeigler and Karl F. Johnson have investigated empirically the relationship between educational innovation and a variety of social, economic and political factors.[19] A large number of variables were factor analyzed and reduced to five basic classifications—urban-economic, educational expenditures, welfare liberalism, social characteristics, and political. Zeigler concluded that per capita income is the only variable significantly related to innovation. He surmised that low income districts need innovation the most but are least likely to attempt it. Zeigler did not conclude that political variables are significantly related to innovation. The variables which he calls political, however, are very different from the community and organizational forces which I have alluded to above. His variables include percentage of individuals voting democratic, voter turnout, length of term for house members, and other similar measures.

One factor which seems to enable the process of innovation to become and remain highly politicized is that there are no widely accepted procedures for measuring the quality of a particular innovation. Researchers are often forced to assume that innovation is, in itself, good. They then proceed to count innovations and use them as the dependent variable in their research studies. The Zeigler-Johnson effort includes this assumption.

The Politics of Educational Innovation by Ernest R. House is a highly readable assessment of where we stand today with regard to large-scale innovation schemes.[20] House feels that many of our current woes result from our assumption that innovations can be standardized, packaged, and distributed widely into diverse school contexts. He labels this assumption "the doctrine of transferability." In Chapter 8 of his book, House discusses this doctrine and its relationship to the Clark-Guba schema discussed above.

Accountability[21]

In a curious way, the general interest of the education establishment in the concept of innovations coupled with government policy which conscientiously encouraged widespread development and testing of innovations contributed to the current fascination with the concept of accountability. As federal funds began to diminish somewhat, and as early results suggested that much federal money targeted for education may have been either wasted or diverted, it became obvious that federal contracts and grants should include provisions for evaluating the outcomes of funded projects. Private foundations also began to include evaluation clauses (or sections) in their contracts and grants. A few universities even set up organizational units which would specialize in project evaluation.[22] Gradually the agencies funding educational innovation began to try to hold the recipients of such funds accountable. Concurrently, as programs in defense, welfare, urban renewal, and other governmental services increased the demands on the tax dollar, accountability became a popular concept among school boards and professional educators (regardless of whether innovations were involved).

The increasing importance of evaluation of educational and social programs requires that the role of the evaluator be considered and defined. In "Evaluation and the Control of Education," Barry McDonald makes a clear distinction between evaluation and research, and then identifies three models of evaluation.[23] He suggests that a "bureaucratic" evaluator subjugates his own values to those of his client and does whatever the client wants; an "autocratic" evaluator is an independent agent who has considerable control over his study and makes policy recommendations; a "democratic" evaluator attempts to make an objective study and then brokers the results to the various audiences of the evaluation. McDonald thinks that it is important and necessary that "democratic" evaluations be attempted more often—especially with today's emphasis on accountability.

Just as the quality of an innovation is hard to measure, so is the quality of a school program or a school district; and there is little agreement on how one would begin to establish that a particular school district or other educational enterprise has indeed been accountable. The notion of accountability connotes incredibly different things to different people. According to Murphy and Cohen,

Like most metaphors concerning reform, this one (accountability) covered a variety of disparate elements; performance contracting, community control, management-by-objectives, educational vouchers, management information systems, and educational assessment . . .

The fate of such reforms is intrinsically interesting for a society in which science is a major source of authority. Particularly noteworthy is the reform's assumption that democratic politics will work better if action is based on scientific information. The idea is that political control has at least partly failed in education because of vested interests, popular apathy, the complexity of modern society, or other reasons. Reformers assert that administrative action will be more effective if scientific data are substituted for—or added to—political intelligence.[24]

Three recent books present three very different notions of accountability and should serve to alert the reader to the complexities of this important area of concern. Leon Lessinger and his associates stressed in *Accountability*[25] the engineering aspects of school reform. Lessinger places heavy emphasis on systems analysis, planning, cost/benefit analysis and related approaches. Perhaps the greatest drawback to this line of attack on educational problems is that systems approaches often require clear, single measurable goals. Persons advocating such approaches often argue that it is either wrong or ridiculous to plan or evaluate programs without first stating unambiguous goals. For political reasons, however, educational goals are often stated ambiguously. In addition, they are multiple and conflicting rather than single. Finally, they are likely to change somewhat from year to year.

In his recent book, *The Politics of School Accountability,* Edward Wynne defines accountability as the "systems or arrangements that supply the public, as well as schoolmen, with accurate information about school output performance."[26] According to Wynne, this information, in the form of quantitative measures, will identify where goals are and are not being met, and will thus lead to action which will get the school program on course again.

Wynne uses an adaptation of the systems approach of David Easton to analyze the accountability system. Although professional educators and the public have roles in this model, Wynne stresses some forces which are usually overlooked—researchers, the state of the art, writers and speakers, and the media. Wynne argues that increased use of quantitative measures, i.e., accountability, could have desirable results: teachers and parents might be put in their proper, advisory relationship, school administrators might begin acting in the public interest, more talented individuals might be drawn into the field of education.

John Wilson discusses one form of accountability—performance contracting—in *Banneker: A Case Study in Educational Change.*[27] He chronicles the events preceding and following the agreement to put a major part of the education of children in Banneker Elementary School of Gary, Indiana, in the hands of a Behavioral Research Laboratories, a private company. The success of this proposed four-year project was to be measured by objective tests, which would also determine the amount of the company's fee. Although the project had a stormy and abbreviated life, it also had some positive results.

Wilson reaches two tentative conclusions about the type of performance contracting done at Banneker: State departments of education will have great operating power and legal authority to prevent or alter performance contracts; schools and contractors will necessarily have to deal persuasively with these departments.

This chapter has presented a brief overview of several points of contact between the field of education and the discipline of political science. The studies mentioned were categorized into the following five areas: power configurations, political socialization, organizational theory, educational innovations, and accountability. Thus the chapter may be taken as a first cut at defining the sub-field of "politics of education."

Notes

1. *Educational Administration Quarterly* (Autumn 1974).

2. Ralph B. Kimbrough, *Political Power and Educational Decision Making* (Chicago: Rand McNally & Co., 1964).

3. Frederick M. Wirt, "Theory and Research Needs in the Study of American Educational Politics," *Journal of Educational Administration* 8, 1 (May 1970): 53.

4. Stephen K. Bailey et al., *Schoolmen and Politics* (Syracuse, N.Y.: Syracuse University Press, 1962).

5. Ibid., p. 108.

6. Harmon Zeigler, *Interest Groups in American Society* (Englewood Cliffs, N. J.: Prentice-Hall, 1964).

7. Mancur Olson, Jr., *The Logic of Collective Action* (Cambridge, Mass.: Harvard University Press, 1965), see especially Chapter VI.

8. *Harvard Educational Review* 38, 3 (Summer 1968). The entire issue is devoted to research reports and discussion on the topic of political socialization. From R. D. Hess "Political Socialization and the Schools," *Harvard Educational Review* 38, Summer 1968, 529. Copyright © 1968 by President and Fellows of Harvard College.

9. Richard M. Merelman, *Political Socialization and Educational Climates* (New York: Holt, Rinehart and Winston, Inc., 1971).

10. John J. Patrick, *Political Socialization of American Youth: Implications for Secondary School Social Studies*, Research Bulletin No. 3 (National Council for the Social Studies, 1967).

11. Ibid.

12. Robert D. Hess, "Political Socialization in the Schools," *Harvard Educational Review* 38, 3 (Summer 1968): 528-535.

13. Ibid., p. 529.

14. Mike M. Milstein and James A. Belasco, *Educational Administration and the Behavioral Sciences: A Systems Perspective* (Boston: Allyn and Bacon, 1972).

15. David L. Clark and Egon G. Guba, "An Examination of Potential Change Roles in Education," Seminor on Innovation in Planning School Curriculum, (October 1965).

16. David L. Clark and Egon G. Guba, "A Reexamination of a Test of the 'Research and Development Model' of Change," *Educational Administration Quarterly* (Autumn 1972): 93-103.

17. See, for example, Ernest R. House, "A Test of the Research and Development Model of Change," *Educational Administration Quarterly* (Winter 1972); and Maurice Kogan, "Educational Research and Development in the United States, Examiners' Report and Questions;" Committee for Scientific and Technical Personnel Educational Policy Reviews, Organization for Economic Cooperation and Development (Paris 1969).

18. David L. Clark and Egon G. Guba, *The Configurational Perspective: A Challenge to the Systems View of Educational Knowledge Production and Utilization* (Indiana University, November 1974).

19. Harmon Zeigler and Karl F. Johnson, *The Politics of Education in the States* (Indianapolis: The Bobbs-Merrill Co., Inc., 1972).

20. Ernest R. House, *The Politics of Educational Innovation* (Berkeley, California: McCutchan Publishing Corp., 1974).

21. For an interesting discussion of the historical roots of the accountability movement, see Raymond E. Callahan, *Education and the Cult of Efficiency; A Study of the Social Forces that have Shaped the Administration of the Public Schools* (Chicago: The University of Chicago Press, 1962).

22. For example, the University of Illinois at Urbana has set up within its College of Education a Center for Instructional Research and Curriculum Evaluation. The University of Western Michigan has set up a similar unit designated the Evaluation Center.

23. Barry McDonald, "Evaluation and the Control of Education," *Safari: Innovation, Evaluation, Research and the Problem of Control* (Norwich, England: University of East Anglia, November, 1974).

24. Jerome T. Murphy and David K. Cohen, "Accountability in Education—the Michigan Experience," *The Public Interest* 36 (Summer 1974), pp. 53-54. Copyright © 1974 by the National Affairs, Inc.

25. Leon Lessinger et al., *Accountability: Systems Planning in Education* (ETC Publications, 1973).

26. Edward Wynne, *The Politics of School Accountability* (Berkeley, California: McCutchan Publishing Corp., 1972).

27. John A. Wilson, *Banneker: A Case Study of Educational Change* (Homewood, Illinois: ETC Publications, 1973).

Part V
Anthropology, Geography, and History

13 Anthropology, Change, and the Social Sciences

Michael Barkun

As an occasional "consumer" of anthropologists' work, it seems to me that their large and impressive literature has been for the most part ignored by political scientists.[1] We have certainly not devoured anthropological monographs with the insatiable appetite that overcomes us in the presence of sociological theory or welfare economics. Nonetheless, it is a literature which has much to say to us and, I think, to which we can make some modest contributions. In the discussion that follows, it is well to bear in mind that it does not purport to be a systematic or exhaustive description of anthropologists' pursuits, that in consequence there are significant omissions, and that in the main it reflects my own recent interests and preoccupations that have led me into ethnographic works.

Obstacles to Dialogue

The lack of significant dialogue between anthropology and political science is in part the result of a more general compartmentalization of intellectual labor, reinforced by the budgetary and administrative "territories" of the modern university. Hopefully, the presence of a new interdisciplinary journal, *Political Anthropology,* will do much to build lines of communication. There are, however, at least two intellectual impediments less easily removed. The first is the methodological prejudice that Mary Douglas calls "Bongo-Bongoism." "(W)hen a generalization is tentatively advanced, it is rejected out of court by any fieldworkers who can say: 'This is all very well, but it doesn't apply to the Bongo-Bongo'."[2] Fieldwork has, at least since the days of Malinowski's ventures into the South Pacific, become something of an anthropological dogma. Given the tendency of late nineteenth and early twentieth century anthropologists to confine their expeditions to Oxbridge libraries, the later insistence upon direct and prolonged contacts had a salutary effect. How many western industrial societies do we know as well as we know the Nuer? A special fusion of rigor and empathy marks the best ethnographies, evoking a people in the totality of its beliefs and experience.

An earlier version appeared in *Policy Studies Journal,* 2 (1973); 30-35. In preparing the revision, as part of a continuing project on millenarian movements, I wish to acknowledge the generous support of the National Endowment for the Humanities.

151

However, the fieldwork dogma has increasingly made social anthropology the victim of its virtues. An insistence upon the particular and the concrete makes comparison appear both unattractive and unprofitable. For any generalization can be demolished by recourse to a single contrary ethnographic report. It appears not to matter that the best ethnographies are themselves generalizations which might be set to flight by the deviating experiences of individuals or groups from the culture in question. Since case studies constitute a kind of epistemological base-line, the search for cross-cultural generalization has been particularly slow and conflict-ridden.

Apart from this concretizing fallacy, the other major difficulty is one shared with other disciplines. Social anthropology, like much else in American social science, has traditionally had a longstanding commitment to the study of social order. Anthropologists have only recently come to question the importance of this claim upon their resources, and, in consequence, have begun to edge toward an examination of disruption and change. There has, of course, been a parallel movement in political science, although I think the proximate causes have been different. Political scientists reacted to the social and political instability of the middle and late 1960s by "discovering" collective violence as a subject of scholarly interest. Anthropologists have had to face the rising levels of turmoil in non-western societies that have come in the wake of independence and modernization. At some more basic level, these two scholarly reorientations may spring from a common cultural source. While this is an intriguing problem in the sociology of knowledge, it need not detain us here. It is simply important to recognize that at least on one level we have much in common. For reasons to be made clear shortly, an emphasis upon social order causes even more complications for anthropologists than it does for students of industrialized societies. The apparent productivity of an order-centered anthropology, however, has until quite recently allowed dilemmas of change to go largely unnoticed.

"Anthropology" is no more monolithic than any other discipline. The particular form which concerns us was shaped in the 1920s and 1930s by British social anthropologists and, somewhat later, by their British and American students. British social anthropology, with its long-standing interest in social harmony, shares the traditional bias toward the study of social order prevalent in American social science and to which mention has already been made. Indeed, Clyde Kluckhohn has aptly characterized it as "a kind of sociology of 'primitive' peoples."[3] Moreover, British anthropologists, from Malinowski and Radcliffe-Brown to their latter-day American disciples, have been predominantly functionalists. Now it is true that anthropological functionalism is less well known than the sociological functionalism with which political scientists are more familiar. Nonetheless, both share a comforting concern for society as an integrated, ongoing whole. By contrast with Parsonian intricacy, anthropological functionalism possesses a refreshing—one might say, almost homely—simplicity. The desire to see society in a holistic fashion led British social anthropology to dwell upon political and legal processes. Given this concentration, it is all the more surprising that its work has generated so little interest among political scientists, for whom such processes have been central.

There is neither need nor space here to catalog the formidable line of anthropological monographs that explore the complexities of power and conflict.[4] For some reason, if political scientists have any contact at all with this literature, it is usually through the medium of E. Adamson Hoebel's *The Law of Primitive Man*.[5] This collection of case studies adequately paraphrases the primary source literature, but how much better to feel the immediate force and vividness of, for example, Malinowski's *Crime and Custom in Savage Society*[6] than to receive it second-hand. In the functionalist perspective, problems of politics and law have a tendency to collapse into one another. One cannot adequately grasp the process of conflict management unless one knows how basic decisions are made, and vice versa. This politico-legal fusion runs against our deep-seated tendency to make a rigid distinction between the "legal" and the "political." If for no other reason, therefore, it is a refreshing experience to immerse oneself in Malinowski, Evans-Pritchard, Mair, or Middleton and Tait. They are, certainly, not entirely successful in rendering reality as a seamless web; but they do demonstrate the critical interpenetration of law and politics in a way that challenges some of the deep-seated categories of political science.

The early functionalists felt they were observing simple societies caught like flies in amber. The absence of written records and the general insensitivity to oral history made the illusion of timelessness appear to be reality itself. This impression of an unchanging round of life was further reinforced by the conventions of British colonial policy, which set the conditions under which most social anthropologists worked. That policy, however mixed its motives, did grant to many subject peoples a relatively high degree of autonomy. Indigenous political and legal systems were encouraged within limits, both to ease the task of local administration and to perpetuate the fragmentation of power. British administrators, too, had a tendency to freeze the customs they found into a perpetual status quo, again the better to rationalize administration. It was in this state of tradition suspended in modernity that non-western, particularly Southern African, peoples were studied. With no discernible past and a politically foreclosed future, it seemed only natural to apply holistic approaches. One could truly see social behavior in the totality of its interrelationships, since colonial constraints were always there to preserve the boundaries.

Eventually, of course, colonial power passed and economic development inexorably closed in about traditional areas. Pretenses of insularity could no longer be maintained, either on political or economic grounds. As if these stunning changes were not enough, the past abruptly reemerged. The newly independent nations required acts of psychological and intellectual as well as political, independence. A principal component has been a "search for a usable past." Clearly, the history of Africa in terms of rivalries among European powers did not provide such a past. However, that view has been supplanted by a revisionist historiography, respectful of oral traditions and anxious to demonstrate that indigenous peoples were not changeless after all. This new history—for example, the so-called "Dar es Salaam School" in East African History[7]—highlights themes of political organization and resistance to colonization previously ignored or obscured.

Functionalism could be useful and persuasive as long as the boundaries of the social organism held. But, as the boundaries collapsed, social anthropology was confronted with the problem of explaining change, and for this purpose functionalism has proven inadequate. The concept of parts integrated to form a smoothly functioning whole, each component tied reciprocally to the others, related well to apparently slow-changing, culturally homogeneous societies. But it failed to account adequately for the disappearance of the old and the sudden appearance of the new.

Order and Law

As anthropologists turn their attentions to the abrasive contact of cultures, new approaches evolve, along with a new appreciation for the importance, not only of patterns, but of breaks in patterns. Two recent works provide apt illustrations of the way in which this changed orientation manifests itself in legal anthropology. Francis Mading Deng's study of law among the Dinka of the Sudan[8] is of particular interest because it is at once an anthropological study and the work of someone whose primary professional identification is with the law. Nonetheless, Deng, who is himself the son of a Dinka chief, has produced a meticulously detailed description of the legal stresses of modernization. The complexity of the Dinka's dilemma grows not only out of the usual problems of a developing society but also from the peculiarly Sudanese situation which has pitted a dominant Arab, Muslim North against a weaker black, Christian, and pagan South. In addressing the problems of cultural clash, Deng has chosen to supplement the conventional apparatus of social anthropology—geared to far more stable situations—with Harold Lasswell's value analysis. The result is one of the few genuinely persuasive applications of the Lasswellian framework to legal problems.

In an equally compelling fashion, Jane Fishburne Collier's study of law in a Mayan Indian community[9] illustrates both the limits of functionalism and the ways in which its defects may be remedied. Social anthropology has had a tendency to view primitive societies as neater and more symmetrical than they are. The necessity of tracing complex kinship relationships no doubt in part accounts for this, but whatever may be responsible, the result is a distaste for contradictions and loose ends. In the field of law specifically, the penchant for orderly description goes together with a concentration upon rules and, most significantly, upon the punitive reactions of the community to rule violators. While there are exceptions to the focus upon sanction and rule violation—Malinowski himself is the most prominent—it seems in the main to be an accurate characterization.

As Professor Collier reports, she began her study of the Zinacanteco Indians with precisely such presuppositions and abandoned them only after they led to blind alleys. "I realized that I would have to reconsider my theoretical framework. Zinacantecos were not concerned with crime and punishment. They cared about ending conflicts."[10] Her focus shifted to the ranges of alternatives open to litigants in specific kinds of situations, together with the pressures and incentives that favored some alternatives over others. The resulting conception of law relies less upon the specification of imposed rules and far more upon the way in which the legal system's subjects themselves manipulate the rules. A case in point is the tension between Indian customary law and official Mexican law. The problem, which might be conventionally thought of in terms of superiority-inferiority, resolves itself into one of the costs and benefits that a litigant must weigh in choosing to invoke a particular system.

This concept of multiple legal systems in a single territory is a potentially powerful tool for understanding law in developed societies. It cuts through the fiction that our own legal system, for example, is homogeneous and integrated. If anything, we experience far more conflicts among opposed value systems than the Zinacanteco. Yet the fiction of uniformity asserts that the American legal system rises in a majestic and consistent hierarchy, each level securing consistency in those below it. Given the scope of American society, the fragmentation of effective power, and the jumble of jurisdictions, we may wonder that we get along as well as we do while upholding a uniformist conception. Legal anthropology at its most sophisticated has, consequently, much to tell us about the business of unravelling jurisdictional and cultural complexities. As students of local criminal justice have already found, each city constitutes a legal culture of its own. While formally subordinated to national constitutional mandates, local consensus and lack of oversight render police, prosecutors, defense attorneys, and judges effectively independent of external pressures much of the time. The perceived values of the community and the need for day-to-day cooperation among interacting professionals are the paramount considerations. Yet on occasion the environment does impinge, through the appellate process, the spectacular individual case, or a federal funding agency. At such times, legal systems confront one another as surely as they do in contacts between tribes or between colonial administration and indigenous population. This is not, by the way, to suggest that anthropological techniques and metaphors offer facile opportunities for moral judgment. At a normative level, we might even sympathize with that hoary British category, "natural justice," trotted out from time to time to control customs "repugnant" to western sensibilities. The point is not that legal anthropology permits legal systems to be analyzed in terms of "good guys" and "bad guys," but rather that it can lay bare complexities and contradictions which we take for granted; as the anthropologist's cliche has it, "The fish doesn't know the water."

Even legal anthropology, however, has limits to its usefulness, the limits of ordered, ongoing societies. As long as the system maintains itself, deals adequately with internal and external stresses, and fails to include substantial change, equilibrium models suffice. Such situations are becoming harder and harder to find, either in simple or complex societies. In any case, we know remarkably little about societal resilience, how far a community can bend in order to accommodate stress. Even those elements of the functionalist tradition that might illuminate the problem have been remarkably little used. Thus Max Gluckman's striking concept of "rituals of rebellion" was first enunciated nearly a quarter of a century ago.[11] It has since suffered the fate of constant citation and ample metaphorical usage without the systematic development its originality deserves. The notion of rebellious actions undertaken with the tacit support of the community, and for which governing norms exist, suggests a gray area between order and revolution. "Rituals of rebellion" continues to be invoked, most recently in the context of student disruptions in American and European universities. Yet its mere invocation tells little about the dimensions of the frontier area between stability and disorder. Ironically, Gluckman's own skepticism about the viability of ritualized rebellion in modern societies has proven no inhibition upon its appropriation by political scientists and sociologists.[12] The problem that arises is not, however, one of intellectual proprietorship. Rather, it is one of careless borrowing for purposes of exotic color, not rigorous analysis. The concept of ritualized rebellion has yet to bear its full fruit. The major questions have not yet been addressed: When and where do rituals of rebellion appear? Under what circumstances do rituals of rebellion slip into outright revolution? What kinds of stress can such rituals handle?

Explaining Change

When such adaptive devices are either nonexistent or no longer effective, stability can no longer be assumed. Significantly, I.C. Jarvie's brilliant, if occasionally strident, critique of functionalism, *The Revolution in Anthropology,*[13] takes as its point of departure the failure of functionalism to explain the Melanesian "cargo cults." These movements arose early in this century and have continued sporadically up to the present. In their periodic sweeps through Melanesian societies, they have combined sudden repudiation of traditional beliefs and practices with the equally abrupt spread of millenarian beliefs: Ships (more recently, airplanes) are about to arrive, bearing both the spirits of the ancestors and the manufactured goods (the "cargo") that symbolize western power. The cults purport to have discovered the magical means by which westerners suddenly acquire manufactured articles. For without direct acquaintance with manufacturing processes, the manner in which ships and planes disgorge cargo are thought to be the product of secret and magical means. Bizarre though the cargo cults appear, it is just such breaks with tradition that cause insuperable difficulties for functionalism. And as the pressures of modernization grow, the need to explain its consequences increases.

Earlier writers were content to describe the means through which homeostasis was maintained. This approach assumed the survival of the society; what was problematic were the particular institutions chosen. As more and more attention is paid to stress, change, and disruption, survival can no longer be assumed. Instead, a society under stress faces a range of alternatives which includes both dissolution and many different forms and degrees of survival. Anthony Wallace, in his seminal paper on revitalization movements,[14] argues that societies under stress cannot continue to conduct "business as usual." They must either reconstruct the cultural system under the guidance of a charismatic figure or face a kind of cultural death. Wallace's "revitalization process" on the surface bears considerable resemblance to systemic-functional theories. A society begins in homeostasis and passes through stages of successively more serious stress, until a charismatic figure restructures the culture in a manner which permits a return to stability. It is this restructuring that marks a break with past theorizing. For Wallace must import a radical kind of innovation into his homeostasis-stress-homeostasis cycle. The charismatic figure enters as a kind of *deus ex machina*.

Explaining innovation is a difficult business. Attempts to do it in terms of such concepts as "stress," "frustration," or "relative deprivation" have proven generally unfruitful.[15] Such responses as the American Indian Ghost Dance, the Ras Tafari in Jamaica, and the Maji Maji uprising in East Africa defy explanations built upon assumptions of continuity and order. The ability of societies to restructure themselves in the anticipation of some coming millennium has been demonstrated in nearly every area of the world, both western and non-western. If it poses particularly severe conceptual problems for anthropologists, that is only because anthropologists have perhaps more than other social scientists dealt with communities that seemed immune from rapid change. As these examples suggest, the phrase "ongoing social system" is a possibility, not a universal condition. To achieve ongoingness in certain precarious circumstances, a community may be compelled to resort to some fairly unconventional expedients. One measure of this lies in the tendency of catastrophic change to so often precipitate movements committed, in Norman Cohn's phrase, to "the pursuit of the millennium." That so many attempts to create a perfected society here and now have been made in the non-western world testifies to the havoc western penetration has wrought in traditional modes of thinking and knowing.

Movements of total transformation are not, however, solely in the anthropologist's domain. While conspicuous in Southern Africa, South Asia, and Oceania, many of the same characteristics can be found closer to home. Thus dependence upon charismatic leadership, expectation of a future millennium, and division of the world into good and evil spheres are also hallmarks of modern totalitarianism. As fears concerning the environment, the availability of energy, and the viability of modern economies mount, we may anticipate that the pursuit of the millennium will once again take hold in the West.

Strategies for Comparative Study

I have attempted, however briefly, to note some recent contributions and limitations of anthropological studies. It would be inappropriate to close without suggesting that the relationship need not be one of mere borrowing. The anthropological literature, rich though it is, has not been without defects. The principle one seems to me to be a continued addiction to case studies and a concommitant unwillingness to venture very far in the direction of comparison and generalization. The emphasis, since Malinowski, upon intensive fieldwork in a single society, usually over many months, doubtless accounts for this. The demands upon researchers' time, and the vast amount of data six months' fieldwork produces, militate against less intensive but more wide-ranging inquiries. Thus one proceeds through the literature society by society and encounters relatively few attempts to draw together the discrete, monographic contributions.

The careful comparative use of anthropological data by lawyers, sociologists, and political scientists, while still relatively rare, demonstrates both the value of the data and the need to integrate it. The utilization of anthropological data within the framework of broader legal studies has been particularly fruitful. Kenneth Carlston found African ethnographic studies of great value in relating law and social structure.[16] Adda Bozeman has drawn from a wide geographic range to lay bare the cultural assumptions of legal systems.[17] Utilizing the Human Relations Area Files, Richard D. Schwartz and James C. Miller related legal institutions and societal complexity in a manner which continues to excite fruitful controversy a decade after the original publication.[18] What is perhaps most interesting about their work, however, is not its comparative use of ethnographic data, interesting though that is, but rather the fact that it points toward an evolutionary approach to legal institutions. The return of an evolutionary perspective again suggests the need to explain change as well as continuity.

If legal institutions and systems must be viewed as changing, how much more so is this true in the case of social unrest itself. Here, too, comparative utilization of anthropological sources has progressed, although, once again, largely in the hands of non-anthropologists. Thus Bryan Wilson's recent very ambitious synthesis draws together a wealth of material from Africa, Oceania, and the Americas about the ways in which these peoples have organized themselves to cope with culture contact.[19] On a more geographically restricted basis, Peter Worsley has systematically analyzed the voluminous Melanesian Cargo Cult literature.[20] Although neither Wilson's nor Worsley's work is without defects—theoretical diffuseness in the former, rigidity in the latter—both demonstrate that anthropological data can be used comparatively to build generalizations without fatally compromising it.

In sum, a largely untapped body of data and low-level propositions exists, which, if carefully and critically applied, can add increased depth to political science research. The ethnographic literature provides a spectrum of societies which exhibit a far wider range of variation than we are accustomed to. It provides as well a set of microcosms within whose confines broader political and social processes may be studied. Social anthropology in its traditional sense is becoming increasingly obsolete. The isolated simple societies of the past are inexorably being drawn into the political and economic mainstream. The insularity that allowed them to be studied, as it were, *in vacuo* has broken down almost everywhere. It becomes more and more difficult to identify communities that specifically demand the anthropologist's investigative and descriptive skills. Yet this very homogenization makes the broader application of anthropological techniques and findings more essential. So long as it was possible to shunt the anthropologist's material over to a pigeonhole marked "primitive cultures," that material could safely be ignored by most political scientists, sociologists, economists, and historians. We cannot any longer relegate it to a residual category simply because the differences between the anthropologists' raw material and our own can no longer be detected with assurance.

American society, for example, is no longer the melting pot it was assumed to be. Ethnic and racial separatism and segregation produce islands of cultural diversity that can no longer go unnoticed. Educational institutions, governmental bureaucracies, and large corporations produce their own distinctive sub-cultures. Are they any less insular for their members than an African tribe? Or less distinctive and demanding? The fiction of uniformity that has played havoc with legal thinking produces similarly distorting effects for the study of politics and economics. Institutions and communities erect boundaries, even though the polity is presumed to be a seamless web. In its extreme forms, erecting boundaries may seem essential for an institution's survival, as it is for those that Erving Goffman calls "total institutions" and Lewis Coser, "greedy institutions."[21] Mental hospitals, prisons, some educational institutions, communes, armed forces—these suggest but do not exhaust the genre of insulated segments of society, amenable to ethnographic study. For we surely are as much in need of ethnographies of courts, universities, and corporations as we are of those few remaining preliterate peoples at the margins of the industrializing world.

If explanations of change are still too few and too simplistic, the need for careful and empathic description remains. In a broad sense, of course, there is never description without some tentative explanation, however covert. And, as we have seen, even the best anthropological descriptions have too often been predicated upon explanations from which meaningful change had been excluded. Sometimes the guiding theoretical orientation was simply taken for granted and never stated openly. At other times, it was put forward as the key to understanding society's ongoingness. When sufficient evidence filtered through, even the basic assumption of ongoingness finally appeared problematic. The search for an explanation that would cover change, not merely continuity, still seems groping and inconclusive. But in the meantime, as the search for a meaningful explanation of change goes forward, the need for adequate description continues too —even though, paradoxically, the very techniques available for description come to us permeated with questionable theoretical assumptions. Anthropological methods and materials, as applied to the problems of complex society, at least have the advantage of novelty, and that advantage in part neutralizes their built-in theoretical bias. There is a freshness, a naivete, that comes with descriptions of the familiar in terms of another discipline. Given the doubts which surround functionalism, it may ironically be the case that anthropological methods, which gave birth to functionalism between the two world wars, can operate more effectively in new surroundings than in their accustomed haunts. It is possible, too, that with the reservations about functionalism in mind, sociologists and political scientists can extract more from anthropological data than could those who originally collected it.

Notes

1. An early and notable exception was David Easton's "Political Anthropology," in Bernard J. Siegel (ed.), *Biennial Review of Anthropology, 1959* (Stanford, Calif.: Stanford University Press, 1959), pp. 210-62.

2. Mary Douglas, *Natural Symbols: Explorations in Cosmology* (New York: Vintage, 1973), pp. 15-16.

3. Clyde Kluckhohn, "Anthropology in the Twentieth Century," in Guy S. Metraux and Francois Crouzet (eds.), *The Evolution of Science* (New York: Mentor, 1963), pp. 396-422.

4. For bibliographies of the legal anthropology literature, see Laura Nader, "The Anthropological Study of Law," *American Anthropologist* 67 6 (part 2): 3-32; Sally Falk Moore, "Law and Anthropology," in Bernard J. Siegel (ed.), *Biennial Review of Anthropology, 1969* (Stanford, Calif.: Stanford University Press, 1970).

5. E. Adamson Hoebel, *The Law of Primitive Man* (Cambridge, Mass.: Harvard University Press, 1954). On Hoebel's work, see Leopold Pospisil, "E. Adamson Hoebel and the Anthropology of Law," *Law and Society Review* 7 (1973): 537-60.

6. Bronislaw Malinowski, *Crime and Custom in Savage Society* (Totowa, N.J.: Littlefield, Adams, reprinted 1966).

7. Donald Denoon and Adam Kuper, "Nationalist Historians in Search of a Nation: The 'New Historiography' in Dar es Salaam," *African Affairs* 69 (1969): 329-49; Terence Ranger, "The 'New Historiography' in Dar es Salaam," *African Affairs,* 70 (1969): 50-61; Denoon and Kuper, "The 'New Historiography' in Dar es Salaam: A Rejoinder," *African Affairs,* 70 (1969): 287-88.

8. Francis Mading Deng, *Tradition and Modernization: A Challenge for Law among the the Dinka of the Sudan* (New Haven: Yale University Press, 1971).

9. Jane Fishburne Collier, *Law and Social Change in Zinacantan* (Stanford, Calif.: Stanford University Press, 1973).

10. Ibid., p. viii.

11. In the form of the Frazer Lecture, Glasgow, 1953. This and related papers were subsequently collected in Max Gluckman, *Order and Rebellion in Tribal Africa* (Glencoe, Ill.: The Free Press, 1963).

12. Ibid., p. 135.

13. I.C. Jarvie, *The Revolution in Anthropology* (Chicago: Regnery, 1969).

14. Anthony F.C. Wallace, "Revitalization Movements," *American Anthropologist* 58 (1956): 264-81.

15. For bibliographies of the millenarianism literature, see Michael Barkun, *Disaster and the Millennium* (New Haven: Yale University Press, 1974); Weston La Barre, "Materials for a History of Studies of Crisis Cults: A Bibliographic Essay," *Current Anthropology* 12 (1971): 3-44; Vittorio Lanternari, "Nativistic and Socio-religious Movements: A Reconsideration," *Comparative Studies in Society and History* 16 (1974): 483-503.

16. Kenneth S. Carlston, *Social Theory and African Tribal Organization: The Development of Socio-legal Theory* (Urbana, Ill.: University of Illinois Press, 1968).

17. Adda B. Bozeman, *The Future of Law in a Multicultural World* (Princeton: Princeton University Press, 1971).

18. Richard D. Schwartz and James C. Miller, "Legal Evolution and Societal Complexity," *American Journal of Sociology* 70 (1964): 159-69; Howard Wimberly, "Legal Evolution: One Further Step," *American Journal of Sociology,* 79 (1973): 78ff; Upendra Baxi, "Comment —Durkheim and Legal Evolution: Some Problems of Disproof," *Law and Society Review* 8 (1974): 645-51; Richard D. Schwartz, "Legal Evolution and the Durkheim Hypothesis: A Reply to Professor Baxi," *Law and Society Review* 8 (1974): 653-68.

19. Bryan Wilson, *Magic and the Millennium: A Sociological Study of Religious Movements of Protest Among Tribal and Third-world Peoples* (New York: Harper and Row, 1973).

20. Peter Worsley, *The Trumpet Shall Sound: A Study of "Cargo" Cults in Melanesia,* 2nd ed. (New York: Schocken, 1968).

21. Erving Goffman, *Asylums: Essays on the Social Situation of Mental Patients and Other Inmates,* (Garden City, N.Y.: Anchor, 1961), pp. 1-124; Lewis A. Coser, *Greedy Institutions: Patterns of Undivided Commitment* (New York: The Free Press, 1974).

14 Geographic Contributions to Policy Studies

John O'Loughlin

Shortly after I had written a brief article on geography and public policy,[1] the *New York Times* printed an evaluation of modern geography by Robert Rheinhold.[2] Pointing to the discipline's new subject matter and analytical techniques, Rheinhold reviewed recent geographic research in central place theory, spatial diffusion models, mental maps, and the "man-land" approach to the study of natural hazards. He emphasized throughout the article the theoretical and mathematical methods employed by geographers today. The difference between the "old" geography, characterized by regional description and "modern" geography, with its nomothetic approach to the study of contemporary problems, was well documented by Rheinhold. However, the recent backlash against the "homo economicus" approach of the locational analysts and a consequent emphasis on the policy applications of geographic work was mentioned only briefly. In this chapter, I will concentrate on the development of a policy-orientation among geographers and outline some of the approaches and techniques utilized by the profession.

Geography's Role in Policy Research: United States and Europe

In the United States, geography is a little known social science. The public often confuse it with geology or more often equate the discipline with the "National Geographic." Recent efforts by the Association of American Geographers (AAG) to introduce new programs of study into high schools and to educate the lay public about the "new" geography have met with only limited success. This is not surprising because for too long geographers were cloistered in their academic towers and had little of interest for the American public. Few geographers were appointed to governmental commissions and the roles that geographers should have played often fell to sociologists and geologists. Despite the development of spatial analysis and geographic expertise in the explanation and prediction of spatial patterns of human phenomena, acceptance of a spatial viewpoint by other academics, governmental bodies, and the public has been slow.

One suggestion on how geography might raise its profile in the United States involved geographers undertaking research that has a policy orientation. Geographic research has not been translated into real-world applications. For example, "research into urban spatial structure . . . has attained a high level of theoretical and technical sophistication but its impact on policy has, so far at least, been minimal."[3] Geography was one of the last social sciences to become aware of social problems in this country, although many such problems beg spatial analysis. Yet, "the Chicago school of sociology . . . has been looking at social problems from what is often essentially a spatial point of view for the last fifty years."[4]

A sharp contrast exists between the position of geography in the United States and its position in European and British Commonwealth countries. Due in large measure to the colonial drive, with its accompanying need for exploration and description of far-off places, geographical societies were founded in London, Paris, Berlin, St. Petersburg, and other European centers. Geography achieved an initial strong foothold in the high schools and chairs of geography were established in the leading universities by 1900. After the First World War, land-use planning concerns came to the forefront, especially in Britain. In the last thirty years, regional planning bills have been enacted throughout Europe. Geographers have assumed important roles on the advisory planning boards, especially in Britain, Sweden, and the Soviet Union.

Even though geographic methods permeate many aspects of planning in Europe, dissatisfaction exists regarding the role of geographers. "Research has tended to respond to available data and techniques with a consequent preoccupation with remedies for past errors rather than prevention of future ones. Second, geographers have been content to influence rather than make decisions. If relevant research is to be translated into planning policy, then geographers must be prepared to participate as decision makers themselves."[5] Planners in Britain assume that the basic structure underlying policy alternatives needs adjustment rather than a complete overhaul.[6] Many British geographers are concerned that these adjustment policies will perpetuate the spatial inequalities that presently exist between regions and within metropolitan areas. Of course, this concern is not confined to Britain but appears in all societies where planning philosophies are being debated and subsequent plans implemented.

Concern with the public policy implications of geographic research in the United States was evident for the first time at the San Francisco meetings of the Association of American Geographers in 1970. Gilbert F. White, one of the speakers at a session titled "Geography and Public Policy," saw three major questions facing the profession: (1) What are the criteria for selecting research problems in the light of possible social implications? (2) What steps, if any, the AAG should take to advance and support the concern with contemporary problems? (3) What are the problems of the tradeoffs between academic freedom and the pursuit of social justice?'' Each academic faces in his institutions the issue of how to reconcile our jealous protection of freedom of inquiry in research and teaching with our conviction that education should be an instrument of social change toward peace and justice.''[7]

The trend of concern with contemporary problems intensified at the 1971 Boston meetings with a session on "Geographical Aspects of American Poverty and Social Well-Being," containing papers on interstate variations in social well-being, mobility problems of the poor, residential segregation in Chicago, and social justice and spatial systems. According to David Smith, two alternative but complementary approaches were evident at Boston: "(first), to begin with existing geographical knowledge and then look for practical applications or (second) to begin with a policy problem and then ask how far geographic knowledge can illuminate it."[8] The Association set up a committee on Geography and Public Policy. Unfortunately, this committee missed a golden opportunity to involve the geographic profession in policy research and implementation, and was disestablished in 1973 because of its non-activity.

In 1972, the AAG received funding from the National Science Foundation for its Metropolitan Analysis project, with the stated goals of providing an accurate comparative assessment of the progress being make toward meeting human needs in America's twenty largest metropolitan areas. For each of these metropolises, a vignette, stressing problems and opportunities in the area, has been prepared by a local geographer. The second part of the project consists of thirteen policy monographs on important metropolitan problems such as commuting problems of the poor, public health services delivery, education, metropolitan government, and the quality of urban physical environments. These monographs will be comparative in nature, each problem being evaluated for a sample of metropolitan areas. The final part of the project is the mapping of census data at three scales for each metropolis. The project represents a major effort on the part of the AAG in policy research. It is hoped that its research results will stimulate greater concern for urban problems among both academics and the lay public and at the same time, that the project's conclusions will assist the formulation of more effective urban policies.

Development of Policy Orientation in Geography

The policy thrust of physical geography received a major boost with the passage of the National Environmental Policy Act in 1969. Section 102 of this act stated that all federal agencies had to include environmental impact statements in all future projects. Because geography has been concerned with the man-environment interface, it would seem as if a golden opportunity exists for the study of social systems affected by proposed projects and the development of methods of measuring the social values in environmental impacts. A good example of geographic work in this important policy arena is the natural hazards research by Burton, White, and their students.[9] By studying peoples' perceptions of recurring hazards and their causes, in cross-cultural settings, they have provided a significant input to governmental plans for alleviating death and destruction in hazard zones.

Recent innovations in aerial photography, radar, and infrared imagery have spawned a new breed of technician-geographers. Using images from both low-level and high-level flights, they have engaged in settlement analysis, land-use inventories, and environmental impact analysis. Unfortunately, much of the imagery is classified and the work of many geographers, being used for intelligence purposes, is not known. Nonetheless, urban imagery for the United States presents opportunities for analysis of poverty pockets, the urban fringe, and the distribution of green-space within the built-up area. Large numbers of geographers with remote sensing, and accompanying cartographic expertise, are being employed by state agencies and large private research firms, as well as the usual intelligence-gathering government agencies.

Like many other disciplines, the first use of geographers and geographic methods to study practical problems was during World War I. Between the world wars, many of these "applied" geographers found employment in other branches of government and in private business. A good example of their public policy work is the Michigan Land Economic Survey of the 1930s.[10] The northern part of the state had been ravaged by the exploitation of its natural resources and the survey was undertaken by geographers at the University of Michigan, in cooperation with the State Department of Conservation. Based on the accurate inventory of resources of the cutover lands, a land management policy was formulated by the state of Michigan. In the business world, geographers were hired, beginning in the 1930s, in marketing research. Alternative sites for the location of retail outlets were evaluated in spatial terms (size and income of market area, distance to nearest competitor, etc.), and the best (most profitable) location picked. This type of research continues today, although now using the latest mathematical and statistical tools. Its main importance for current policy research in geography is the continuing search for the "best location", often termed the geographers' unsolved problem.

Socio-Spatial Justice and Geographic Policy Studies

Since the discovery of poverty and related aspects of the American scene by geographers in 1969-70, a veritable explosion of literature on the spatial dimensions of social justice has appeared. This literature can be placed in three groups: (a) liberal formulations, (b) revolutionary approaches, and (c) geographic expeditions. The liberal method is characterized by an emphasis on problem-solving, and a more equitable spatial distribution of power and services. Initially, work of this genre focused on descriptive models of social injustice in a spatial (especially urban) context. In many instances, the real-world situation was compared to a model, based on spatial efficiency criteria, in order to measure the inequities in the present system. For example, Earickson using a simulation model assigning patients to physicans, indicated that the present health care system in Chicago is not spatially efficient and that 90,000 patient-miles would be saved if physicians were relocated in the metropolitan area.[11] More recently, research has tended to focus on prescriptive models of change and social engineering proposals. "Scientific models ideally could perform (societal action and control) functions, first by indicating which alternative actions can be accommodated within the bounds of currently accepted scientific knowledge, and second by specifying the foreseeable side effects of these actions."[12] Peet sees the geographer's greatest potential contribution in the eradication of American poverty largely in planning for the location of social and economic institutions which provide services and opportunities for low income people.[13] This approach again raises the question of "best location," which, of course, varies depending on the constraints placed on an optimizing model. Another major research thrust of this "liberal" group is the explanation of spatial patterns of social pathologies. Using the standard cartographic and multivariate techniques, they have analyzed the spatial distributions of crime, diseases, political power, access to services, and poverty.

A second approach, which depicts the liberal formulations as helping to perpetuate present inequalities, is the Marxist perspective. (The Association of American Geographers established a Committee on Marxist Perspective in 1974.) As stated by Harvey, present geographic theories of urban form and process are "counter-revolutionary," that is, they explain the present patterns and suggest ways to reduce present spatial maldistributions. For example, urban land use theory, derived from the Von Thunen concentric model, accurately predicts the location of slums in American cities. But since the societal objective is to get rid of such blight, Marxist geographers argue that we should wish this theory to become "not true." "The simplest approach here is to eliminate those mechanisms which serve to generate the theory. The mechanism in this case is very simple— competitive bidding for the use of the land."[14] "Revolutionary theory," then, is change-oriented and seeks to create truth rather than find it. Most of the applications of Marxist theory in spatial terms has involved the ever-present ghettoes and slums of American cities, seen as the products of a neo-colonialist system. As yet, this body of literature is still unknown to the majority of geographers but is gaining in importance as the "liberal" paradigm provides little new or incisive in urban research.

Field work in geography, a teaching and research device since the development of modern academic geography, has assumed a new and important role in recent years. Urban geographic field expeditions, where academic geographers live and work in inner city communities, have appeared in Detroit and Toronto. Their goals are to "map and describe the human condition. (They) concentrate on material that does not appear in the census."[15] Analyses of school-districting plans, local recreation, housing, police services, auto deaths of children, urban renewal plans, etc., have appeared in field notes but only recently made inroads to the "establishment" journals. Concern exists among urban explorers that in the search for "relevance" and "policy applications" the more important questions of "relevancy and policy for whom" are often overlooked. A way has been suggested to avoid the pitfalls of decisions from authorities unaware of real community needs. It is the development of a priority of needs based on investigative work of the urban scene at the micro-level. Research resulting from urban exploration has been criticized for its "non-scientific" character.[16] In reply, Bunge, originator of the concept of an urban expedition has written "there is no such thing as a dispassionate scientist. . . . Urban exploration, the use of geography in the protection of children, survival geography, because of the overwhelming need, cannot wait for a gradual acceptance."[17]

The sub-field of geography most immediately concerned with policy questions, political geography, has shown signs of emerging from the research doldrums into which it sank after the Second World War. (This was partly a response to the confusion of political geography with the discredited theory of "geopolitics," which had achieved great prominence in Nazi Germany.) Oliver P. Williams, a political scientist, has provided a framework for the analysis of metropolitan politics and policies, using an essentially spatial approach.[18] He defines the concept "urbanism" as the convergence of people on a particular location within the city so as to facilitate interaction among themselves and with other parts of the urban matrix. Now, location becomes important, as the most powerful groups will gain the choicest sites and powerless groups will be left the unattractive locations. A major policy problem for social scientists is how to improve the "access" of powerless groups, that is, how to make their location more instrumental in increasing their power. For example, residential segregation benefits blacks, because an increasing number of electoral districts have black majorities. By utilizing the location-black population coincidence, often by a bloc vote, blacks can increase their political power and thereby improve their "access."

Contemporary Policy Questions in Geography

In the final section of this short chapter, four contemporary policy questions are briefly reviewed. The vexing question of "best location" was mentioned earlier. Great progress has been made in recent years in the development of optimizing location-allocation algorithms, but the basic problem of the definition of "best" still remains. A major criticism of models of location-allocation (locating a set of facilities to serve a population) is that they are based on economic efficiency criteria, with little consideration of social needs. The criteria (or constraints) of equity (assuring equal access by all groups) and efficiency (distance-minimizing solution) are often in conflict. Efficiency constraints are far easier to incorporate than equity considerations, which are based on social and moral values. Unfortunately, most algorithms used by geographers have placed efficiency ahead of equity: there is no technical reason why social considerations should not be met in the assignment of populations to optimally located service centers. Among the social criteria, cited by Harvey, that might be considered are need, valuation of services (individuals who command scarce resources have a greater claim), merit (based on the degree of difficulty to be overcome in contributing to production), and contribution to the common good.[19] Of these, need is the easiest to measure and by a weighting procedure can be incorporated into a territorial distributive algorithm. Among the policy applications of these spatial assignment models have been the allocation of people to hospitals in Guatemala,[20] pupils to schools in Georgia[21] (where racial integration criteria were met), and children to day care centers in the Model Cities of Columbus, Ohio.[22] The model's most spectacular policy application was in Sweden where a geographer, Sven Godlund, was designated by the government to select the sites of three new specialized medical centers and the sites of six existing hospitals that were to be upgraded.

Reapportionments of electoral, school, and service districts have been suggested by geographers, based on varying social and compactness criteria. A combination of the transportation algorithm (used initially in commodity flow studies) and the Weberian model (a weighting procedure) has been suggested by Goodchild and Massam as one method of grouping small territorial units into optimal regions.[23] Unlike the Weaver-Hess algorithm, commonly used for delineating reapportioned districts, the transportation-Weberian model meets all three Court requirements of compactness, equal population, and contiguity, in electoral districting.

A geographer, Richard Morrill, was appointed "Special Master" by a Federal District Court in Seattle to reapportion the congressional and legislative districts for the state of Washington in 1972 after both Democratic and Republican plans had been rejected by the court.[24] A geographer, rather than a political scientist, was nominated because the court "felt that political scientists would want to study the whole complicated history of conflict and decision-making in the case, but that the drawing of equal population regions was a technical task, subject to demographic and geographic rather than political criteria."[25] Morrill was asked to draw up his plans within the constraints of one percent population deviation, to maintain the integrity of counties, cities, and census divisions as much as possible, to produce compact districts, to avoid crossing natural geographic barriers, to reflect the unity of character or interest in districts (e.g., Indian reservations and black neighbors), and to minimize the changes of the existing apportionment. Morrill's plan was accepted by the court and implemented for the 1972 elections.

Another reapportionment plan by geographers that received a lot of publicity was the plan for decentralization of Detroit's public schools, the joint result of research by the Detroit Geographical Expedition and black community of Detroit.[26] The Board of Education had proposed eight plans for school decentralization, all of which placed the majority of black students under white control. The geographic team identified 7,311 ways of redistricting the city and proposed a plan of four black and four white dominated districts, sharing community control and maximizing integration.[27]

Concern with landscapes of the future and the impact of proposed policies on future spatial patterns has led geographers into forecasting and simulation. According to Hagerstrand, forecasting stems from analysis of observed spatial structure and observed trends of change. This in turn provides us with a method of guiding choices between possible lines of action, and the study of general goals for development irrespective of feasibility.[28] Geographic forecasts (usually for metropolitan areas and economic regions) vary from formal mathematical models to goal-oriented social policies. As spatial predictive models become more accurate, policy questions of the advisability of implementing change will become increasingly important: do we want the situation as forecast to become a reality? If not, what policies should be adopted to prevent this?

A fourth policy question, which is stimulating research into the locational aspects of urban power and conflict, concerns externality effects on urban neighborhoods. The impacts of governmental decisions have received more attention than private impacts, partly because of the unequal distribution of the negative externalities. Neighborhoods try to attract services with positive impacts, such as fire stations and discourage services with negative externalities, such as sewage-dumps. It has been noted by Wolpert that facilities imposing negative impacts are sited at least-protest sites.[29] However, major problems in research on externalities revolve around measurement questions. Obviously, the effects of a facility, both positive and negative, decline with distance away from its site. But to an even greater extent, externality effects have to be measured on the basis of the preferences and perceptions of the residents affected.

Regional scientists from the University of Pennsylvania have adopted a community focus in evaluating public facility location plans. In particular, they have reported on neighborhood conflict because of highway location and urban renewal plans. From this they have proposed that inner-city communities develop alternate strategies for dealing with land use changes in their areas. In the struggle over decisions between planners and the community, Wolpert et al. feel that "unless planning commissions and policy-making groups are augmented by a cadre of public defenders and advocates who support the cause of inner-city neighborhood development, then greater decentralization of control is an essential stage toward cooperative resolution of equity issues."[30]

In this short chapter, I have tried to indicate the many policy areas in which geographers are working, as well as the techniques and methodologies used by the geographic profession. Almost all policy decisions have a spatial dimension. Cox and Reynolds have distinguished between decisions which are "fundamentally locational" such as urban renewal and those that are "derivatively locational" such as a redistribution of income policy.[31] Social scientists are discovering the spatial dimensions of social problems after years of wandering in the aspatial wilderness. It is the hope of an increasing number of geographers that these social scientists, working in interdisciplinary teams, use geographic techniques in the analysis of policy issues and decisions.

Notes

1. John O'Loughlin, "Geography and Public Policy," *Policy Studies Journal* 2 (Autumn 1973): 35-38.

2. Robert Rheinhold, "Modern Geography Transformed, Gains Scholarly Respect," *New York Times*, June 11, 1973: 33, 62.

3. Andrew T. Blowers, "Relevance, Research and the Political Process," *Area* 6, 1 (1974): 33.

4. Richard Peet, "Social Issues in the Social Geography of American Poverty," in Richard Peet (ed.), *Geographic Perspectives on American Poverty,* Antipode Monographs in Social Geography No. 1, 1974, p. 12.

5. Blowers, "Relevance, Research," p. 32.

6. John Eyles, "Geography and Relevance," *Area* 5, 2 (1973): 159.

7. Gilbert F. White, "Geography and Public Policy," *Professional Geographer* 24 (May 1972): 103.

8. David M. Smith, "Alternative 'Relevant' Professional Roles," *Area* 5, 1 (1973): 2.

9. See, for example, Ian Burton and Robert W. Kates, "The Perception of Natural Hazards in Resource Management," *Natural Resources Journal* 3 (1964): 412-441, or Gilbert F. White *Human Adjustment to Floods*, University of Chicago, Department of Geography, Research Paper No. 29, 1945.

10. The project is described in Preston E. James, *All Possible Worlds* (Indianapolis: Bobbs-Merril Company, Inc., Publishers, 1972), Ch. 14, "Applied Geography."

11. Robert Earickson, *The Spatial Behavior of Hospital Patients*, University of Chicago, Department of Geography, Research Paper No. 124, 1970.

12. Gunnar Olson, "Some Notes on Geography and Social Engineering," *Antipode* 4, 1 (1972): 2.

13. Peet, "Social Issues," p. 10.

14. David Harvey, *Social Justice and the City* (Baltimore: The Johns Hopkins University Press, 1973), p. 137, Chapter 4, "Revolutionary and Counter-Revolutionary Theory in Geography and the Problem of Ghetto Formation."

15. William Bunge, "The Geography," *Professional Geographer* 25 (Nov. 1973): 334.

16. Peirce F. Lewis, "Review of Fitzgerald: Geography of a Revolution," *Annals, Association of American Geographers* 63, 1 (March 1973): 131-132.

17. William Bunge, "Fitzgerald from a Distance," *Annals, Association of American Geographers* 64, 3 (September 1974): 485.

18. Oliver P. Williams, *Metropolitan Political Analysis: A Social Access Approach* (New York: The Free Press, 1971).

19. Harvey, *Social Justice and the City*, Chapter 3, "Social Justice and Spatial Systems," pp. 96-118.

20. Peter Gould and Thomas R. Leinbach, "An Approach to the Geographic Assignment of Hospital Services," *Tijdschrift Voor Economische en Sociale Geografie* 57 (1966): 203-206.

21. Donald W. Maxfield, "Spatial Planning of School Districts," *Annals, Association of American Geographers* 62, 4 (December 1972): 582-590.

22. Lawrence A. Brown et al., *Day Care Centers in Columbus: A Locational Strategy*, Ohio State University, Department of Geography, Discussion Paper No. 26, 1972.

23. Michael F. Goodchild and Bryan H. Massam, "Some Least-Cost Models of Spatial Administrative Systems in Southern Ontario," *Geografiska Annaler* 52, Series B, No. 2 (1969): 86-94.

24. Richard L. Morrill, "Ideal and Reality in Reapportionment," *Annals, Association of American Geographers* 63, 4 (December 1973): 463-477.

25. Ibid., p. 463.

26. Cited in Ronald J. Horvath, "The 'Detroit Geographical Expedition and Institute' Experience," *Antipode* 3, 1 (1971): 73-85.

27. J. W. Shepard and M. A. Jenkins, "Decentralizing High School Administration in Detroit: An Evaluation of Alternative Strategies of Political Control," *Economic Geography* 48 (January 1972): 95-106.

28. T. Hagerstrand, Public Address delivered at the Twenty-Second Symposium of the Colston Research Society, University of Bristol, April 6-10, 1970. Published in M. Chisholm, A. E. Frey and P. Haggett (eds.), *Regional Forecasting* (Hamden, Conn.: Archon, The Shoe String Press, 1971).

29. J. Wolpert, "Departures from the Usual Environment in Locational Analysis," *Annals, Association of American Geographers* 60, 2 (June 1970): 220-229.

30. J. Wolpert, A. Mumphrey, and J. Seley, *Metropolitan Neighborhoods: Participation and Conflict over Change*, Commission on College Geography, Resource Paper No. 16, Association of American Geographers, 1972, p. 43.

31. Kevin R. Cox and David R. Reynolds, "Locational Approaches to Power and Conflict," in K.R. Cox, D.R. Reynolds, and S. Rokkan (eds.), *Locational Approaches to Power and Conflict* (New York: Sage Publications, Inc., 1974).

**Part VI
Social Philosophy**

15

Policy Studies and Ethics

John Ladd

There are a number of ethical issues that suggest themselves in connection with policy studies. Many of them are not new. Indeed, some of them go back to Plato. For in advocating that political matters be studied in a disciplined, rational, and scientific way by experts especially trained for the purpose, Plato might be said to be the originator of policy studies. There is no question that he would have enthusiastically welcomed recent developments in this area, especially the growing use of mathematical models and methods. Therefore it would not be surprising if many of the difficulties inherent in Plato's political theory did not have their counterparts in contemporary policy studies. For that reason, it seems worthwhile to raise the same sort of questions that are often asked of Plato's technocratic state: are policy studies essentially totalitarian, élitist or paternalist enterprises? I do not mean to say that they are. But I think that it is imperative that we try to say why they are not, if they are not.

There are also obvious affinities, not only historical, but logical and ethical, between various inquiries included under policy studies and classical utilitarian theory. Again, it can be argued that policy studies have inherited many ethical problems from their utilitarian ancestry. Even Rawls' theory of justice, which is non-utilitarian in crucial respects, retains some of the problematic assumptions of utilitarianism that typify many areas of policy studies. All of these theories share in common the aim of developing an analysis of enlightened, rational decision-making in the area of public policy; and all of them are concerned in one way or another with questions relating to the just distribution of goods and benefits, the calculation and comparison of utilities and probabilities, basic value-theory, and so on.[1]

My comments in this short chapter cannot do justice to all the ramifications of the relationship between ethics and policy studies. What I say must be brief and selective. It will reflect my own thinking on social and political problems, which, I might observe, is radically anti-utilitarian. I am not convinced that rational decision-making procedures of the sort just mentioned are either possible or desirable.[2] Be that as it may, there are still a lot of unanswered questions concerning the moral implications of the various techniques, concepts, models and theories employed in policy studies. I want to suggest in a very general way what some of these questions are.

I am tempted to begin with Laurence Tribe's provocative question:

177

"Policy Science: Analysis or Ideology?"[3] But after reading his interesting article, it is not clear to me precisely what he means by these terms. His question, it seems to me, rests on a false dichotomy, for in a sense ideology and (political) analysis are inseparable. (Perhaps that is his point!) However, it is crucial at the very outset to recognize that policy studies (analysis or science) belong to what Aristotle would call "practical sciences," that is, inquiries that fall under *practical reason*.[4] Where pratical reason is involved, theory and practice cannot be separated; for practical inquiries, such as policy studies, cannot even be understood, much less practiced, without taking into account their relationship to action, for example, decision-making and policy formation. Moreover, this relationship to action is not just casual or contingent, it is logical (conceptual) and necessary, and in that sense unavoidable. Hence, for *logical reasons*, it is impossible to engage intelligently in the study of policy questions, for example, to make policy analyses, and ignore the practical and moral implications of what one is doing. In this sense, insofar as the latter belong to ideology, ideology and analysis are inseparable.

Practical questions as such, including policy questions, arise in the context of human purposes, aspirations, and needs; they presuppose already existing social structures, institutions, and practices; and they refer to existing agencies and organizations. Deliberation, if it is to eventuate in action, can only be about what is possible for us, as Aristotle points out.[5] Being a practical science, policy studies cannot, therefore, be separated from these contexts. In effect, that means that in our deliberations and planning we cannot limit ourselves to immediate questions of means to ends; we must also be prepared to examine critically the context in which the action is contemplated and to evaluate it morally. Every condition and presupposition must be subjected to moral scrutiny, and inasmuch as the moral quality of its conditions and presuppositions determine the moral quality of a practical science, *all* of them, not just some of them, must survive the test of morality. We must be ready, therefore, to answer moral questions, say, about the economic system, the organization and division of labor, or the decision-making machinery that, as the case may be, make up the background of our policy study. By the same token, if we find that our inquiry is premised on some unfortunate historical circumstance or social practice that is morally objectionable, then we should revise our procedures in that light. Perhaps the aberrations of systems-analysis as practiced by McNamara's "whiz kids" early in the Vietnam war could have been avoided had one recognized the necessity of a constant moral reexamination of the factors that have just been mentioned. In sum, from the moral point of view, it is absolutely necessary that we avoid becoming unwitting and unwilling supporters of the status quo, be it political, social or ethical.

All too often, however, the most troublesome questions about the moral presuppositions of a policy study are dismissed or postponed to some other day. Undoubtedly, the challenge they pose creates a certain amount of anxiety, not only because the questions themselves are difficult to answer and the answers are controversial, but because they are also dangerous; a candid answer might undermine the whole study—and cost someone his job. Yet it is becoming increasingly clear that, like Watergate, these questions cannot be swept under the rug.

The easiest and most favored way of avoiding difficult questions about morality is to postulate a rigid and absolute distinction between means and ends. If questions of means are separated from questions of ends, then it is possible simply to adopt a division of labor, a separation of function: some will have the job of studying the means, i.e., the social scientists and technocrats, and others will have the job of determining ends, i.e., the "ideologists." The doctrinaire separation of means and ends is not new; it is part of the utilitarian heritage. Obviously it accords well with the stupendous development of new formal techniques and mathematical models. And it is given a respectable intellectual mantle by the Weberian theory of a value-free social science as well as the Weberian theory of bureaucracy.[6] All of these facets confer an aura of respectability on the means-ends dichotomy that makes it difficult to question, perhaps even imprudent to do so.

Nevertheless, there are many good reasons for rejecting this unquestioned dichotomization of means and ends, as postulated in theory and practiced in fact.[7] To begin with, it makes havoc both of our conception of ends and of our conception of means. By dividing questions of means from questions of ends, people are encouraged, if not compelled, to view ends, in contrast to means, as unscientific, not susceptible to rational evaluation or debate, and wholly capricious and arbitrary; in other words, as subjective. From the point of view of "science," i.e., "rationality," one value system is as good as another, and the "choice" of ultimate values is itself, almost by definition, not a matter of reason. For that reason, political and social scientists, if they want to be *scientists*, cannot concern themselves with value, but only with empirical realities. Ends and values belong to the poets, the priests, and the ideologists.

The dichotomization of means and ends not only distorts our conception of ends, but also conceals the value-laden side of the technical concepts and procedures that we use in determining means. In the policy sphere, for example, it is clear that many of the concepts used are value-laden; this is not only obviously true with regard to general notions like poverty, housing, health, traffic, pollution, urban renewal, safety, welfare and cost, but it is probably equally true of more specific concepts employed in more specific areas, e.g., "traffic flow."

Finally, the very selection and formulation of "policy" problems to be explored as well as the choice of criteria for evaluating success in solving them reflect value-commitments of one sort or another, commitments that are sometimes conscious, but more often unconscious. Against our fondest expectations, if we look honestly at what we are doing, we find values and valuations seeping in at every level. In view of this fact, it is tempting to conclude that the notion that public policy studies (or any parts thereof) can be "value-free" serves primarily as a coverup to protect the social scientist from moral self-scrutiny or moral questioning by others.

One natural result of the means-ends separation is that it lends credence to the proposition that the end justifies the means, in some version or other. Indeed, one might ask to what extent this proposition is the operative principle in policy studies. In their reply to the customary moral objections to it, its adherents usually point out that only a good or worthy end justifies. But granting this qualification, we still face the perhaps insuperable task of framing a sufficiently complete and inclusive conception of the end (the *summum bonum* or the common good) to meet the usual difficulties of a teleological ethics. The task is, I submit, an impossible one; for it is not possible to satisfy all the moral requirements in question without introducing considerations involving means. Even Mill, like Aristotle before him, had to include virtue as a constituent, rather than a mere means, to happiness. When we turn to concepts like the common good or public interest we will find that they, too, cannot be defined without reference to means. For example, justice is generally held to be an intrinsic component of the common good or of public interest, yet, by its very nature, justice is as much concerned with means as it is with ends. I hope that it is obvious that policy studies cannot ignore considerations of justice; if I am right, then it cannot accept the divorce between means and ends in any simple sense.

Again, the conclusion that values are subjective and arbitrary, a consequence of the means-end dichotomy that has already been pointed out, provides an excuse for political and social scientists to "choose" their own value-principles according to what is most convenient for them; for example, it allows them to select value-principles to fit the demands of a particular theory or a particular methodology. Welfare economics and social theories based on the theory of games are cases in point. Their methodology requires the identification of values with preferences or satisfactions, an identification that is questionable from the point of view of ethics or, at the very least, one that needs further philosophical clarification and defense.[8] The elegant logical properties of "values" defined in terms of, e.g., preference, does not automatically guarantee their moral adequacy or even their moral import. It seems clear to a moralist that the appeal of "preference" as a value or moral category is due to the economist's predilection for the market model, the category of supply and demand, etc.

Indeed, the structuring of moral issues in terms of formal models and techniques so as to make them susceptible of analysis represents a curious anomaly, the inversion of the means-end principle, where the means (i.e., analytical elegance and computability) justify the ends (i.e., values as preferences).

Neutralism is a pervasive feature of American life, especially in an institutional or professional context. "That is not my job!" is the most familiar reply when people are confronted with moral issues. There is a wholesale abdication of moral responsibility in the political and social sphere: we treat our actions and activities as instrumentalities over which we, as actors, claim to have no control. We take for granted that our instruments themselves are morally neutral. Thus, we have all heard it said: "guns (or automobiles) don't kill, only the people who misuse them kill," "computers don't make plans, only people who use them make plans," "social science doesn't tell us what to do, only the official who makes decisions does that," and so on. When applied to the activity of persons, e.g., of the social scientists, the same kind of neutrality is claimed that we confer on physical objects like machines. This is something like what Sartre calls "bad faith."

As I have argued throughout this chapter, the neutrality or moral immunity that is claimed for one's activities, e.g., as a social scientist, is illusory. No one of us, including the professional or bureaucrat, can escape moral responsibility that easily, that is moral responsibility of the kind that demands due concern, foresight, and care for the consequences of one's actions or emissions for the safety and well-being of others and, in particular, for their moral integrity as individual persons.

A few brief observations on the concept of moral responsibility are in order here, for the whole neutralism/immunity syndrome is the result, at least in part, of a mistaken view of responsibility.[9] Responsibility, in the sense of a condition that gives rise to duties and obligations, seems to be of two sorts, or rather there are two entirely different and opposing conceptions of it: one, which I call *official* or *task-responsibility,* and the other, which I call *moral responsibility.* Official or task-responsibility is institutional; it is the kind of responsibility that goes with offices, jobs, and functions; for example, it is a policeman's responsibility to preserve order. A characteristic logical feature of this kind of responsibility is that it is divided up and limited like the jobs that it is associated with. "This is my responsibility, not yours." "That is your responsibility, not mine." "That is their responsibility, not ours," and so on. Lines are drawn between those responsible and those *not* responsible. One person's official or task responsibility excludes or cancels out that of another. The advantages and disadvantages of *not* being responsible are considerable. I escape blame if I am *not* my brother's keeper.

Moral responsibility, on the other hand, has a different logical structure from official or task responsibility: one person's moral responsibility does not abrogate that of another person. In a sense, we are all responsible for each other. So I cannot claim that my responsibility is diminished or cancelled out simply because someone else is also responsible. The tragic case of Kitty Genovese, where all the witnesses to her murder felt that *someone else* ought to do something about it, illustrates the substitution of a morally spurious, limited type of responsibility for genuine, unlimited moral responsibility. The abdication of responsibility under the misconception that responsibility is always limited presents a serious problem for a democracy or for a moral community in which all persons are ends in themselves (Kant). In particular, there is a constant threat to morality in the practice of dividing (assigning) responsibility according to positions or jobs; for the result is that we, as social scientists, planners, public officials, or public representatives, have only task-responsibilities, our responsibilities are limited. The moral responsibility for things always lies with *someone else*. Against that, I would like to argue that moral responsibility is not the kind of thing that is subject to *respondeat superior* or *respondeat alterius*. It is something that each and every one of us has by virtue of being an autonomous moral being. Morally speaking, all of us are responsible for justice and for the common good, not to mention that of our neighbors. The rulers, the officials, and the experts have no monopoly in that regard. Nor do they have special moral privileges or immunities by virtue of their position.

In closing and for sake of discussion, I want to point out a basic reservation (question) that I have with regard to some of the objectives of policy studies. It seems to me that, like utilitarianism, policy studies often operate with a very limited picture of what morality and politics are all about; namely, they conceive of morality and politics as principally concerned with the production and (just) distribution of *consumer goods* for society; for example, the production and distribution of happiness, welfare, primary goods (Rawls), or the satisfaction of needs or preferences. A natural consequence of this picture is the functional division between producers and distributors, on the one hand, and consumers, on the other hand. At another level, it is reflected in the functional division between decisionmakers (managers) and the public for whom the decisions are made (clients, subjects, *tutelae*). In any case, we have those who are on the giving end, i.e., are active, and those who are on the receiving end, i.e., are passive. This conception of political morality, aptly called *paternalism* by Kant, denies the inherent right of every individual, no matter who he or she is, to participate fully and equally in active morality, in particular, in the decisions of his or her society. The idea that some people are, as it were, merely second-class citizens in the moral community is one of the chief sources of moral frustration, apathy, and hopelessness among the under-privileged, which includes, of course, not only the poor and the minorities, but also the young. A clear understanding of the relationship of the individual to public policy, not only as a receiver (consumer), but as an active moral agent seems to me to present the most important challenge to policy studies from the point of view of morality. Another way of putting my point, in language that is more familiar and popular, is to say that policy questions must be understood as basically, not administrative questions but political questions, calling for the active participation and consent of the citizenship.

Notes

1. For an up-to-date discussion and bibliography of utilitarianism, see Dan W. Brock, "Recent Work in Utilitarianism," *American Philosophical Quarterly* 10, 4 (October 1973).

2. On this question, see the critique, from an "Aristotelian" point of view, of John Rawls, *A Theory of Justice,* considered as a Platonic theory, by P.H. Nowell-Smith, "A Theory of Justice," *Philosophy and Social Science* 3 (1973): 315-329.

3. Laurence H. Tribe, "Policy Science: Analysis or Ideology?" *Philosophy and Public Affairs* 2, 1 (Fall 1972).

4. Aristotle, *Nichomachean Ethics,* bk. 6, Chapters 2 and 5. The locus classicus for a discussion of the practical syllogism is *De Motu Animalium,* 700 b. For an application of this notion to rational decision, see John Ladd, "The Place of Practical Reason in Judicial Decision," C.J. Friedrich (ed.), *Nomos VII: Rational Decision* (New York: Atherton, 1964).

5. Aristotle, *Nichomachean Ethics,* bk. 3, Chapter 3.

6. For further detail, see John Ladd, "Morality and the Ideal of Rationality in Formal Organizations," *Monist* 54, 4 (October 1970).

7. The inseparability of ends and means is, of course, a recurring theme in the writings of John Dewey. See, for example, his *Human Nature and Conduct* (New York: Holt, 1922) and *The Theory of Valuation* (Chicago: Chicago University Press, 1939). I owe many of the arguments given here to Dewey.

8. For philosophical critiques of, e.g., Kenneth Arrow's theory, see articles by R.B. Brandt, K. Baier, and John Ladd in Sidney Hook (ed.), *Human Values and Economic Policy* (New York: New York University Press, 1967).

9. Some of the discussion that follows contains points that are ex-

plained in more detail in John Ladd, "The ethics of participation," in J. Roland Pennock and John W. Chapman (eds.), *Nomos XVI: Participation* (New York: Atherton Press, forthcoming).

16 Philosophy and Policy Studies

Eugene J. Meehan

Humanity is in one hell of a mess and worsening seems a more reasonable prognosis than improving, given the course of recent events. Populations explode; food supplies do not. Resources are wasted at prodigous rates with little significant benefit to mankind. Habits and institutions likely to be very expensive if not positively lethal are cultivated avidly by large populations. Antiquated normative structures and antediluvian social institutions seem to be collapsing under the pressure of changing human needs and capabilities. The United States provides the extreme prototype. Two centuries of operating with an economic system founded on individual selfishness produced immense expansion, along with side effects whose human and material costs are increasing implacably and rapidly. The real catastrophe, however, may be the socialized incapacity of those who suffer the consequences to judge the consequences to be catastrophic. A political apparatus that "functioned" well in an era when its functions were limited to modest tax gathering and refereeing the conflict of competing interest groups has become more and more expensive and ineffective as it struggles with the problems churned up by a large-scale society in which the conditions of life of the individual are primarily a function of governmental action rather than individual effort. An individualistic ethic that operated reasonably well in a society blessed with a powerful family structure (which supplied personal, social, economic, and even political norms) and faced with compelling incentives to regular work turned counterproductive as the family disintegrated but was not replaced. The educational institutions which might have cushioned the transitions and provided the alternatives society required turned out to be a massive bureaucratic sham, perhaps the most gigantic and expensive institutional pretence since the Holy Roman Empire. James Coleman has shown us how little is taught in and by the schools, Christopher Jencks added insult to injury by pointing out that what is taught in the schools tends to be useful only within the schools, and Ivar Berg reinforced both by demonstrating the weakness of the relation between the content of the academic curriculum and the requirements of the occupation, even in science and engineering.

These and other widely agreed aspects of contemporary society are compelling evidence that the institutions responsible for making and improving policy, whether public or private, social or economic or political, have performed very poorly indeed where they have performed at all.

185

Areas of major human concern have been ignored; the consequences of positive policy have often been so unfortunate that it is moot whether the drift course of events might not have been an improvement; there is little evidence to show that men have learned very efficiently from their experience how to perform better in the future—unlike the fabled child, mankind in the aggregate blisters its fingers repeatedly on the same smoking metal. The weakness is universal, for such strictures apply equally to capitalist, socialist, and communist societies, to rich nations and poor, to public and private agencies alike. There are exceptions, obviously, but mankind in general, however organized, simply does not know or has not been able to agree upon either what ought to be done or how best to do it. That, I believe, is the context in which the contribution to policy-making and evaluation of an academic discipline such as philosophy, or any other social institution, can best be evaluated.

What has philosophy to do with such matters? Very very little! With some relatively minor exceptions, those concerned with making or criticizing policy (analytically, the two tasks are identical) will find little or nothing in philosophy that will help them perform more effectively and much that is actually misleading or counterproductive—where philosophy has influenced policy it has tended to play Fagin to society's Oliver Twist, as in the model supplied for development of the educational system. Even such ostensibly practical philosophers as Machiavelli or Burke are in fact little more than a source of interesting assumptions which must be tested against experience prior to use. To treat philosophic speculation as an adequate basis for action would be as improper as using Aristotelian science as a working base for solving a problem in engineering. Of course, lack of relevance or efficacy need not mean a lack of influence, as the patent medicine industry or the works of Karl Marx (quite properly categorized by Paul Samuelson as a second-rate Ricardian) attest.

The focus of the thesis should perhaps be underscored to minimize misunderstanding. I am not trying to impugn the competence of philosophers within their own domain. Indeed, I have no idea how the products of philosophic activity could be differentiated qualitatively beyond their esthetic characteristics or perhaps the internal consistency of the presentation—laboratories cannot judge the soothing effect of competing patent medicines. In any case, such considerations are not related to the present discussion, though it is perhaps germane that philosphers themselves seem to share my uncertainty about the criteria of quality to be applied to their own products. Moreover, the argument does not require a denial of the value of what philosophers actually do, though in fact I am fully prepared to do so and supply justification. The central point of the essay is simply that when the products of philosophy are measured against the human need for ways of improving the human condition, they emerge almost grotesquely irrelevant. Granting that there are many other dimensions of human interaction with the environment beyond the search for knowledge, as there are many other human needs beyond the need for knowledge, I do not believe that philosophers can bypass the argument merely by saying "That is unfair because philosphy is not concerned with such matters." Few philosophers have been prepared to concede that what they are doing has no relation to human affairs beyond the enjoyment or amusement it provides them, and most have been rather pretentious in their claims. If that concession is made, it is hard to distinguish any reasonable grounds for allocating scarce resources for the edification of such intellectual grasshoppers. If, on the other hand, philosophers claim to deserve support because they contribute significantly to the supply of valuable services available in society, the burden of identifying those services and justifying their importance rests with them. As I hope to make clear, they are not, in most cases, entitled to support because of their contribution to making, improving, or even studying policies and policy-making.

Requirements for Policy-Making

How much philosophy or any other activity can contribute to policy analysis and criticism depends on the minimal requirements for competent and corrigible policy; that in turn is contingent on the meaning of "policy." Unfortunately, the definitional problem cannot be solved by a simple appeal to common usage. In many and perhaps most discussions of the subject, the meaning of "policy" is simply left undefined or assumed; in other cases, policies are identified variously and not always consistently with the actions of persons or corporations, with laws or administrative regulations, with actions, ideals, intentions, or aspirations, or with official statements. The way around this morass is to find a meaning for "policy" that refers to significant dimensions of human activity, that lies within human capacity, and that is close enough to current usage to incorporate valuable work already completed in the field. In the context that current usage supplies, the most promising line of development treats a policy as a guide to action or choice—as analogous to the prescribed treatment for a particular illness. Since many of the necessary conditions for making reasoned and therefore corrigible choices have already been established, that procedure would allow policy analysts to make use of the available critical structure with little modification. Other facets of the meaning attached to "policy" in current usage which seem to warrant attention could be identified and pursued, of course, though preferably under some other rubric.

Analytically, reasoned action or choice involves performance of two basic tasks: first, connecting the present capacity to act of a specified actor (who may be a collectivity) to a set of alternative future outcomes with some measure of reliability; second, weighing those alternative outcomes in terms of a transitively-ordered set of preferences (already available or created for the occasion). Reasoned actions always involve both empirical and normative factors and the empirical component is prior—there can be no normative judgment until the options have been established. Structurally, human actions involve an actor, an action, and a set of consequences flowing from the action. The consequences are the central focus of reasoned action or criticism of action because efforts to criticize human endeavor in terms of the actors involved or the intrinsic characteristics of the action lead unavoidably to inconsistency. Criticism of action in terms of consequences, stated as changes in the conditions of life of the humans affected by action, is both analytically necessary and methodologically possible. Consequences, adequately stated, are expressed as the differences produced in the environment by human action or anticipated as a future result of human action. They can be set forth in the general form "Situation A *instead of* situations B, C, D, etc." providing a base for comparison leading to reasoned choice. Actions are precisely equivalent to choices and inaction counts as choice so long as the capacity to act is present. The indicator of action can therefore be either a change or failure to change when the capacity to produce change is present.

The set of assumptions and processes required to perform these two basic tasks in ways that are amenable to intellectual control and improvement, brutally compressed, are as follows. Assuming that all of man's knowledge of the world is based on the flow of information coming through the perceptive system, the key to survival and improvement is the human ability to organize patterns of perceptions in useful ways, to test their usefulness by comparing them to other useful patterns and by acting upon them knowingly, to store, recall, combine, and recombine the patterns into structures that are more than additive (to create), and to use those patterns to improve the human condition—an evaluation also made possible by the use of patterns developed by the same procedures but from a different base. The three essentials for successful development of human capacity, which are also the minimal conditions for human learning, are (1) the organizing capacity of the central nervous system, (2) the feedback loop between man and environment supplied by the perceptive apparatus and an assumption of temporal continuity in the environment, and (3) the ongoing-in-time character of the human enterprise. Since the procedures exhaust human capacity, they must suffice to produce and criticize both the purposes that man seeks in the environment and the means used to achieve them; there is neither possibility nor need for separate networks for reasoning about empirical and normative problems though each may involve different elements of the total structure. The human capacity to create or to organize can be taken as given. Men do produce patterns for organizing experience; how they do it is not known, though the process is not logical in the deductive sense. While the process remains unspecified, roadblocks to creativity can be identified and removed and aids to creativity can be supplied; there is simply no guarantee of success, no formula that can be applied by anyone.

Man's natural endowment suffices for (but cannot guarantee) creating the empirical and normative patterns required to satisfy the three fundamental human needs with reference to the environment: first, to anticipate future events, so that he can adapt to them; second, to control (produce or inhibit) future events so that the environment can be adapted to human preferences; and third, to choose among the alternatives that the human capacity to control the environment creates. The set of instruments required, the basic patterns, can be identified both structurally and functionally. The simplest unit is the concept, used to organize perceptions into the "things" or entities men perceive. While some concepts, "yellow" for example, are considered simples, most are already compounds that group observables by their shared attributes. Such classifications can be used to generate expectations about the future if class membership is assumed on the basis of incomplete observation of attributes; given the assumption, unobserved class attributes can be inferred and attached to the observed specimen. For example, if an observer sees a bird of a particular size and color, by assuming that it is a robin he can infer (and expect) that the bird will eat certain kinds of food, nest in particular ways, and so on. If his assumption is warranted and the classification has been developed properly, those expectations will presumably be satisfied by further observation—otherwise the classification would be modified or the grounds for the assumption changed. Expectations can also be generated by a pattern which links the values of two or more variables by rule —connecting rain with clouds of a particular shape and color, for example. If the variables in the pattern are further assumed to be causally connected, so that changing the value of one will *produce* changes in the value of the other according to rule, then the instrument can be used to control the environment—as turning a switch to a particular position can turn off a light. The instrument required for reasoned choice is a transitively ordered priority structure in which all of the elements from which a choice must be made can be identified, and a rule that links the two conceptually.

In the aggregate, human knowledge is an immense collection of partially and imperfectly integrated patterns. No pattern, whether empirical or normative, can be provided with an absolute justification; the reasoning that is used to justify or support a pattern must be predicated upon evidence obtained from comparisons. Structures that are used to generate anticipations about the environment or means for controlling it are tested against use for specified purposes in specified situations; normative patterns are tested by comparing the conditions of life obtained through their use with the conditions of life that would be produced using the available alternatives. So long as patterns are held tentatively, so long as each application is regarded at least in principle as a test, the knowledge structure remains alive and viable. While the structures and procedures involved may seem overly simple, they can account for and explain the success of such successful intellectual enterprises as science as well as improvements in the normative apparatus (the criteria used to evaluate industrial safety, for example) in the same way that the operation of a complex computer can be explained in terms of opening and closing simple two-position switches.

Given this epistemological setting, the meaning of "policy" can be specified accurately and fruitfully and the limits that must be honored when policies are made or criticized are widely agreed—though often specified in different language than the terminology used here. At a minimum, reasoned and corrigible policy-making or choice requires an identifiable actor with a genuine (rather than formal or legal) capacity to alter the environment in specifiable ways, a set of patterns (theories or explanations) that can project the various outcomes which the actor can produce by his actions, an agreed set of concepts for identifying the normatively-significant dimensions of those outcomes, a priority structure that covers the various alternatives open to the actor, and a rule of action that applies the priority structure to the particular case. *That rule of action is the best candidate available for the label "policy."* Construed as a guide to action, a policy becomes the instrument that applies a priority structure to a particular choice. The policy differs from the priority structure in the same way that the desire to minimize disfigurement in hospital treatment differs from the particular treatment prescribed for a particular case in order to satisfy that set of priorities.

The separation of policy and priority structure is analytically essential. Various policies can be used to apply a priority structure to the environment, and they may sometimes lead to the same result in the same situation. Policy disagreements may therefore refer to either the rule of action or to the underlying priority structure. For example, a child offered a choice between two coins may prefer more resources to less but use a variety of rules of choice to make its decision: choose the largest coin, choose the brightest coin, choose the most valuable coin, and so on. Over time, reasons may be found for using one rule rather than the other, even if the priority structure remains unchanged. The rule "Choose the largest coin," for example, would be seriously counterproductive if applied to a choice between a small but valuable gold coin and a large and nearly worthless copper—one choice is actually included in the other, hence making the wrong choice gives up a significant surplus of the resources ordered in the preference system. In practice, complex issues such as housing or welfare will involve a very large number of rules, and therefore provide endless opportunities for inconsistency. The practice of referring to such aggregates as "housing policy" or "educational policy" is seriously misleading; the aggregates cannot be dealt with by reasoned action until they are broken into constituent elements nor can they be criticized without disaggregation.

The argument that supports a choice will refer to the outcomes that could have been achieved by a specified actor in a specified situation. Since each outcome can in principle be conceptualized in endless different ways, argument over choices will require a set of agreed common denominators; otherwise, the arguments may not intersect. Ultimately, human choices are weighed in terms of their consequences for human populations; *reductio ad absurdum*, no people, no choice problem, and no choice. Such concepts as "national security," "public interest," or "quality education" are never more than intervening variables in reasoned choice, and before they can be used they must be connected by appropriate theories to some defined human population. Unfortunately, the concepts presently used for discussion of aggregate populations are rarely usable for policy analysis. If the impact of choice is to be measured accurately, populations must be defined so that each member of a class or aggregate is affected in the same way, including all side affects of any normative importance, by a common action in the environment. Otherwise, systematic comparison is a logical impossibility; aggregates can be compared only in terms of their distributed properties.

Analytically, though not empirically, the policy-making process usually begins with some concrete situation, defined in terms of the conditions of life of some specified human population, that attracts attention on normative grounds—requires change or maintenance. That is the sense in which systematic analysis is always the servant of normative judgment. To deal with the situation, an actor must be found or created (and creating jurisdictions for normative purposes is one of the more important collective functions in any society) with the capacity to alter the situation; hopefully, the actor will be chosen so that maximum improvement is achieved at least cost, though in practice that is often inordinately difficult. The actor's priority structure must rank the situation high enough to produce intervention; the first choice in any choice is a choice among choices, though that initial selection is ordinarily suppressed, and situations that are normatively deplorable may remain unchanged if resources, capacity to act, priority structure and jurisdiction or responsibility are not linked in a way that will produce action. Within the limits of existing knowledge, available resources, and time, the alternatives available to the actor are then projected to the fullest extent possible, using the normative variables embedded in the accepted normative structure. If the situation is already covered by the priority system, a rule is devised that will apply it to the situation, and then tested for acceptability in continuous use. If it is not, reasons must be sought for preferring one alternative to the others, and if the search is successful (any reason is superior to no reason, and if no reason is forthcoming, the choice is simply a matter of indifference given the accepted value system), the result is incorporated into the priority structure of the actor.

What is crucial is that *all* of the known implications of each alternative line of action be taken into account lest it seem reasonable to kill the patient in order to cure the disease. Moreover, the actor or critic must be sensitive to the possibility that other dimensions of the human condition should be included in the balance of costs and benefits, and that such change may alter the whole preference structure as well as the particular decision. The great value of technological achievement, in this context, is that it increases the means available for altering specific conditions in the environment to achieve preferred outcomes and therefore offers the possibility of varying costs and benefits while achieving the same basic results. The overall strategy for the policy analyst is simple but effective: go to the environment with a purpose, take the environment as you find it, pursue the best purpose you can locate with the best tools available in the light of best knowledge, and bear in mind the possibility that better tools may be developed for achieving the purpose being pursued and other purposes more worthy of achievement may be generated in the quest.

The Contribution of Philosophy

Given this conception of the meaning of "policy" and the nature of inquiry, the needs of the policymaker or critic can be specified both usefully and quite accurately. Policy analysis necessarily involves both empirical and normative inquiries. In empirical inquiry, the essentials will include: (a) concepts that can be used to organize and relate observables in ways that will permit the development of justified expectations with reference to the environment and means of controlling events that occur in the environment in foreseeable ways; (b) the patterns or instruments needed to achieve these purposes (classifications, forecasts, theories or explanations); (c) appropriate logics for calculating the implications of change (the patterns are logics linked to observation by appropriate transformation rules); and (d) observations or descriptions which provide the raw materials from which patterns are formed and to which they apply, and the set of constraints which serve to bound the enterprise. While some of the activities required are clearly inappropriate to philosophy, would require philosophers to cease to be philosophers, there are two areas in which philosophy might reasonably be expected to contribute: first, in the area of conceptualization and, second, in the development of an appropriate epistemological/methodological base for inquiry.

Neither the conceptual apparatus developed in philosophy nor the set of procedures that philosophers employ in conceptualization are of much use to the policymaker, and some of the conceptual apparatus must actually be demolished as a precondition to progress in the field. That is, such long-established and widely used concepts as "power," "freedom," "justice," or "equality," are analytically worthless in the study of human affairs; in the aggregate, they make up a fish net so badly conceived and executed that its use is merely an exercise in futility *so long as the goal is to catch fish*—the latent function of the apparatus in academia is another matter. Moreover, the kind of semantic analysis which contemporary philosophers used to attack philosophic essentialism contributes little or nothing to the development of suitable concepts and indicators for the study of policy. The important question is not "What use has been made of a concept in the past?" but "What is the most useful use that can be found for this concept and why is it useful?" or "How can this concept be used for improving the human condition or if it cannot what concept can be developed for that purpose?"

In the field of methodology or philosophy of inquiry, some very useful work has been done, but it is very uncertain how much contribution has actually been made to non-philosophic inquiries. The philosophy of science, for example, has been active for more than four decades but has contributed little or nothing to scientific practice and is in fact ignored by scientists with no discernable ill effects—nor do philosophers of science claim that science would be better performed if their philosophy was honored. Even if it is conceded that the quality of social science improved during the period when philosophy of science flourished, and that serious attempts were made to translate the products of philosophy of science into social science terms, it remains problematic whether the improvement was due to the influence of philosophy of science or simply a parallel development generated primarily by working inquirers in social science seeking to increase the quality of their own performance. Nevertheless, this remains the one area in philosophy which the empirical inquirer can examine with profit; unfortunately, the tendency for philosophy of science to become increasingly philosophic with time has eroded the value of the field —decreased the amount of intellectual profit to be had from each unit of time spent.

With respect to the more narrowly normative dimensions of policy-making, the major analytic requirements are: (a) a set of concepts that can be used to identify the normatively-significant dimensions of the alternative outcomes from which choices are made—they will refer to the attributes of specified human populations; (b) a priority structure that will order attainable outcomes—the ordering must be transitive but the structure need not be integrated (a set of deductions from some common set of axioms); (c) a justification for the preference ordering; (d) rules for applying the preference ordering to particular situations (policies); and (e) sets of observations that can be used to refine and correct the preference ordering and the policies that apply it. While philosophers might reasonably contribute in any of these areas without losing their union cards, the two major points at which assistance is most likely to appear are in the development of suitable concepts for identifying the normative dimensions of action and of appropriate arguments for justifying particular preference-orderings, and at the next level for justifying that justification. Both tasks seem quite close to the classic philosophic tradition. And most philosophers would argue that if their discipline has little to offer the empirical inquirer beyond methodological improvement the field of normative inquiry has by tradition belonged to them, and in that province they have performed well. Most empirical inquirers seem to agree! Yet by reference to the needs of the policymaker, or even the individual actor, what philosophers have to offer in the normative realm is far less adequate, far more misleading, and in the long run far more pernicious in impact, than their contributions to empirical inquiry. The field has been preempted using concepts that are useless for comparing the conditions of life of either individuals or groups, using priorities stated as unconditional absolutes rather than comparisons, supported by arguments that are unconvincing outside the hothouse atmosphere of philosophic academia; in no way can it be argued that philosophy has provided useful guidelines for day-to-day living, or the foundations on which such guidelines might be constructed.

There are various reasons why this state of affairs has been allowed to develop. For one thing, the need for normative guidance more sophisticated than the content of traditional church and family norms is relatively recent, particularly in the field of collective action. Moreover, members of the academic guilds have been loath to force their colleagues to come to grips with everyday problems, thus demonstrating either their value or their futility and fatuity. A "live and let live" attitude characterizes, and has characterized, academic life; it works to the advantage of the older disciplines, whatever the quality of their performance, because it inhibits precisely the kind of destructive criticism needed to weed out what is meaningless or useless. In the educational system, the efficacy of different modes of study, texts, curricula, or faculties, is rarely tested against the needs of clients or the benefits to society at large. Evaluations tend to refer to the needs of the producers, the good intentions of those who manage the apparatus, the length and weight of the tradition that girds particular practices. The fact that philosophy is not alone, no more useless or less useful than literature or political science or Greek is irrelevant. *Tu quoque*! is not an adequate substitute for *mea culpa* where systematic criticism is concerned; recognition of error is the essential first step in the improvement of any performance. Finally, philosophy has benefited greatly and undeservedly from the gross incompetence of extremists who sought to eliminate all normative questions from social inquiry in the name of science. While the effort to rid social science of philosophic essentialism may have been laudable, raw empiricism is a mere purgative, offering little nourishment with extended use. The patent stupidity of the attack combined with the academic penchant for the ignorance fallacy to buttress the philosopher's dubious claim to be worth attending.

The reasons why philosophy is not useful for policy analysis have nothing to do with the characteristics or intentions of philosophers or even their competence as philosophers; it is a function of the nature of philosophizing as it is practiced by philosophers, of the kinds of activities in which philosophers indulge and the way in which they are performed. Practical uselessness is a product of a long-standing separation of philosophy from ordinary human affairs. The prime feature of the situation is the divorce of philosophy from observation—whether the divorce is cause or symptom is irrelevant, the impact is the same in both cases. The status of philosophic activity within the discipline is virtually unrelated to its consonance with observation or its usefulness in the daily affairs of men. Like economics, philosophy gains from its language a certain plausibility with respect to real world affairs, but it lacks a solid foundation in sustained and systematic inquiry and its products are employed for human purposes at peril. It deals with observables, but not by reference to observations, a crucial distinction. Even the philosophers of science remain primarily philosophers, concentrating on the formal and logical characteristics of scientific inquiry rather than the purposes, procedures, and products of the working scientist—that has been a major weakness of the Nagel-Hempel approach to the subject.

In general philosophy, intense activity sustained over long periods of time has generated an object of inquiry that bears precious little resemblance to the observed world in which ordinary mortals live. Speculation, literary activity, exegesis, and glossing has produced a body of philosophic material which tends to serve as the primary grist for the ongoing philosophic mill—protected against testing in use or the cauterizing touch of observation. Philosophers come very close to being dogs in pursuit of their own tails.

The procedures employed in the study of this strange object of inquiry, and the criteria of acceptability applied to the results, combine to account for the uselessness of philosophy as practiced and to suggest that it is not likely to change. They also provide an important lesson regarding the role of observation in the quest for knowledge. Philosophy is exemplar of the science whose propositions consist almost entirely of theoretical terms, of the metalanguage constructed without adequate concern for the primary language on which it is parasitic, of the scholastic undertaking whose products are consequential within the discipline and nowhere else. Such traits cannot survive in a discipline committed to specific observation and testing in use.

The kinds of questions that philosophers ask about their private universe are best illustrated from the leading journals. A one-year sampling of the major essays in the *Journal of Philosophy* and the *Journal of the Philosophy of Science* can be found in the Appendix to this chapter. The absence of concern for observables, and the utter lack of relation to the policy analyst's concerns, is obvious. And journals with ostensibly greater concern for everyday affairs, such as the journal entitled *Philosophy and Public Affairs*, retains a primary concern for the "philosophic" dimension of public affairs, label notwithstanding; with one or two notable exceptions, its contents have differed only rhetorically from those published by the older philosophical quarterlies.

The substance of philosophic activity is equally affected by the separation from observation and the absence of any commitment to testing in use. Criticism focuses almost exclusively on the internal characteristics of argument; the performance characteristics of the object of study are ignored—indeed, most of the objects of study are the work of others and do not, strictly speaking, have performance characteristics. The strategy of inquiry commonly followed in the discipline reverses the direction of movement characteristic of observation-based fields of study, beginning with the general and not with the particular and specific. There is a tendency to seek for overarching conceptual structures into which everything can be fitted rather than the conceptual apparatus needed to deal with particular situations. The treatment of materials tends to be static and timeless, concentrating on structure, in contrast to the concern with dynamics and process that characterizes the sciences. The results of inquiry tend to be presented as absolutes, ideals, unbounded and universal structures rather than the relative and limited conclusions characteristic of competent empirical inquiry. Discussion, in brief, focuses on the category rather than the specific case, on the aggregate rather than the particular, on the universal rather than the limited. That is the principal reason why so little of philosophy can serve as a guide in practical affairs—statements are generalized to a level at which they have no particular implications, hence cannot guide action.

The criteria of evidence and accepted standards of argument in philosophy also contrast sharply and unfavorably with those on which scientific inquiry and reasoned choice depend. Acceptability is unrelated to applicability to human affairs; observation and testing in use are not treated as a necessary conditions for acceptance. Lacking applications that can serve as a critical base, philosophic criticism focuses necessarily on the internal, structural, and historical aspects of argument—accepted usage, logical properties, clarity of meaning, internal structure, and so on. Philosophy tends to be built entirely within the metalanguage. But a metalanguage is only a proposed working logic for a first-order or working language, and the acceptability of the logic is contingent on its consequences within the working language—no logic is perfectly applicable to human activity, even if that activity is only verbal or linguistic. Moreover, in the absence of observations philosophers are forced to rely on such factors as literary allusions, imaginary instantiation, consistency with received tradition, literary style, and even citation to authority, for evidence on which to base their criticisms.

Given that conception of what constitutes evidence, the quality of the ensuing argument is unlikely to be high. Perhaps the best illustration available of the kinds of argument that philosophers are prepared to entertain seriously can be found in contemporary moral philosophy. In what is perhaps the most widely discussed volume in the field since Toulmin's *The Place of Reason in Ethics*, or Stevenson's *Ethics and Language*, John Rawls[a] argues for acceptance of two principles of justice by asserting that rational men placed in a peculiar and imaginary situation that he calls the "original position" would choose those two principles in preference to any others available to them. Leaving aside the question whether the "original position" has been or can be stated adequately, and even conceding that rational men in that condition of knowledge would in fact choose Rawls' two principles, that still does not constitute a reason for accepting the two principles as guides to action—and some extremely good reasons can be offered for refusing, not least the line of reasoning offered on their behalf by Rawls—in effect, an argument from ignorance of a special kind. Despite the curious nature of the argument, the volume has been taken very seriously indeed, subjected to widespread criticism, used as a topic for discussion in various meetings and symposia, and so on. No one, so far as I can determine, considered the argument peculiar, specious, or unworthy of attention. Yet if that same form of reasoning was applied to such topics as abortion or the death penalty, who would be willing to take the results seriously, to use them as a basis for action? It is very curious.

With some minor exceptions, the needs of the policymaker and critic are not being fulfilled and cannot be fulfilled by what philosophy is currently producing or has already produced, though some value can be had

[a]John Rawls, *A Theory of Justice* (Belknap Press, 1971).

from the study of methodological developments, particularly in philosophy of science. Whether or not performance of these functions is a legitimate or necessary purpose of philosophy, that purpose is not being met at present. Is the situation likely to change in the near future? It seems not. Those already trained in philosophy would have to overcome the impetus of their habits, reinforced by their fears; the expense would be substantial to those involved. The young might succeed, and are worth encouraging, but they are playing against a stacked deck. The impetus to change is weak; the reward structure, in philosophy as elsewhere, is dominated by the elderly. Moreover, the principal objections to current philosophic practice are intellectual and not readily appreciated; even if the message passed those barriers, there is no guarantee of acceptance—I no longer believe that building a better mousetrap will lead to its adoption; a good public relations program may do more for an inadequate mousetrap. Indeed, prestigious ritual has sometimes prospered because of lethal intellectual objections; Tertullian's "I believe *because* it is absurd" has its modern counterparts. While fear of status loss might produce change even among the old, and there are some signs that a tax-weary population is beginning to wonder why society should provide an unending feast for a horde of unproductive locusts, the results of change are more likely to be substitution of another batch of locusts than eradication of the species. If entitlement can be linked to performance in the educational structure, change may occur, though if philosophy is only a sterile and harmless amusement for learned men, as C.D. Broad once said, society may wish to retain it, along with other remnants of vanishing species—eagles and grizzly bears and professors of Greek. Few philosophers are prepared to accept such slight honorific recompense for a lifetime of work, excepting that curious class of savants called logicians who seem to rejoice in their own uselessness. Neither past history, the competence of the critics of philosophy, nor the quality of the educational system (the prime product of the philosophic tradition) suggest that change is imminent. A fantasy to which I am much attached recalls the scene in medieval England in which the monks, forcibly ejected from their warm sanctuaries in mid-winter, ride their donkeys through the countryside in search of food and shelter; if philosophers continue to refuse to address themselves to human concerns, they too may meet their Henry VIII, in the form of a state legislature, most likely, and find themselves out on their individual asses in the collective cold. But it is only a fantasy. Meanwhile, those concerned with policy analysis must have their intellectual tools and they will have to produce them for themselves, whether empirical or normative. They are not likely to come from philosophy.

Appendix

One-Year Sampling of Major Essays in the Journal of Philosophy *(1972)*

Opacity in Belief Structures

Quine in Perspective

The Empirical Meaningfulness of Interpersonal Utility Comparisons

Knowledge and Justified Presumption

Empirical Realists and Wittgensteinians

Senses and Kinds

The Parsing of "Possible"

Functionalism, Machines, and Incorrigibility

Is Raising One's Arm a Basic Action?

Truth and Mass Terms

Knowledge, Causality, and Justification

Propositional Verbs and Knowledge

Philosophical Aspects of Molecular Biology

Tarski's Theory of Truth

Some Observations Concerning Logics and Concepts of Existence

Attribute Identities in Microreducations

Individuals and the Theory of Prediction

Can the Self Divide?

On Alleged Refutations of Mechanism Using Godel's Incompleteness Results

Positive, Comparative, Superlative

Grammar Psychology and Indeterminacy

Indeterminacy of Translation

A Justification of Reason

200

One-Year Sampling of Major Essays in the Philosophy of Science *(1972)*

What's Wrong with the Received View on the Structure of Scientific Theories

Towards an Aristotelian Theory of Scientific Explanation

An Analysis of Festinger's Cognitive Dissonance Theory

Einstein's Discovery of Special Relativity

A Critique of Popper's View on Scientific Method

Three Types of Referential Opacity

Inductive Logic and Causal Modalities; A Probabilistic Approach

Reporting, Evaluating, Describing

The Determinism of Quantum-Mechanical Probability Statements

Explanation and Teleology

Thomas Reid's Discovery of a Non-Euclidian Geometry

Functionalism and the Elimination of Theoretical Terms

Biological Foundations of the Psychoneural Identity Hypothesis

The Logic of Projectability

Degrees of Interpretation

Determinism, Laws, and Predictability in Principle

Quantum Mechanics and Interpretations of Probability Theory

On Arguments Against the Empirical Adequacy of Finite State Grammar

Contextual Falsification and Scientific Methodology

Reduction in Genetics—Biology or Philosophy?

Statistical Explanation

17 Legal Philosophy and Policy Studies

Martin P. Golding

The purpose of this brief chapter is to point out or, more loosely, suggest the ways in which legal philosophy is of special import for the field of policy studies. This task is made somewhat difficult by the fact that there appears to be considerable disagreement on the scope of policy studies and on its contents and methods. What unifies—possibly all that unifies—the various workers in this field, which is also designated by the terms "policy science" and "policy analysis," is an interest in the subject of policy. But while dictionary definitions of "policy," and also stipulative or technical definitions, are easy to come by, a glance at the literature shows that many divergent items go under the name. Perhaps this seeming confusion is only natural in an emerging discipline.

Two main trends within policy studies can, however, be identified: the descriptive and the prescriptive. The former is concerned with describing such matters as the factors which initiate policy-making processes, the roles played by various actors and organized groups in arriving at policy decisions, the methods employed by decisionmakers and their research staffs, the impact of policies, etc. Some studies focus on specific policy decisions; others focus on the policy-making process in general, and attempt to identify elements which enter into all such processes, or most of them. While both types of study of necessity employ one or the other kind of model and conceptual framework, it is far from clear that researchers in the field can claim to have discovered any (descriptive) uniformities that hold within the policy domain. The prescriptive trend is concerned with the improvement of the policy-making process. This endeavor clearly presupposes the identification of values or interests (instrumental, mediate, or ultimate) which policies ought to promote, or—if such normative inquiry appears too formidable or ' "unscientific"—at least criteria and standards (e.g., efficiency) by which one may evaluate alternative policy proposals for the accomplishment of any given end. Policy researchers have, for these purposes, borrowed from other disciplines, for example, economics and operations research. But here, again, a good deal of divergence can be found, and there seems to be no uniformity of approach or result. Nevertheless, despite this unsettled situation, and perhaps because of it, legal philosophy may have useful points of contact with policy studies in both its descriptive and prescriptive components.

Any account of the scope of legal philosophy must begin with the recognition that there are no sharp lines which separate it from other branches of philosophy: social and political philosophy, ethics, and even philosophical psychology. The philosophy of law takes up many of the same problems as do these other branches, although it often does so within a narrower, legally-oriented, focus. Secondly, legal philosophy frequently utilizes the insights and results of the various social sciences. Sociology and anthropology, for instance, are as indispensible to the legal philosopher as they are to the policy theorist. There are few problems of legal philosophy that do not entail at least some reference to empirical generalizations about human conduct and social organization.

Before I turn to the specific content of legal philosophy, I should like to emphasize one general way in which a knowledge of legal philosophy can be of significance for policy studies. It is clear that law must always occupy a place at the very heart of research on the policy process: law as a profession, as a body of rules, as a group of institutions, and as a socio-cultural institution in its own right. Law, in each of these aspects, plainly is infused with substance that has many moral and evaluational dimensions toward which sensitivity can be enhanced through acquaintance with legal philosophy, particularly on its ethical sides. (This proposition is compatible with the most hardboiled positivist or realist position.) This type of sensitivity is a desideratum for the descriptive as well as the prescriptive component of policy studies. The fact that legal philosophers are often in sharp disagreement about the presuppositions or implications of some legal phenomenon in no way undercuts this point; it rather strengthens it. The competing ethical perspectives of philosophers of law, and the different ethical theories on which reliance is placed, can provide the policy researcher with a variety of patterns of analysis and systematic frameworks for the study of policy-making processes. A bit of experimentation along these lines should prove fruitful.

Now to specifics. Legal philosophy, as a mode of inquiry concerning law, deals with two sorts of question: *analytical* (or conceptual) and *normative* (or justificatory). The first sort of question arises from the fact that the law employs various key concepts, uses certain key terms, in the formulation of rules, principles, standards, and doctrines. A grab bag of handy examples of such concepts includes: rights, duties, contract, person, property, offense, causation, negligence, intention, and due process. Furthermore certain key concepts are used in describing or talking about laws and legal institutions, e.g., the concepts of a legal rule, authority, punishment, responsibility and so on. (These terms may also be used in the formulation of rules, etc.) The task of the legal philosopher is to supply an analysis of such concepts or (what is the same) an elucidation of the meaning(s) of the key terms. A variety of types of analysis is possible. One may, for instance, concentrate on analyzing the "behavioral" meaning of legal concepts. Alternatively, one may attempt to show how certain concepts are functionally related in the process of judicial reasoning. No one variety of analysis excludes the legitimacy of other types. Philosophers in the main, however, have tended to supply analyses of a more "conceptualist" sort. Their aim has often been that of exposing the obscurities which surround these concepts and, in turn, proposing clearer meanings for the key terms; they have been concerned with the "rational reconstruction" of legal concepts.

The normative questions of legal philosophy deal with the justifiability of the various rules and institutions of the law, with primary, though not exclusive, emphasis on their ethical basis. Here it should be noted that philosophers are particularly interested in the "meta" question of what general forms of justification are available for this task. But aside from attending to how particular rules, etc., might be justified, philosophers have been especially concerned with certain rather general issues. Why have a legal system in the first place? Is there a moral obligation to obey the law, and when is disobedience justified? (These questions, and others like them, are, of course, familiar fare in political philosophy.) The normative questions of legal philosophy sometimes also take the form of problems of *institutional design*: e.g., How should legal institutions be designed so as to conform to standards of justice?

These different facets of legal philosophy, as well as their import for policy studies, may be illustrated by looking at one of its problem-areas, philosophical issues in the criminal law. The normative question of the justification of punishment received its first detailed examination in Plato's *Laws*. (The author of this chapter can personally testify to the fact that it comes as a surprise to many people, even academics and even advanced students in criminology, that the rehabilitation theory of punishment is not a modern idea, but was first systematically expounded by Plato.) Recent writers on the subject have pointed out that this is not a unitary issue, but rather is composed of several, separable questions: (1) Why have penal laws in the first place? (2) Who should be punished as a way of enforcing the law? and (3) How and how much should someone be punished? Although there are no agreed-upon answers to these questions, putting them in this way enables one to see in clearer light the prima facie relevance or irrelevance of such traditional theories of punishment as social protection, general and special deterrence, retributivism, and rehabilitation. For they do seem, at first blush, to be unequal in their *direct* relevance to each one of these questions, and it may be necessary to assign to each of the traditional theories its due role within the (now) complex problem of the justification of punishment.

It would be stating the obvious to show how all this is of the utmost importance to prescriptive treatments of so-called "crime-control policy," even treatments which are concerned solely with the improvement (which of course entails a value judgment of some kind) of policies designed to achieve a preestablished, and perhaps arbitrarily given, end. But it is also the case that the above approach to the problem of punishment can be of great use to purely descriptive studies of crime-control policies, for it provides alternative models or frameworks for such studies. (This is, of course, a two-way street; the philosophy of law would profit considerably from more attention to descriptive studies of crime-control policy. One should not, however, make the mistake of thinking that legal philosophers do not already acknowledge the importance of empirical inquiry for their own work!)

For further illustration, let us consider the second of the above questions: Who should be punished? This not only raises the vexing issue of responsibility, but also the issue of the punishment of the innocent. How shall legal processes be designed so as to prevent the punishment of the innocent, and how much looseness in procedure is tolerable to secure a high level of protection for the public? Both issues are vital to a study of criminal law from a policy perspective, and the literature of legal philosophy can promote sensitivity to the moral dimensions and implications of alternative policies. The subject of responsibility also provides an extraordinarily rich area which is of moment for the student of policy-making. What is the meaning of "responsibility" and what are the conditions of responsibility? These analytical questions have been examined in fine detail in recent thought. Each one of the standard criteria of culpability (*mens rea*), purpose, knowledge, intention, recklessness, negligence, etc., have been analyzed in a searching manner. It is interesting to note, in this connection, how analytical and normative questions frequently interpenetrate, for there is an intimate relation between the criteria of culpability and their opposites, namely, the grounds of exculpation. These are also grist for the analytical mill. But why should a legal system allow for excuses and defenses at all? Analysis of the grounds of exculpation quickly implicates a consideration of this normative question, and vice versa. It would take us too far afield to expatiate further on these matters, but it should again be emphasized that there are few topics in the area of policy and the criminal law—even such a topic as the efficiency of the police—which do not sooner or later lead head on to philosophical (analytical and normative) questions. It would be a delusion to think that these questions can be completely avoided.

It is probable that mere mention of the term "legal philosophy" will immediately call to mind the long-standing debate between positivism and natural law. I dare say that most policy theorists in the field of law adopt a "realist" or "behavioral" approach. It is easily understandable that one should wish to avoid "sterile" controversies, but appearances to the contrary, there is much to be learned from this old debate and fresh perspectives of a useful kind may be acquired. The realist tends to view legal rules as *predictions* of behavior. A good deal can be said in favor of this approach, but it also may have considerable shortcomings: it tends to overlook the fact that much behavior is rule-governed and rule-guided; it substitutes an "external" point of view on matters whose understanding also requires an "internal" point of view, as H.L.A. Hart has called them. The predictive approach—widely current in the social sciences—needs to be supplemented by a fuller understanding of what it means to say that a legal system exists in a society.

This is what the old debate between legal positivism and natural law is basically about. It deals with an analytical question, the explication of the concept of law, that has normative overtones. What are the conditions for the existence of a legal system in a society and what are the essential elements of legal systems? Does every body of law have a minimum content? The question "What is law?" is not, and can never be, a purely *straightforward* empirical question, for the marshalling of data already presupposes some conceptual framework in terms of which the inquiry is carried out. Strange as it may seem, it is the descriptive policy student who probably most needs to take a side on this old debate, if only as a methodological postulate.

As is well known, the positivists have held that the conditions for the existence of a legal system do not include among them any moral or ethical component. (They of course do not deny that the law is influenced by moral ideas; nor do some of them at least, particularly the followers of the utilitarian Jeremy Bentham, deny that the law *ought* to be made in accordance with certain ethical conceptions.) Positivists have tended to emphasize the centrality of sanctions and the imperative character of laws. In their analyses of the concept of the existence of a legal system, they have also tended to put great weight on the existence of a law-making agency and the effectiveness of its law-creating activity. The great success of legal positivism has been in its providing conceptual tools for rationally reconstructing full-blown, developed legal systems: each element of a system can be assigned its location within a chain of laws and acts of law-making and law-applying. The positivist approach should be of particular use to the descriptive policy analyst. It provides a model in terms of which one can investigate the respective roles, in the formation of legal policy, of formal and informal (official and non-official) agencies, organizations and actors.

Natural law theorists, on the other hand, have held that the satisfaction of certain moral standards or ethical goals is a necessary condition for the existence of laws and law-making. They have tended to accord the idea of "rational purpose" a central position in their analysis of the concept of law. Recent natural law thinking has stressed the problem-solving character of law-making. Prescriptive policy study, therefore, has an affinity to the natural law approach. It should be pointed out that, as employed by natural law theories, the idea of rational purpose is a substantive rather than a purely formal or technical notion, for legal problem-solving is constrained by the requirements of justice and the common good. I think that policy theorists might find it instructive to compare their procedures with those of the natural law thinkers.

This is hardly the place for a detailed examination, but it is clear that the debate between positivism and natural law represents two rather different ways of conceiving the existence of a legal system. Natural law thinkers tend to distinguish rather sharply between systems of social control that are based solely on force and systems that have some kind of intrinsic moral appeal. It might be suggested that such a distinction has some usefulness even for descriptive policy studies, despite the more obvious attractions of the positivistic approach. The debate over whether a legal system must of necessity satisfy certain moral requirements is, of course, not the only problem involving the relations between law and morality. There is also the normative question of whether, or to what extent, the law should enforce morality. This is the evergreen question of public control *versus* individual freedom. Is it possible to formulate a principle which delimits the public and private spheres? There has recently been a good deal of fresh philosophical discussion of this question, particularly on the legitimate uses of the criminal law in a pluralist democracy. It is hard to see how the prescriptive policy theorist can avoid serious consideration of this question.

There are many other topics in legal philosophy which could be mentioned, but I think enough has been said to show the significance of legal philosophy for policy studies. I should like to stress, in closing, that this is a two-way street. A subject of special interest to the author is that of philosophical issues in conflict resolution, particularly the various forms of third-party dispute settling and the roles played in them by standards of procedural justice. Here, close cooperation between the policy student and the legal philosopher may not only be mutually profitable but may also be indispensible.

Brief Bibliography

Fuller, L. *The Morality of Law*. Rev. ed., 1969.

Fuller, L. *Anatomy of the Law,* 1968.

Ginsberg, M. *On Justice in Society,* 1965.

Golding, M.P. *Philosophy of Law,* 1975. Contains bibliography.

Golding, M.P. (ed.). *The Nature of Law*, 1966.

Hart, H.L.A. *The Concept of Law,* 1961.

Hart, H.L.A. *Punishment and Responsibility,* 1968.

Hughes, G. (ed.). *Law, Reason, and Justice,* 1969.

Kantorowicz, H. *The Definition of Law,* 1958.

Kelsen, H. *The Pure Theory of Law,* 1967.

Kent, E. (ed.). *Law and Philosophy,* 1970. Contains bibliography.

Morris, H. (ed.). *Freedom and Responsibility,* 1961. Contains bibliography.

Summers, R.S. (ed.). *Essays in Legal Philosophy*, 1968.

Summers, R.S. (ed.). *More Essays in Legal Philosophy,* 1971.

In addition, many texts and collections of readings on jurisprudence are also of interest: e.g., texts or collections by Cohen and Cohen, Dias, Fitzgerald, Friedmann, Lloyd, Paton, and Pound's collection of writings in the field.

Part VII
Mathematics and Natural Science

18 Uses of Applied Mathematics in Political Science

Robert Ferber

Two broad forms of applied mathematics would seem to have wide applicability to problems of political science. These are the use of the techniques of statistics to collect and analyze data bearing on political science and the use of mathematical modeling techniques to describe the political process and political behavior. Great strides have been made in the former case, but the use of mathematical models is for all practical purposes in its infancy. Indeed, mathematical models in political science seem to be quite rare.

This chapter will offer some comments on the use of these two very different approaches in political science with particular reference to the feasibility of different sorts of approaches to particular types of political science problems.

Current State of Affairs

In terms of quantitative data, the use of statistics in political science seems to have increased dramatically in the past twenty-five years. Analyzing this trend, James Hutter finds that in the three-year period from 1946 to 1948 less than 12 percent of the articles in the *American Political Science Review* used statistical or mathematical techniques as compared to 65 percent approximately two decades later in the three-year period from 1968 to 1970.[1] The percentage of articles in seven major political science journals containing such approaches was not much less during this later period, namely, 58 percent. While these percentages represent tremendous increases, a look at the figures behind them indicates that the increase in the use of statistics in mathematics has actually not been nearly as impressive. Thus, in little over one-fourth of these articles only the simplest of descriptive methods were used, such as percentages, means or rankings. Only about 10 percent of these articles made any use of mathematics, those uses being primarily algebra or matrix algebra. While the results are not clear on this matter from the Hutter article, it appears that probably not much more than a quarter of the articles utilized fairly sophisticated techniques, such as the various forms of multivariate analysis.

As a follow-up to Hutter's study, and to obtain more up-to-date information, the writer made a similar investigation of the quantitative content of the 1973 issues of the *American Political Science Review,* Volume 67. This review revealed substantial progress in the use of quantitative methods by political scientists. Of the forty-six articles in that issue, excluding communications and comments, only one-fifth made no use of quantitative methods (other than to cite a number here and there in the text), about a third (14) used fairly simple quantitative techniques, such as cross-tabulations and simple correlation coefficients, and fully half used such fairly sophisticated approaches as multiple regressions and other forms of multivariate analysis. Indeed, multiple regressions seemed to have been about the most commonly employed statistical tool.

Considering the fact that most of the articles in *APSR* that did not use quantitative methods were not of the sort that would require such techniques, unless *APSR* is completely atypical of political science journals, this would suggest that impressive progress has been made in applying quantitative methods to political science. No doubt, however, much more progress remains to be made. This chapter attempts to point out some of the principal quantitative techniques that might be applied to political science, based in part on work in political science and based in part on applications of these techniques in other fields.

The World Is Multivariate

The growing use of multivariate methods in political science is paralleled by the increasing use of these methods in other social sciences. It demonstrates the increasing awareness that numerous factors enter into the determination of attitudes and behavior, in political science as in other social sciences, and the effect of any one can only be ascertained by relating it in a framework that enables the effects of related variables to be taken into account at the same time. Indeed, the tendency to seek relationships between variables on the basis of two-way comparisons (such as voting behavior versus education or voting behavior versus age) is on the same level of sophistication as the old allegation that the earth is flat.

To omit other relevant factors invariably produces a biased estimate of the variable being studied, for to the extent that it interacts with other variables, the resulting effects are distorted. Usually (though not always) the apparent effect will be magnified, which means that the researcher is likely to triumphantly blandish positive results but which are not likely to weather careful scrutiny. Thus, a two-way comparison is invariably likely to find a clear relationship between age and voting behavior, but might this effect really not be due to education and the fact that the younger people tend to have more education? Without including education in the analysis (as well as other possibly relevant variables), there is no way of telling.

To be sure, it is never possible to include all relevant variables in an analysis. Fortunately, however, numerous past studies indicate that this is not necessary, that only if a relatively few key variables are included, exclusion of others tends to have virtually no effect on the results. Pinpointing these key variables is not always easy, but this is one of the tasks of research.

While this is not the place to go into the different forms of multivariate methods in any detail, suffice it to say that by now methods of this type exist for dealing with almost any type of problem situation. In a very broad sense, multivariate methods may be said to consist of two types. One type is where one or more variables can be singled out as "dependent" or the "effects," and the objective is to identify what other variables, usually denoted as "independent variables," determine or are associated with the dependent variables. Thus, a study may seek to identify what variables explain how different people voted in a particular election as well as the relative importance of these independent variables. In this case, the individual voter is the unit of observation, the dependent variable is the manner that each individual voted, and the independent variables might include such characteristics as age, education, occupation, and attitudes on a variety of issues taken up in the election. By means of multiple regression analysis or by a related technique, numerical estimates can be obtained of the statistical importance of each of these variables on voter behavior.

Various other multivariate techniques exist for dealing with such "cause and effect" problems. These include path analysis, where the interrelationships among the dependent and independent variables are fairly complex, canonical correlation for the case where one is studying a set of dependent variables all at the same time (such as how an individual voted on a number of different candidates); and simultaneous equations, for the case of many dependent variables that are interrelated with each other and with the independent variables.

Another type of multivariate analysis is that seeking to find similarities between sets of variables. For example, it may be interesting to know how well people of different backgrounds hold similar attitudes on a variety of public issues. From answers to a number of questions by these subjects, such methods as factor analysis or cluster analysis can be used to determine the extent to which these people fall into groups or "clusters." A method such as factor analysis can also be used to reduce a number of variables to a smaller number by eliminating the similarities among them.

From the point of view of the nonquantitative specialist, one of the beauties of these techniques is that with the availability of computers, it is now possile to make use of these techniques without knowing the underlying mathematics. A number of good books are available that enable a person to understand these techniques with only a knowledge of elementary statistics,[2] though it is wise to consult a specialist to check that no errors are being made.

Finding Out What Is Going On

Using surveys to get insights into people's behavior and attitudes may well have originated in political science, in the polls taken to attempt to predict the outcome of elections. By now, this is not only a tool of scientific research but is also used widely by politicians to gauge how voters are responding to their pleas and to the issues raised by their opponents. While these polls are often done haphazardly, the fact remains that surveys of voter behavior and attitudes can be extremely useful and are quite common in political science as well as other fields. The purpose of this section, therefore, need not be to call attention to the value of surveys but rather to indicate some further possibilities, which tend to be overlooked.

A major objective in survey work is to ascertain how people's behavior changes over time, an interest shared by all social scientists. As a rule, such information is sought by means of recall interviews on successive one-time interview studies, meaning that different samples are interviewed in each time period. Overlooked by this procedure, however, is that all it yields is so-called marginal distributions, namely, results which may camouflage the real changes underway in a population.

To take an example, suppose that interviews are made in January and in June of people's attitudes toward a new bond issue. Suppose, also, that 52 percent of those interviewed favored it in January and 55 percent in June. If different samples were involved each time, as is usually the case, one might naturally be led to conclude that very little change has taken place in the attitudes of the voters on this issue. In fact, enormous changes may have taken place but are concealed by the use of different samples each time. For example, suppose that the same 100 people were interviewed in each of the two periods. Table 18-1 shows how these results might have been obtained even though less than half of the sample held the same views in the later period.

In other words, from this table we see that in fact only 47 of the 100 people retained the same attitude, while 25 had switched from "yes" to "no," and 28 had switched from "no" to "yes."

While this example may seem extreme, the studies that have been made of this question suggest that it is not atypical, that is, opinions within a group may change substantially but the full extent of this change is hidden when one simply looks at totals for a particular period, because of compensatory swings. Clearly, however, for both policy and analytical purposes, substantial changes in opinions between two periods have a very different

Table 18-1
Tabulation of Interview Results

| | January | | |
June	Yes	No	Total
Yes	27	28	55
No	25	20	45
Total	52	48	100

significance than if very few changes take place, regardless of what the totals show for each period.

An even more fruitful approach to the study of political behavior and attitudes is made possible by panel or longitudinal studies. In such studies, samples are selected and the members of the samples will be interviewed many times, sometimes over a number of years, so that a considerable body of information is obtained about people's attitudes and behavior on a subject as well as on motivations underlying this behavior and on socioeconomic and other characteristics of the individuals that may affect this behavior.

Studies of this type can be invaluable in political science for throwing light on the nature of political attitudes and behavior, how these change over time, and on the influences working on them. Voter behavior is a particularly appropriate field for studies of this type. While voting does not take place with the frequency of consumer purchases, the collection of similar information on voting behavior should be of unique value to the political scientist, especially if the voting of panel members can be linked with changes in their social and economic position and with attitudes toward selected issues and political parties. The design and data collection phase of such a study present some difficulties, but none is insuperable and the resulting information would constitute an invaluable source for the study of voting behavior.

Models of How Nations Vote

Interesting possibilities would seem to exist for studying interrelationships among the behavior of the different nations through the use of econometrics and the techniques of simultaneous equations. This approach may be used, for example, to analyze the factors influencing voting behavior of different nations in the United Nations. Thus, it might be hypothesized that on a particular issue the vote of a nation will be influenced by certain cultural, economic, and political characteristics of that nation and also by the manner in which a key nation votes that is considered a leader of that particular group of nations. Thus, the general relationship for "follower" nation i may be of the form:

$$V_i = f(X_i, Y_i, Z_i, V_k) \qquad i = 1, \ldots, m - 3 \qquad (1)$$

where $\quad X_i, Y_i$ and Z_i are certain characteristics of that nation

$\qquad V_i$ is its vote on the particular issue

$\qquad V_k$ is the vote of "leader" nation k for the group to which nation i belongs.

For the sake of simplicity, let us assume that there are three such groups, one "leader" nation in each group, and that there are m nations altogether. Hence, there would be $m - 3$ equations of the form (1).

In the case of the "leader" nations, let us assume that their vote is affected primarily by the same set of cultural, economic, and political characteristics in that nation, plus the votes of the "leader" nations of the other two groups, which we denote by V_1 and V_m. The general equation for a leader nation may then be expressed as:

$$V_k = f(X_k, Y_k, Z_k, V_1, V_m) \qquad (2)$$

There would be three such equations, one for each of the "leader" nations.

Overall, therefore, these two general formulations yield a set of m equations in the m unknowns, V_i (from $i = 1$ to $m - 3$), V_k, V_1, and V_m.

Given information on the voting behavior of the nations over a period of years, and on the cultural, economic, and political characteristics considered most relevant, these equations could be solved under certain conditions to yield estimates of the relative importance of each of these variables in influencing the voter behavior of each nation.

While this model is a very simple one from a political point of view, it should illustrate how such techniques might be applied. In practice, the model could probably be made much more realistic by introducing dynamic elements, such as adding voting behavior of the country in the recent past as an additional variable, a technique that makes such equations much more amenable for forecasting purposes. Regardless of the form of model, the fact remains that political actions of both nations and other political bodies are frequently interdependent and are best explained in terms of a model that recognizes these interdependencies.

Diffusion of Political Ideas

Operations researchers and rural sociologists have made basic contributions in recent years in explaining the diffusion of product innovations. As a rule, this approach takes the form of the development of a mathematical model to describe the diffusion process, followed by the application of this model to data collected as part of the same study or in some other connection.[3]

The same approach could easily be applied to the diffusion and acceptance of political ideas over time. Thus, what is the time path of the acceptance of a new political idea? What differentiates people who accept this idea in its early stages and those who are receptive to it only at a much later time? In other words, who are the innovators and who are the laggards? Are the innovators on one issue also the innovators on other issues?

The necessary data for these studies could be obtained either by the usual types of surveys or by longitudinal analysis. Such studies have been done for some time in the fields of sociology and of marketing,[4] and these techniques are directly applicable to political behavior, since the communication of a political idea or a new candidate is operationally in essence a form of social marketing.

Longitudinal data are even more valuable for studying the diffusion of political ideas, since sampling variation does not then become a source of interference. To be sure, other sorts of bias may arise, such as panel conditioning, but there are ways of dealing with them. However, by following the same voters or governmental bodies over time data can be compiled on when certain ideas are adopted by different units in the sample, thereby providing a unique basis for analysis of diffusion of political ideas.

Simulation of Decision Processes

An intriguing use of quantitative methods, one that paradoxically involves no mathematics (other than counting), is the attempt to simulate thought processes in individual decision-making. The procedure involves close observation of decisionmakers as they make particular decisions, supplemented by numerous questions on reasons why and causal factors, all of which are then used as a basis for representing, either in English or in algebraic notation, the decision process in some sort of logical flow diagram. This diagram can then be transformed into a computer program (though this is not necessary), and is then used to test the validity of the representation by applying the same procedure to later decision situations and checking how the results correspond with what the decision maker actually did.

This approach can be illustrated by a study done by W. M. Morgenroth that simulated with remarkable accuracy the pricing process of a particular firm in an oligopolistic industry. By observing how prices were altered by means of discussions with executives in the industry, the researcher was able to develop the heuristic model shown in figure 18-1, which provides a rigorous though nonmathematical explanation of how prices are formed.[5]

This type of approach has clear applicability to many different aspects of political science behavior. How does a legislator decide which way to vote on a particular bill? How does a voter decide whom to vote for? More broadly, how does a government decide how to react in a particular type of crisis? How does a political party choose whom to run for office? Questions such as these can be investigated by this procedure and the results used to obtain a better understanding of how decision processes are formed and influenced.

Quantification without Mathematics

These four illustrations, particularly the last one, serve to indicate that a minimal knowledge of pure mathematics is required for many applications of quantitative methods to political science and other social sciences. The simulation approach described in the previous section requires no mathematics at all. For many other techniques, the advent of computers and the availability of program packages for a wide variety of different types of quantitative analysis mean that the researcher need not be a statistician or mathematician. He does have to be aware of the possibilities and the pitfalls of different quantitative methods, and of how to interpret results. More than anything else, he has to be able to take a firm approach with programmers and other technicians and not allow them to fit his problem to whatever program or technique they may be interested in at the moment. Like swimming, one does not have to be an expert to enjoy it and benefit from it—and with a few simple precautions, the danger of drowning is minimal.

Notes

1. J. L. Hutter, "Statistics and Political Science," *Journal of the American Statistical Association* 67 (December 1972): 735-742.

2. For example, W. W. Cooley and P. Lohnes, *Multivariate Data*

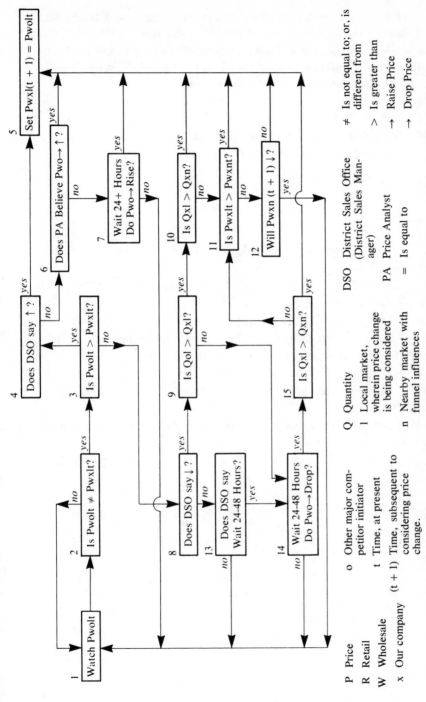

P   Price
R   Retail
W   Wholesale
x   Our company

o   Other major com-
    petitor initiator
t   Time, at present
(t + 1) Time, subsequent to
    considering price
    change.

Q   Quantity
l   Local market,
    wherein price change
    is being considered
n   Nearby market with
    funnel influences

DSO District Sales Office
     (District Sales Man-
     ager)
PA   Price Analyst
=   Is equal to

≠   Is not equal to; or, is
    different from
>   Is greater than
↑   Raise Price
↓   Drop Price

Source: W. M. Morgenroth, "A Method for Understanding Price Determinants," *Journal of Marketing Research* (August 1964): 19.

Figure 18-1. Model 1, Mark XI, Revised. A Binary Flow-Chart Depicting the Price Decision Process. Region W, Division W.

Analysis (New York: Wiley & Sons, 1971); N. Draper and H. Smith, *Applied Regression Analysis* (New York: Wiley & Sons, 1966).

3. For an example, see I. Bernhardt, "Diffusion of Catalytic Techniques through a Population of Medium-Sized Petroleum Refining Firms," *Journal of Industrial Economics* 19 (November 1970).

4. See, for example, E. M. Rogers, *Diffusion of Innovations* (New York: Free Press, 1962).

5. W. M. Morgenroth, "A Method for Understanding Price Determinants," *Journal of Marketing Research* (August 1964): 17-26.

References

Coplin, W. D. (ed.), *Simulation in the Study of Politics*. Chicago: Markham Pub. Co., 1968.

Draper, N. R. and H. Smith. *Applied Regression Analysis*. New York: Wiley & Sons, 1967.

Kmenta, J. *Elements of Econometrics*. New York: Macmillan Co., 1971.

Madge, J. *The Tools of Social Science*. New York: Doubleday & Co., 1965.

Meier, R. C. et al. *Simulation in Business and Economics*. Englewood Cliffs, New Jersey: Prentice-Hall, 1969.

Naylor, T. H. *Computer Simulation Techniques*. New York: Wiley & Sons, 1966.

Reed, R. C. *A Mathematical Background for Economists and Social Scientists*. Englewood Cliffs, New Jersey: Prentice-Hall, 1972.

Tatsuoka, M. *Multivariate Analysis*, New York: Wiley & Sons, 1971.

19 What Can Natural Science and Policy Studies Contribute to Each Other?

D. J. Montgomery

From Natural to Political Science[a]

What natural science, together with parts of engineering and applied mathematics, can contribute to policy studies may perhaps be classified under four headings:

1. *Providing technical information.* The importance of this input need not be labored. The material base of a modern industrialized society is science and engineering. Policy alternatives cannot be formulated, nor can their consequences be assessed, until the technical factors have been analyzed. Controls for nuclear weapons, strategies for energy conservation, ethics of genetic engineering are empty exercises unless based on a knowledge of the practicable, and this knowledge is achieved principally through science and engineering.

2. *Generating analytical techniques.* Here again the contributions are obvious. Some fields of long-standing application are statistics—whose very name betrays its political origin—and analysis of real variables (especially constrained extrema of several variables). Less venerable techniques are matrix analysis, numerical analysis, programming methods, computer-aided projections, and other trappings of operations research and decision theory. The mathematical techniques seem to me to serve a reassuring rather than a creative function, in that they tell us that if we can develop sensible input-output measures or meaningful social indicators, we will not be handicapped in the mathematical manipulations for extracting the logical implications therefrom. The creative—and hard—part is to propose functions that reasonably reflect human behavior and ultimately help to improve it.

3. *Suggesting concepts and descriptive methods.* The techniques of mathematics and natural science that are likely to be useful in policy studies are primarily quantitative ones. Hence whenever we deal with social variables, such as national income or poverty level, that by their nature require quantification, we have available a battery of techniques and methods that have proved themselves useful in science and engineering. What may be of profound consequence, moreover, is that natural science may demonstrate

---

[a]For additional material on the relations between natural science and policy studies, see chapter 20 in this volume by Gene Coggshall on science policy. A future issue of the *Policy Studies Journal* will contain a symposium on "Science Technology and Policy" to be edited by Avery Leiserson.

the necessity and possibility of quantifying concepts traditionally held to be nonquantifiable. The quantification will give these concepts operational meaning and thus enable them to have increased impact on actual decisions.

Let us give illustrations. In the analysis of population-limitation policies, one must ask sooner or later what it is that human beings ultimately value. Ethicists often list major values—freedom, justice, survival, and so on—on which there is pretty good agreement for a given civilization. The bind arises when policy options must be considered, for the values often conflict. Under the threat of excessive population, how much of our freedom to breed must be given up to maintain a pleasant environment in the community? How much will distributive justice be affected by having a large number of children in a family? And how much will changes in the equity-equality equation in the name of justice drive down productivity and thereby lower everyone's material standard of living? As a way of resolving ethical dilemmas, ethicists have sought a way to rank the major values. But the values do not form an ordered set. The importance of any one value depends on the degree to which the other values are achieved. Why survive if slavery is to be the price? Yet what good is freedom to the starving man? Ethics answers only that all the major values are essential, that none can be completely set aside. Few would quarrel with this statement, but it offers little guide when we have to chose among competing policies.

Clearly quantification is called for. The natural scientist will not be dismayed by attempting quantification of entities previously unquantified; that is the story of his life. First, he might try to identify a set of major values that is exhaustive and nonoverlapping, for example:

Material needs at the personal level (symbol P, "*P*rovision of material goods")

Material needs at the societal level (symbol E, "quality of the material *e*nvironment")

Nonmaterial needs at the personal level (symbol F, "*f*reedom to thrive spiritually")

Nonmaterial needs at the societal level (symbol J, "social and distributive *j*ustice")

Next, we must devise a function S of these four variables P, E, F, J that we may think of as a *satisfaction index* measuring the "quality of life," a concept which surely can be given meaning only in terms of satisfaction of the component needs. Then, to use this scheme for deciding among alternative deployments of resources to achieve a societal goal, we must estimate the satisfaction index S for each of the alternative deployments. The sign and the size of the resulting index will be an input to the decision makers, who can take it into account in rendering their judgments. At this stage of the formulation there is no procedure for ordering different values, nor is there any need—the methodology is directly useful.

If nonetheless it is desired to order values, a meaning can be given to that concept by further quantification. Suppose that P, E, F, J can be reduced to a common measure (say money equivalent, or welfare units, or some yet-to-be-discovered currency). We could say that under given conditions one value, say E, is more important than another, say P, at fixed F and J, if the increase is S resulting from a prescribed increment in E is greater than the increase in S resulting from an increment of the same size in P. In words, at fixed levels of freedom and justice, and at some given combination of E and P, the quality of the material environment would be "more valuable" than the provision of goods, as for example when income is ample and environment is noxious. The reverse might be true, of course, when income is meager and the environment is salubrious.

The approach of the preceding paragraph is perhaps more reminiscent of economics than natural science. The physical scientist likes to identify attributes of systems that are independent of the state of the system. He would like to be able to say, for instance, that one society holds F as a higher value than does another society, irrespective of the particular P, E, F, J. An analogy from mechanics will serve to illustrate this point: The physicist characterizes a particle by its rest *mass*, a parameter ascribed to it that permits predicting its motion, and that does not change with time or position. It accordingly makes sense to say that one particle is more massive than another no matter what the motion, though we cannot make corresponding statements with respect to speed, momentum, or energy. In value theory we should like to fish out of each society's behavior some parameters associated with P, E, F, J that describe the dependence of S on these four variables. The parameters themselves could then be compared between societies, just as mass can be compared between particles. Thus we would have succeeded in defining values operationally, in a way that permits ordering them. We accordingly define values as parameters that are assigned to societies or component thereof, these parameters serving to permit prediction of certain aspects of the behavior of the society. These values will be powerful aids in estimating the satisfaction index S resulting from alternative deployments of resources leading to different sets of P, E, F, J, and hence will be a guide to policy making.

This example has been presented not as a scheme feasible at the moment, although there would seem to be no insurmountable obstacles to making it useful on a limited scale. We are endeavoring to show what has to be done in decision analysis and policy formulation if discussion of ethical values is to consist of something beyond rhetoric. We view as a counsel of despair the notion that the decision maker cannot go beyond the ethicist's statement that "all major values are essential."

4. *Developing a perspective*. A first way in which natural science may

help to provide a perspective in policy studies flows out of its limitations. Many working scientists define their activities as *devising and utilizing schemes for describing and predicting phenomena within limited ranges of experience*. This definition has substantial operational content. Two crucial points are the *absence* of the word "truth" or "model" or "explanation," and the *presence* of the restriction "within a limited range of experience." The first point keeps us from straying into the morass of rhetoric and mysticism, the second one from suffering distress upon failing to discover a universal formula. None of this is to say that there is not elegance—or beauty, if you will—in science. Indeed, a good case can be made that creativity in science is largely dependent on sensitivity to logical elegance. But it is to say that time should not be wasted on such tiresome controversies as evolution versus creation, or reductionism versus vitalism. Just see which scheme, or which mixture of schemes, more adequately predicts phenomena in the appropriate area. Hear the other guy out, tell him that he may be right, and get on with the job in your own style.

A second way in which natural science may offer a hand to its younger brothers is in the matter of historical perspective. Natural science had some centuries to be conceived and nurtured before it flourished. Yet it deals with only the narrow part of experience where things are simple enough to be identified and labeled with reasonable agreement among competent observers. Social science, a much later arrival, must deal with subtle and complicated phenomena, often without much agreement. Is it not unrealistic to expect that a set of useful concepts and a handbook of solid data could have been distilled out of a complicated subject by a small band of observers in a limited time? A physical scientist, or a biological one, can reach for a handbook carrying the concentrated results obtained by armies of investigators over the entire world and during centuries. The social scientist is relatively in the stage of alchemy. We note that even though the search for the philosophers' stone failed to reach its avaricious goal of transmuting lead into gold, it succeeded in ameliorating everyday life by transmuting petroleum and air and water into plastics and fibers at one level of technology, and matter into energy at another. The history of natural science shows that in its realm the effort devoted to rational inquiry has been worthwhile, and gives us heart that corresponding attention in the realm of societal affairs will be rewarding. The wealth of concepts and techniques developed through centuries in the natural sciences stands at the disposal of the social sciences. One must be eclectic, of course—the history of science warns that concepts helpful in one region of discourse may be useless or worse in another. Let us taste of natural science what looks nourishing, but let us not be too eager to swallow it all. Rationalism must not become scientism.

From Political to Natural Science

We now give a hint as to what political scientists interested in policy studies might contribute to natural science. It is unlikely that there will be substantial contributions *in the small,* that is, in matters concerned with the details of scientific methodology. Natural science has had decades and decades of experience in working out techniques for treating its subject matter, and there are only a few areas likely to be candidates for aid from policy studies. These areas are characterized by highly complex interacting systems, such as biophysics or metallurgy. On the other hand, there could be major contributions to natural science *in the large*. Science is a matter of finding out how things work, with social utility or disutility by and large set aside. What makes a scientist productive is his success in selecting problems that can be attacked fruitfully from his strategic position at the moment, that is, from the resources of his time and his ability, of current theoretical understanding, and of experimental facilities at his disposal. A large part of these resources are furnished by the society through political processes. But these resources are limited, and hence must be managed. Science, as a process, is indeed a management task; how are time, talent, equipment to be deployed to maximize scientific progress? This is a policy question for the individual investigator, and he needs help from policy studies in understanding both that the question exists and how it is to be resolved. And since the society furnishes many of the resources, it will ask: What portion of societal resources is to be allocated to natural science, and how is the allocation to be made? This is a persistent policy question for the society, and it calls for major attention from policy studies.

Natural science may be able to serve political science, even to the extent of furnishing paradigms; but political science can show natural science how to thrive in the complex and changing world.

20 Sources in the Field of Science Policy

Gene Coggshall

Science policy, and more generally the study of the effects of science and technology on society, did not become an active field of study until after World War II. The proliferation of research and development following the war, together with the awareness of possible nuclear destruction, caused many to abandon the model of the scientist alone in his lab, divorced from the larger society, unaffected by it and not affecting it. This "ivory tower" model has been replaced by the model of accountable scientists and technologists in need of some notion of their relation to the greater society. It is toward refining this latter model that a growing number of scientists and humanists are directing their efforts.

For this chapter I will limit my discussion to U.S. science policy (with the understanding that questions of science policy in developing nations raise quite dissimilar problems to those in the United States and other high-technology nations). I find it useful to divide the study of relationships among science, technology, and society into these smaller, interrelated areas: science policy studies (limited to the sociology of science and technology and to the interactions of these social groups of scientists and technologists with the larger society and with government programs); technology assessment; the humanities, science, and technology; science, technology, and law; and the impact of new biology and biomedical technology.

It goes without saying that my method of subdividing the areas of concern to those studying science, technology, and society interrelationships is both simplistic and incomplete. For instance, I might use the subdivision "science, technology, and public policy," a title that many university programs have taken. In this instance, however, it seems to me that public policy is of concern to many of the researchers in all the areas I've chosen to delineate. Or I might mention the implications of new work in sciences other than biology. Yet there seems to be substantially more concern with biology than, say, physics. It should be understood, of course, that new work in any of the sciences concerns scholars in the field of science, technology, and society.

Although I don't intend to spite those books, journals, and programs that I neglect to mention below, I'm sure there will be readers or friends of readers who will note deficiencies in my lists. Literature has burgeoned beyond the capacity of any individual to keep abreast of the field. I only cite below a few books with which I'm personally familiar. For the interested scholar, this article should be just a beginning point, a tour guide to the beginnings of more tours.

Science Policy Studies

Scientists and engineers are not, by-and-large, activist groups. Until recently, their participation in the American political process was limited to a small number of vocal individuals and to established professional bodies. Even now their role as official advisors to the federal government is small, having reached a peak (perhaps) in the 1960s but now beginning to descend, as advisory duties in the executive branch are retrenched within the NSF. While the Congress has recently initiated the Office of Technology Assessment to advise the legislative branch, that body has yet to become fully functional.

In local environmental disputes, scientists and engineers have become increasingly vocal. In their role as "experts" these scientists and engineers often disagree and sometimes add little clarity to the policy problem. Yet as political decision-making grows in complexity, due in large measure to burgeoning scientific and technological change, the need for technical expertise in government has increased. With it has come greater interest in science policy studies.

As any sub-group of society attempts to take an active role in policy-making, it finds a concomitant need to understand itself. Thus, science policy studies are often closely related to studies of the sociology of science. New emphasis is being placed on the study of the history of science, and experts in this field are taking longer, closer looks at the science-society interrelationship itself.

The following sources will be helpful to the scholar interested in science policy studies.

Monographs

The Government of Science. Brooks, Harvey. Cambridge, Mass.: MIT Press, 1968.

Men, Machines, and Modern Times. Morison, Elting E. Cambridge, Mass.: MIT Press, 1966.

The Military Technical Revolution. Erickson, John. N.Y.: Praeger, 1966.

Technology and Man's Future. Teich, Albert H., ed. N.Y.: St. Martin's Press, 1972.

Serials

AAAS Bulletin. American Association for the Advancement of Science, 1515 Massachusetts Avenue NW, Washington, D.C. 20005. (Quarterly.)

Analytical Journal of Works on Science Policy. 8 Rue de la Science, Brussels 4, Belgium. (This is an eight-part series of abstracts on scientific policy published over two years.)

Center for Science in the Public Interest, *Newsletter*. 1779 Church Street NW, Washington, D.C. 20036. (Quarterly.)

Energy Policy. IPC (America), Inc., 205 E. 42nd St., New York, New York 10017.

History of Science. W. Heffer and Sons, Ltd., Cambridge, England. (Annual.)

ISHA Bulletin. Institute for the Study of Science in Human Affairs, Columbia University, New York, N.Y. (Now defunct, but see especially Bulletins 4 and 6.)

Public Science. (Formerly *SPPSG Newsletter*.) MIT Press, Room ES3-450, Cambridge, Massachusetts 02139. (Monthly.)

Reviews of National Science Policy. OECD, 2 rue Andre-Pascal, Paris 16ᵉ, France. (Each issue is devoted to one member country.)

Science and Government Report. Kalorama Station, Box 21123, Section B, Washington, D.C. 20009. (Twenty-two issues annually.)

Science and Public Affairs. (Formerly *Bulletin of the Atomic Scientists*.) 1020-24 East 58th St., Chicago, Illinois 60637.

Science Policy. Science Policy Foundation, Benjamin Franklin House, 36 Craven Street, London WC2N 5NG, England. (Bimonthly.)

Science Policy Bulletin. Battelle Memorial Institute, Columbus Laboratories, 505 King Avenue, Columbus, Ohio 43201.

Technology Assessment

America's growth has been tied inextricably to the growth of technology. We are now a high-technology culture. It goes without saying that increased reliance on technology has been a mixed blessing. It is the nature of American culture that its technology is self-perpetuating (the so-called "technological imperative"); it seems as if we can no longer choose to do without the old technology or prevent the use of the new. And it seems equally obvious that the uses of new technologies (and more, the uses of *combinations* of new technologies) are difficult to predict. "Technological forecasting" (predicting both the development of new technologies and their initial uses) is a perilous affair. More important, and surely more perilous, would be predicting the social impact following the implementation of new technologies and new technological systems.

Yet such technological developments as cable TV, the birth-control pill, and the nuclear power plant clearly had exceptionally far-reaching implications for the American society; they deserved attention before they were fully implemented, and they deserve continued monitoring after development. Such attention (together with economic factors) has effectively delayed the deployment of the SST; the second- and third-order effects of the "pill" are still being felt, yet it is clear that its impact on American society has been much wider than generally predicted; and nuclear power plant development, which began with great ease and high hopes, is increasingly under fire from several directions. All of these technologies have been, or will be, subjected to varying processes of "technology assessment."

"Technology assessment" is the study of the impact of developing technology (or technological systems) on society. It does not limit itself to first-order consequences (the effect of the SST on air travel), but seeks to discover and to predict the magnitude of as many second- and larger-order effects as possible (the environmental impact of SST vapor, the effect of sonic booms on kindergarten learning, the impact of SST production on satellite aerospace industries, etc.). The purpose of such speculation is not to alert developers to new areas of market potential (although it may be argued that good technological assessment might be put to that use). It is, rather, to alert both developers and policymakers to the possible impact of the technology or system on the larger society and to open the option of proper regulation *before* production and marketing has reached full scale. Also, technology assessment studies the non-user of the new technology or system as well as the potential user with an eye toward possible redress of accompanying disadvantages.

The term "technology assessment" is relatively new. It originated about eight years ago and gained acceptability during the past year or two, about the time that Congress, in an attempt to deal with demands for technological expertise inherent in many of the bills before it, set up the Office of Technology Assessment. The newness of the field is reflected in the paucity of its literature and the variable quality of that literature; a lot of it is low-grade ore. Much of the journal literature is oriented more toward technological forecasting and "futures" study than toward technology assessment proper. Following are sources helpful to the student of technology assessment.

Monographs

"The Assessment of Technology." Bowers, Raymond and Brooks, Harvey. *Scientific American* 222, 2 (Feb. 1970), 13-21.

Technology and Public Policy: The Process of Technology Assessment in the Federal Government. Coates, Vary T. Washington, D.C.: Program of Policy Studies in Science and Technology, the George Washington University, 1972.

Technology Assessment—Annotated Bibliography. U.S. Congress (Subcommittee on Science, Research and Development), 91st Congress, Second Session, July 1970.

Technology Assessment, Understanding the Social Consequences of Technological Implications. Kasper, Raphael G. New York: Praeger, 1972.

Technology: Processes of Assessment and Choice. Report of the National Academy of Sciences to the Committee on Science and Astronautics, U.S. House of Representatives, July 1969.

Serials

Britannica Yearbook of Science and the Future. 425 North Michigan Ave., Chicago, Illinois 60611. (Annual.)

Futures: The Journal of Forecasting and Planning. 32 High St., Guilford, Surrey, England. (Quarterly.)

The Futurist: A Journal of Forecasts, Trends, and Ideas about the Future. World Future Society, P. O. Box 19284, 20th St. Station, Washington, D.C. 20036. (Bimonthly.)

Technological Forecasting and Social Change. American Elsevier Publishing Co., Ltd., New York, N.Y. (Quarterly.)

Technology Assessment. International Society for Technology Assessment. Published by Gordon and Breach, One Park Avenue, New York, N.Y. 10016. (Quarterly.)

The Humanities, Science, and Technology

For some time, scholars have voiced concern over the increasing split between the humanities and science/technology. Specialization in education has produced the scientist or engineer too busy with his discipline to study the liberal arts, and the humanist equally ignorant of the other's work. Until recently, both sides have uncomfortably accepted the split as a fact of life in our modern, specialized world.

But it is becoming clear, as the model of the ivory tower falls into greater disrepute and education addresses itself more and more to the social benefits of scholarship, that each side should be re-learning the other's language. Recently, the National Science Foundation and the National Endowment for the Humanities have begun a joint program of grants to encourage interdisciplinary studies among humanists and scientists. Cornell University recently received a grant from the Endowment to begin such a program; in this instance, the subject of rational systems of decision-making was chosen as a common starting point for teaching and research.

Professional ethics, the problems of jargon and semantics, and the methods of making decisions, to name but a few, are areas in which humanistic insight should temper scientific judgment and scientific discovery should advance humanistic knowledge. Yet there are virtually no journals, and few texts, that deal with interaction among the humanities, science, and technology.

Below are listed several beginning monographs, together with some serials that may be expected to publish articles in the field.

Monographs

Induction and Intuition in Scientific Thought. Medawar, Peter Brian. Philadelphia, Pa.: American Philosophical Society, 1969.

Science and Human Values. Bronowski, J. New York: Harper & Row, 1958.

The Structure of Scientific Revolutions. Kuhn, Thomas S. Chicago, Ill.: University of Chicago Press, 1970.

Technological Man. Ferkiss, Victor C. New York: Braziller, 1969.

Serials

Computers and the Humanities. Queens College, Flushing, New York 11367.

Daedalus. Journal of the American Academy of Arts and Sciences, 280 Newton Street, Brookline, Massachusetts 02138.

History of Science. (See Serials, Section I.)

Science in Progress. Yale University Press, New Haven, Connecticut. Reprints of Sigma Xi national lectures. (Annual.)

Science Studies. Macmillan Journals Ltd., Subscription Department, Brunel Rd., Basingstoke, Hampshire, England. Reports research in the social and historical dimensions of science and technology. (Quarterly.)

Technology and Culture. Society for the History of Technology, University of Chicago Press, 5750 Ellis Avenue, Chicago, Illinois 60637. (Quarterly.)

Science, Technology, and Law

Law, despite its intrinsically conservative nature, has been greatly changed by the advent of technology. The nature of evidence, questions of privacy, and even courtroom procedures have undergone radical change because of new technologies. And with the onset of ecological legislation, the courts have become battlegrounds for warring scientific and technological factions, to the point that the judge is even called upon to assess alternative technologies.

Environmental law is beginning to develop boundaries and well-developed literature and accompanying professional journals. But law necessitated by technological innovation is as yet often poorly defined.

To meet the challenge of scientific and technological change, law schools are increasing course offerings in science, technology, and law. Also increasing is the number of lawyers with backgrounds in science and technology. Greater attention is being given such disparate subjects as the theft of computer data, population control, the use of biomedical technologies, and technological surveillance.

Below are sources useful to the beginning scholar in this area.

Monographs

The Regulators: Watchdog Agencies and the Public Interest. Kohlmeier, Louis M., Jr. New York: Harper & Row, Publishers, 1969.

Environmental Planning: Law of Land and Resources. Reitze, A. W., Jr. Washington, D.C.: North American Int'l., 1974.

Radio, Television, and the Administration of Justice: A Documented Survey of Materials. Special Committee on Radio and Television, Association of the Bar of the City of New York. New York: Columbia University Press, 1965.

Databanks in a Free Society. Westin, Alan F., and Baker, Michael A. New York: Quadrangle Books. 1972.

Serials

Environmental Law. 10015 Terwilliger Blvd., Portland, Oregon 97219.

Jurimetrics Journal. American Bar Center, 1155 E. 60th St., Chicago, Illinois 60637. Discusses the application of electronic data processing equipment to the law. (Quarterly.)

Law and Computer Technology. World Peace through Law Center, Hill Bldg., 838 17th St. NW, Washington, D.C. 20006 (Monthly.)

Law and Contemporary Problems. Duke University School of Law, Duke Station, Durham, North Carolina 27706.

Lex et Scientia. The International Journal of Law and Science, Westminster Publications, Inc., 381 Park Avenue South, New York, N.Y. 10016. (Quarterly.)

Natural Resources Lawyer. American Bar Association (Section of Natural Resources Law), Chicago, Illinois.

The Impact of New Biology and Biomedical Technology

Of all the sciences, biology now seems to hold the most promise of radically changing man and his culture in the near future. Biology and biomedical technologies are pushing the understanding of man through complexity into radically enlarged understanding. And with the understanding will inevitably come the ability to control; human life and human possibilities are every day being extended, with both positive and negative implications for the future. On the one hand, the ability to cure disease and prolong active life is increasing daily. On the other hand, the ability to tinker with man's genes and possibly create all manner of "test-tube babies" lurks ambivalently over the horizon. Simultaneously, the study of ecology is raising questions of mankind's viability.

With any change in man's physiology or his procreation will naturally come a change in his culture. How man will choose to use, or not to use, his new power is of great consequence to his existence. Realization of these consequences has led to a great deal of work in such diverse areas as medical ethics, problems of the aging, use of "mood-altering" drugs, legal and moral implications of new methods of procreation, and the questions of "letting die." The amount and importance of such work will probably increase, particularly as the debate over national health insurance advances, as ecological considerations reach greater immediacy, and as new biomedical technologies are deployed.

Below are examples from the literature of this area.

Monographs

Biology and the Future of Man. Handler, Philip, ed. New York: Oxford Univ. Press, 1970.

Control of Human Behavior. Ulrich, R., Stachnic, T., and Mabry, J. Glenview, Ill.: Scott, Foresman & Co., 1966.

Essays in Social Biology, Vols. I, II, and III. Wallace, Bruce. Englewood Cliffs, N.J.: Prentice-Hall, Inc., 1972.

Experimentation with Human Beings. Katz, Jay. New York: Russell Sage Fdn., 1972.

A New World in the Morning. Young, David P. Philadelphia, Pa.: The Westminister Press, 1972.

Serials

Bioscience. American Institute of Biological Sciences, 3900 Wisconsin Avenue NW, Washington, D.C. 20016. (Monthly.)

Environment and Behavior. Sage Publications, Inc., 275 South Beverly Drive, Beverly Hills, California 90212. (Quarterly.)

Hastings Center Report. Institute of Society, Ethics, and the Life Sciences, 623 Warburton Avenue, Hastings-on-Hudson, New York 10706.

Social Biology. University of Chicago Press, 5801 Ellis Avenue, Chicago, Illinois 60637. (Quarterly.)

Some Other Sources

Many U.S. colleges and universities are beginning innovative teaching and research programs in the area of science, technology, and society. The Harvard University Program on Technology and Society was one of the leaders of such programs until its termination in 1972; its numerous publications are of considerable help understanding the field. (A series of monographs are available through the Harvard University Press, 79 Garden Street, Cambridge, Massachusetts 02138.)

Other programs now number more than seventy-five. Below is a sampling of the larger programs (alphabetically by state).

Values, Technology, and Society
Walter G. Vincenti, Director
Program in Human Biology
Donald Kennedy, Chairman
Stanford University
Stanford, California 94305

Science, Technology, and Government Program
Lowell H. Hattery, Director
The American University
Washington, D.C. 20016

Science, Technology, and Public Policy
John M. Logsdon, Director
George Washington University
Washington, D.C. 20006

Committee on Technology and Society
College of Engineering
University of Florida
Gainesville, Florida 32601

Program on Science, Technology, and Public Policy
Joseph Haberer, Director
Purdue University
Lafayette, Indiana 47907

Center for Law and Health Sciences
Boston University School of Law
Boston, Massachusetts 02215

Science and Public Policy
Eugene B. Skolnikoff, Director
Massachusetts Institute of Technology
Cambridge, Massachusetts 02139

Program in Engineering for Public Systems
Clifford R. Kuhl, Admin. Ass't.
University of Michigan
Ann Arbor, Michigan 48104

Technology and Human Affairs
Robert P. Morgan, Chairman
Washington University
St. Louis, Missouri 63130

Program on Science, Technology, and Society
Raymond Bowers, Director
Cornell University
Ithaca, New York 14850

Program in Technology and Society
Norman Balabanian, Chairman
Syracuse University
Syracuse, New York 13210

Science, Technology, and Public Policy
T. Dixon Long, Director
Case Western Reserve University
Cleveland, Ohio 44106

Humanities Perspectives on Technology
Douglas D. Feaver, Director
Lehigh University
Bethlehem, Pennsylvania 18015

Science, Technology, and Society Program
Robert Dunham, Vice-President for Undergraduate Studies
Pennsylvania State University
University Park, Pennsylvania 16802

The Cornell STS program (address above) also publishes a "guide to the field" of science, technology, and society studies. This guide includes other college and university programs, research centers, sources of support, and a survey of foreign institutions engaged in science/society studies.

The Harvard program (address above) published several interesting bibliographies; the following two bibliographies may also be of some use.

Science and Society: A Bibliography. Hugh E. Voress, Library Branch, U.S. AEC, July 1971. (Available from the Supt. of Documents, USGPO, Washington, D.C. 20402. Stock number 5210-0272.)

Science for Society: A Bibliography. John A. Moore, Department of Life Sciences, University of California (Riverside), 1970.

**Part VIII
Law**

21

Law, Political Science, and Policy Studies

Ernest Jones

Basic Concepts

What can law contribute to political scientists interested in policy studies? And what can political scientists interested in policy studies contribute to law? Appropriate responses to these questions invite specification of what is meant by "law" and by "political scientists interested in policy studies."

If specification of "law" is perceived as a problem of profitable interrelationships of law, as a discipline, and political science, as a discipline, then "law" would designate the research of legal scholars (principally law professors and law students but including others with legal training). Whether law as so conceived, or as otherwise conceived, appropriately is referred to as a discipline need not concern us here.

If, on the other hand, specification of "law" is approached not solely as a problem of the interrelationships of one discipline to another but from the broader frame of reference implied by asking what can legal systems contribute to political scientists interested in policy studies, then "law" would designate legal systems and institutions of legal process, basic functions of legal process and the behavior of legal functionaries (executive, administrative, and legislative, as well as judicial personnel, lawyers, law professors, law students, legal scholars, etc.). This broader frame of reference is more likely to stimulate a richer flow of recognitions of contributions to political scientists engaged in policy studies. It should be noted, however, that posing the questions with which this paper began in terms of "contributions" skews attention upon positive, to the neglect of negative, outcomes of interactions between "law" and political scientists engaged in policy studies. Negative outcomes are sufficiently important not to be ignored, even in a symposium apparently intended, at least in part, to stimulate interdisciplinary policy studies; and some references to such outcomes will presently appear.

Turning now to specification of "political scientists interested in policy studies," the language quoted will designate political scientists not merely interested in but engaged in policy studies. While there is value in merely thinking about contributions by and to law, this paper will focus on value outcomes attending acts of engaging in policy studies, as related to law broadly defined.

241

Relevant Literature

Since the questions posed in the first paragraph of this chapter have received some attention in the literature it may be helpful to summarize several of the most representative discussions. Papers by Thomas A. Cowan (a law professor), Harry W. Jones (a law professor), and Robert B. Yegge (a law school dean) cited in the list of references have been selected for this purpose.

While Cowan addresses the question of how law can contribute to social science in general, his remarks also have obvious relevance for political scientists, even if they are of less relevance to political scientists engaged in policy studies. In Cowan's view since the methodology embraced by social scientists is dehumanized, law and the theory of legal proof may help social scientists resolve the dilemma of being scientific but nonhumanistic, or of being humanistic but non-scientific. As the life sciences have gained by collaboration with medicine so the behavioral sciences may gain by collaboration with law. In four ways behavioral science may benefit: (1) by increased precision of social science models derived from the law-trained investigator's art of verbal inquiry and questioning; (2) by adding the art of cross-examination to the social scientist's kit of investigative tools; (3) by acquiring a method of controlled experiment, namely, legal coercion; and (4) by acquiring access to an immense reservoir of value judgments on human behavior in the history of law itself and in its present body of empirical rules of decision.

While Jones' essay advances the thesis that students of politics do and must concern themselves with law and lawyers, its principal thrust is to explore the possibilities of fruitful collaboration between political scientists and law professors, particularly as related to differences of perspectives of law professors and political scientists. Such differences in perspective he attributes largely to differences in locations within a university. Law schools, unlike departments of political science, are not oriented "toward general education or the training of other scholars" but "towards the production of professional practitioners." This orientation emphasizes the teaching mission at the expense of undercutting the research mission of law schools. While any aspect of public policy or political behavior may be of interest to some law professors, the prevailing focus of interest is upon disputes and the settlement of disputes, hence upon the adjudicatory functions of legal process whether located in administrative, executive, legislative, or judicial arenas. Moreover, according to Jones, law professors tend to be "fact-minded, problem-oriented, and something of a social activist." Their fact-mindedness is evidenced by distrust of generalizations; their problem-orientation by the selection of specific problems, problems already shaped in society, for research. Both the characteristic of fact-mindedness and that of selecting specific problems for research are reflections of the focus upon adjudicatory functions of legal process, as witness the excessive reliance upon law library research (largely a repository of reasons for adjudicatory decisions), and the testing of legal generalizations by conceiving of them as predictions of future adjudicatory decisions.

Jones draws attention to the increased interest of law professors in empirical research, to the need for interdisciplinary collaboration in such research, and to the lack of an effective pattern for such collaboration. He concludes by presenting examples of law professor research interests deemed by him to contribute most to understanding governmental and political processes. Among the examples included are judicial administration studies; criminal law administration studies; the contributions of sociological jurisprudence and social interest theory towards a clearer understanding of judicial functions; the contributions of legal realism towards understanding judicial functions and the relation of rules to decisions; "ongoing studies of the values served by the legal order"; the descriptive and analytical work respecting the practice, procedures and policies of federal and state administrative agencies; the work of James Willard Hurst on the interactions of legislation and economics, law, and public opinion; and the normative analysis of substantive legal rules, principles, and policies.

Yegge's first paper, *What Has Social Science to Offer Law*, is concerned with the contributions of the methodology and knowledge of the social sciences to the practice of law, and the contributions of the perspectives of the social sciences in the assessment and restructure of legal institutions. Because the "dominant career mind-set" of lawyers is client-oriented social science must have some practical application to be meaningful to them. Yegge also suggests that it helps if the social scientist can communicate with lawyers, sans jargon. Finally, he identifies the lawyer-legislator, the lawyer-administrator, and the lawyer-civic-leader, as constituting a class of lawyers with a common concern for the law as an institution, and as most receptive towards the possible assistance of social scientists in improving the administration of justice.

Yegge's second paper, *What Has Law to Offer Social Science*, identifies the following contributions of law: (1) advising social scientists conducting research respecting such matters as the right of privacy of informants; (2) raising questions about legal phenomena "of intense interest to social scientists"; (3) providing lawyers as data, as generators of data, and as keepers of data; (4) providing an action model—the quest for knowledge to resolve problems, to reconstruct institutions; and (5) teaching social scientists the importance of specificity in describing and defining the mutual expectations among people, and in providing a model for rigor in language and precision in definition. Yegge also warns that while collaboration of lawyers and social scientists is desirable and possible, pervasive colleagueship and any attempt to merge "beyond a common interest in the subject matter," might be disastrous.

Yegge's final paper, *Caveats to the Interface of Law and Social Science*, continues the theme of negative outcomes of law-social science collaboration. Thus, some "goals of social science might be frustrated should its disciplinarians yield to lawyer-centered pressure for immediate practical resolution of problems." "Lawyers are not used to questioning the assumptions which 'the law' has made about human behavior," and they frequently "proceed to verify their own preordained conclusions." Some lawyers are not receptive to social scientist approaches to legal phenomena. Lawyers do not have a legal theory. What they call theory is "a complex set of doctrinal, organizational links." Lawyers are "singularly ignorant" of social scientists' conceptions of research in the sense of generation of new knowledge. What lawyers call research is "legal documentation."

While I have not made a systematic search of the literature for discussions of the questions posed in the first paragraph of this chapter, I believe the papers summarized above are representative. Note, however, that when compared with the conceptions of "law" and of "political scientists interested in policy studies," as defined in first several paragraphs of this chapter, each of the papers summarized is quite limited in its undertaking, and general about matters respecting which specific knowledge is needed. For example, Cowan's paper addresses the interrelationship problem from only one side, law's contribution to social science; lumps all social sciences together for this purpose; and does not approach law comprehensively but selectively, thereby emphasizing only some of its contributions.

Jones' paper is really mis-titled. Instead of "Law and Politics" it would have been more accurately entitled as "Problems of Law Professor - Political Scientist Collaboration in Research." It does not pretend to explore systematically law's contribution to social science, or to political science, and it does not distinguish policy studies by political scientists from their other research activities. Jones' paper is quite insightful, however, respecting law professor-political scientist collaboration in research, albeit not necessarily policy research.

Yegge's papers show more attention to systematic and comprehensive understanding of law-social scientist interrelations, because they approach the problem from both directions, cognizant of negative as well as positive outcomes. Unfortunately, however, his discussions had to find room in the limited space accorded the President's Message in the *Law and Society Review*.

It should be reasonably apparent, then, that although many insights likely are scattered among the writings of numerous disciplines, systematic and comprehensive understanding about the problems posed in the first several paragraphs of this chapter is not to be found in the literature.

Reciprocal Contributions

The balance of this chapter will present some off-the-top-of-my-head suggestions of how law, broadly conceived, might contribute to the policy studies of political scientists; and how the policy studies of political scientists might contribute to law.

If law is conceived as the aggregate legal system and each of its components the question of law's contribution to policy studies of political scientists can be restated as several questions. How does the legal system as an aggregate entity contribute to such studies? How do particular legal institutions contribute? How do such basic functions of legal decision making as the intelligence, recommending, prescribing, invoking, applying, appraising, and terminating functions contribute? How do legal functionaries (executive, administrative, legislative, and judicial personnel, lawyers, law professors, law students, legal scholars, etc.) contribute? Finally, how do propositions of law (from whatever source derived, as statutes, executive orders, administrative regulations, caselaw precedent, etc.) contribute?

Since it is apparent that these questions open a pandora's box of tentative impacts of law upon policy studies of political scientists, only brief, illustrative examples of possible answers to such questions are attempted. In addition to serving as a field of inquiry and as one of the most important consumers of the policy studies of political scientists, the aggregate legal system contributes in innumerable, largely unknown ways to the ordering of society thereby making it possible for political scientists to engage in policy studies. Legal institutions, such as grants and contracts, supply resources needed to carry out policy studies. Legal functions, such as the intelligence function, not only serve as subjects of investigation by policy scientists, but constitute a continuing flow of intelligence to policy scientists. Legal functionaries facilitate policy studies by answering questions, offering advice, opening doors, collaborating as researchers, and in numerous other ways. Propositions of law, such as statutes, authorize the provision of research resources enabling policy studies to be made.

Assuming political scientists engaging in policy studies are particularly interested in collaborative research activities with legal scholars (principally law professors), what can the legal scholar contribute? The papers by Cowan, Jones, and Yegge offer some answers to this question. Some observers (like Schwartz, 1973, and Jones, 1968, at 70) appear to believe that social science treatments of law suffer because of "insufficient knowledge of what law professors know." Presumably the reference to law in such opinions is to the kind of legal research and writing in which law professors have traditionally engaged. The bulk of such research focuses upon the evolution of propositions of law as by-products of adjudication. Much of it, so it seems to me, is of doubtful value for policy studies. But some of it, perhaps the best of it, approaches the study of the evolution, invocation, and application of litigation doctrines (propositions of law whose chief functions appears to be in adjudicatory decision making) in a non-doctrinaire way, i.e., with an acute sensitivity to considerations of public policy. Such research undoubtedly can make solid contribution to policy studies of political scientists. In fact, when a law professor engages in legal research in a non-doctrinnaire way he is engaged in a policy study.

It is, however, easy to exaggerate the value of even policy-oriented legal research of law professors. Few law professors know the methodology of empirical research. In consequence they rely principally upon search of library sources, logical analysis, and arm-chair speculation. In general, therefore, I suspect that political scientists engaged in policy studies who wish to collaborate with a law professor would be wise to select one who is well aware of the limitations of what he thinks he knows from his traditional research, and who is open and receptive to other research strategies.

How can the policy studies of political scientists contribute to law? The opportunities for doing so appear to be virtually unlimited. Since the design of the legal system is by no means permanently fixed, policy studies can contribute by inventing new designs. New legal institutions are constantly needed and policy studies might help meet this need. Basic decisional functions of legal systems, such as intelligence and appraisal functions, are in constant need of policy studies. The same obviously holds true for legal functionaries. Finally, propositions of law, since they represent verbally-frozen policies based upon assumptions that daily become more obsolete in consequence of social change, are in continual need of policy studies.

In expressing an opinion about possible contributions to law of policy studies of political scientists, I am making some assumptions that perhaps should be made explicit. First, policy studies are to be distinguished from social science research. Much social science research is not undertaken to meet the needs of the legal system or of its principal components, but to extend the basic theory of a particular discipline. Hence it does not pose questions or necessarily produce data and findings of direct relevance to the needs of the legal system. (As an example of the limitations of social science research in the formulation of legal policies, see Ellsworth and Levy 1969.) Moreover, much social science theory is static and non-developmental, and because it is focused on cause and effect or probability relations, oriented toward explaining past or present events. To be most valuable policy studies should be future-oriented and undertaken not solely from the perspective of a scientific observer, but from the dominant perspective of an active participant in the policy functions of legal process.

Second, I am assuming that political scientists engaging in policy studies are willing to subordinate their identifications with the discipline of political science and to accept an identification as a policy scientist with the role of an important functionary of the legal system.

Finally, I am assuming that political scientists engaged in policy studies will not hesitate to draw upon the theories, knowledge, and methodological tools of other disciplines if to do so would enrich a particular policy study.

References

Cowan, Thomas A. "What Law Can Do for Social Science." In William Evan (ed.), *Law and Sociology* Free Press, 1962, 91-123.

Ellsworth, Phoebe and Robert Levy. "Legislative Reform of Child Custody Adjudication." *Law and Society Review* 4 (1969):167.

Jones, Harry. "Law and Politics." In Malcolm Parsons (ed.), *Perspectives in the Study of Politics* Rand McNally, 1968, 63-76.

Nagel, Stuart. "Law and the Social Sciences: What Can Social Science Contribute?" *American Bar Association Journal* 51 (1965):356; "Epilogue." In Nagel, *The Legal Process From a Behavioral Perspective* (Dorsey, 1969) 377-386; and "Some Proposals for Facilitating Socio-Legal Teaching and Research." *Journal of Legal Education* 24. (1972) 590-602.

Schwartz, Richard. "Getting a Paradigm Together." *Law and Society Review* 7 (1973):323.

Yegge, Robert B. "What Has Social Science to Offer Law." *Law and Society Review* 3 (1969):484; "What Has Law to Offer Social Science." *Law and Society Review* 4 (1969):5; and "Caveats to the Interface of Law and Social Science." *Law and Society Review* 4 (1969):163.

22 Experimental Jurisprudence and Systems Engineering in Determining Policy

Frederick K. Beutel

In examining the usefulness of experimental jurisprudence and systems engineering in determining policy,[1] it might be pertinent to spend a moment on the meaning of policy-making as it applies to modern government and law.

Nature and Application of Policy-Making

Policy-making as it applies to law and government has a number of meanings varying all the way from the policeman who turns his back on a fight on the beat to the president of the United States who declares a blockade of Cuba. It is present in all branches of government.

In the popular sense, it is often considered to be the means by which high officials of the executive department of states or the nation determine how to direct the government in such matters as going to the moon, conserving natural resources, guiding foreign relations, and generally enforcing the Constitution.

It is also very present and active in the legislative branches where it becomes the basic excuse for reorganizing the legal system, creating new laws, reducing taxes, or reforming the criminal law. Limited only by the Constitution, the legislator is empowered to implement any policy he desires by passing laws which are then to be enforced by administrators.

In the administrative departments, policy-making is also present and active in the determination of the extent to which practices may be instituted to enforce or change the effect of existing laws. Here one finds the legal latitude within which the officials may act varying all the way from complete discretion limited only by the Constitution and the delegation of powers found therein and in the enabling statutes, to those persons like prosecuting officials who are supposed to enforce the law as written. The legal boundaries of such policy-making have been discussed at length by Davis[2] and need not be repeated here.

Although there is much lore to the contrary, the judicial system has the least latitude of all branches of government in making policy. First, judges are limited in their pronouncements to disputes which come before them in the form of cases, and, second, they are bound by law to interpret the written constitutions and laws applying to the cases before them. Socially, they have the least leverage on governmental action affecting the ordinary citizen because it is a fair estimate that not one-hundredth of one percent of individual actions controlled by law ever get to court.[3] When a dispute does get to count, the judges' discretion lies in the interpretation which they can put on the words of the laws and the implications of the evidence in the record.

In the modern state where almost all laws and administrative regulations having the force of laws are written, the judicial policy-making should be legally limited to interpretation. But, in light of the common law tradition, the doctrine of *stare decisis,* the social importance of some of the cases coming before the courts, and the fact that law is taught by the case method, many have mistakenly believed that the courts are the chief policy-making organs of our government.

This, in brief, is the legal or constitutional picture of the policy-making powers of government officials. What are the facts?

In the first place, in modern governments there is no activity of any official in which policy can be made which is not touched or covered by some or a lot of laws. The very authority of the official to consider any activity is covered in the laws creating the powers of his office. Beyond this, any act which he contemplates, any change in administrative directions, will immediately impinge upon some existing law which is the product of earlier policies. For example, a policy to place a man on the moon, which was about as new as possible, immediately encountered—to name only a few—patent laws, trade regulations of manufacturing, appropriations by Congress, military regulations and policies, real estate laws, administrative laws, civil service regulations, and private enterprise including all its supporting laws. Any other contemplation of the creation or enforcement of a new law impinges a myriad of federal, state, and local laws. The implementation of any new policy demands for its success a thorough knowledge of existing laws and their operation as they touch upon the execution of the contemplated policy.

It is not enough for the policymaker to know the state of existing laws as they affect his intended project. He must also know the impact of the administration of those laws on the social situation which his new policy will eventually be expected to change. Here one encounters the difference between "*Law in Books and Law in Action.*"[4]

Up until Pound wrote his famous article about sixty years ago, it was assumed that the law as it appeared in the books was somehow the state in which it was applied in action. Now, under the influence of the sociological jurists, the realists and their many studies, we know that this is not the case. Since World War II, many sociologically-based studies have showed conclusively that Pound's distinction was not only sound but, further, that there is little correspondence between the policy behind the numerous laws and the results which they were getting in society. Although empirical study of law's application to society is still in its infancy, we now know that, in general, there is no one-to-one connection between the purpose of laws, the policies which they represent, the "values" or "ideals" which they purport to support, and the results which they get in society.[5]

This involves two major factors—(1) the extent to which administrators of the law divert the policy intended and (2) the social changes caused by their administration of the law.

Anybody who reads the daily papers now knows that, in addition to "Watergate," which has clearly demonstrated a criminal attempt to change the policy of the laws by obstructing justice in enforcing them, there has been widespread violation of election laws, invasion of civil rights of individuals, diverting the purposes of the FBI, the CIA, and the Department of Justice, and an infiltration of government regulatory agencies by lobbyists of the businesses being regulated, who were appointed to administrative positions in the agencies for the purpose of rendering them impotent to perform the tasks set for them by law. Among these, one will easily recognize the Federal Aviation Agency, the wage/price agencies, oil "control" administrations, and many more which casual research can develop. This raid was led by a president of the United States, many of whose minions were still in high government positions, including the Cabinet, long after Nixon resigned.

This represents only the tip of the iceberg. The news media are full of instances, more real than fancied, where conflict of interest in state and local officials is diverting the very substance of the legal policy and rolling up fortunes for government officials and their friends derived from both criminal and civil violation of the laws which they were appointed to enforce. In addition, well-documented empirical research has shown lesser examples of this tendency of administrators to divert "policy" of the laws.[6] On the criminal side, over 70 percent of all court convictions are based on guilty pleas, most of which are clearly the result of plea bargaining,[7] a process which careful reading of the criminal statutes usually will not reveal.[8] In the enforcement of the bad check laws, the plain provisions of the laws requiring enforcement of severe penalties are knowingly ignored by law enforcement officials who substitute illegal collection of the checks.[9] Of a more general nature, many members of the bar in their practices are found to ignore the requirements of legal ethics.[10] Thus, perversion of the policies and purposes behind laws by substitution of the administrators' own policies and purposes in its application to the public, completely ignoring the plain provisions of the law, is a common phenomenon.

Regardless of the deviation in the enforcement policy of the officials, the effect of the application of the policy through law may not have the social impact which the policymakers expected. A few examples will suffice: The recent sale of grain to Russia was a disaster because the administration did not foresee the legal and economic effect of the deal on the market prices and farming regulations; the forced integration of the races in the schools has not produced the expected benefits;[11] and the unexpected results of the "noble experiment" in the Eighteenth Amendment are well known to all.

In the judicial field, although the courts, as indicated above, are limited both in subject matter and by the provisions of controlling written laws, the nice technicalities of interpretation have given them such latitude in decision-making as to justify, to some extent, their reputation as capricious policymakers. This has been discussed at length elsewhere and need not be repeated here.[12] It should be noted, however, in passing, that the Supreme Court has recently, in dealing with a question of due process in a chattel mortgage foreclosure case,[13] overruled a considered decision of this Court barely two years old without pointing to any change in either societal perceptions or basic constitutional understandings which might justify this total disregard of *stare decisis,*[14] simply because there were two justices participating in the second case who were not in on the opinion in the first.[15] This sort of thing supports the belief that the court makes policy, and encourages the court packers.

The entire picture of the extent to which laws fail of their purposes or their policies, or are frustrated by diversion of enforcement, is not yet known. There are few, if any, government agencies set up to "feed back" this information to the policymakers, and the complicated nature of our civilization renders the democratic process especially impotent in this field.[16] What little research has been done in the area indicates that laws range from complete impotence to varying degrees of inefficiency in accomplishing their purposes.[17]

The present haphazard methods of implementing policy can no longer be tolerated. Modern science in the form of experimental jurisprudence now offers a tool to perfect the connection between the policy and its impact on society.

Experimental Jurisprudence

Experimental jurisprudence is the application of the techniques of experimental science to the creation and operation of law. It recognizes that every law and applied administrative activity, no matter what its policy source, is simply an experiment. As the pragmatists might state it, "There are no absolutes."[18] The validity of each law or social action must be tested by the results of its enforcement in society.

The procedures and methods of this experimental legal science, which are new and, to some extent, tentative and experimental themselves, are set out in eight steps as follows:

1. The nature of the phenomena which law attempts to regulate should be studied. In particular, the social problem to which a specific law is directed should be carefully isolated and examined.
2. The rule of law or other method used to regulate the phenomena or intended to solve the social problem should be accurately stated.
3. The effect on society of adopting the rule should be observed and measured.
4. There should then be constructed a hypothesis that attempts to explain the reasons for this reaction.
5. This description, when broadened to apply to other analogous situations, might be considered a jural law that describes or predicts results which would occur on application of a similar regulatory law to similar problems.
6. If analysis shows that the law is inefficient, there could then be suggested new methods of accomplishing the originally desired result.
7. The proposed new law could be enacted and the process repeated.
8. A series of such adoptions of new laws and the study of their results might throw important light upon the usefulness of the underlying policies behind the enactment, thus effecting a possible alteration in or abandonment of these objectives, or, in the long run, even induce a revision of our present scale of social and political ethics.[19]

It should be noted that this technique focuses upon a study of the individual law or other official action and the results when it is applied to society. If it fails to accomplish its purposes, steps 6 and 7 require revision and reenactment better to effectuate the underlying policies, and further studies involving steps 1 through 5.

The design of such studies and their execution may require the use of any or all social or physical science techniques now in existence or even the invention of new ones. The prompt execution of such studies may also require a redesign of many of our present governmental structures. The process, as in any experimental science, is continuous, and the movement is from the solution of one problem to another. Theoretically and practically, the process will result in (1) the validation of the underlying policy, (2) its alteration, or (3) rejection and replacement by a new policy to be again implemented and tested.

Does this mean that, after a proper scientific testing, the policymaker is again returned to the witches' brew or closeted conference of policymaking based upon "values," ideals, morals, religion, prejudices, popular demands, and the like? Before attempting to answer this question of the ultimate policy base, or whether it can be replaced by science, it might be well to go on with the description of the experimental process.

The policymaker attempting to devise new policies from which to evolve new laws of this stage already has a number of scientific aids. (1) The clearly demonstrated failure of the old policy warns him not to repeat the old mistakes. (2) The hypotheses and jural laws developed in steps 4 and 5 of the previous studies will guide him in the steps his new policy should take and may even show new directions available to take. (3) There are other experimental devices at his command.

A good example of steps 1 and 2 are found in a legislative development after a recent bad check study in the state of Nebraska.[20] The study showed that the felony provisions of the bad check laws were filling the penitentiary with bad check writers at great expense to the state but this had no effect on criminal reform. It also showed that the harsh penalties did not reduce the number of bad check writers while the illegal collection practices of law enforcement officers did. In light of these findings, the legislature abandoned the popular policy of trying to control crime by increasing the penalties. Felony provisions in many cases were abandoned and provisions were made for releasing penitentiary inmates convicted only of bad check writing.[21] It is now possible to restudy the enforcement of the new bad check laws in Nebraska and to assess the usefulness of the change in the law.

Other experimental devices are available. After the policymaker has exercised his best judgment in light of the revealed facts, he may desire to try alternative policies or alternative laws to effectuate the policy chosen. A brilliant example of this technique, which is applicable in many other places, is found in Rosenberg's study of *Pretrial Conference and Effective Justice*[22] where the directors of the research devised three different procedures for handling pretrial conferences in actual cases and simultaneously conducted all three under scientifically devised controls which gave them a test of the efficiency of each method. After this, they were able to make recommendations for future procedures, which were adopted by the courts of New Jersey.

Another experimental device where the state of the law prohibits direct experimentation is a simulated run based on models. A good example of this was part of the Chicago jury study examining the theories of the defenses of insanity in criminal cases.[23] Here a stupid law advocated by the Attorney General of the United States, and now adopted by Congress and in over thirty states,[24] prohibited recording of real jury deliberations even under judicial scrutiny (a return to a sort of voodoo superstition about juries). The experimentors then taped the evidence in real insanity cases and submitted the tapes to simulated jurors drawn from real jury panels in

Chicago.[25] The cases were then tried under the different legal rules of the *McNaughten* and *Durham* cases by a number of such juries and under court supervision. After this, it was possible to compare the effect of the different legal instructions on the same and different juries and to evaluate the two different rules of law.[26] This is a useful technique adopted from the kindred scientific discipline of systems engineering, which also has many other techniques useful in social engineering.

Systems Engineering

Systems engineering is the name usually given to the scientific process of radically improving human or mechanical organizations used in the solution of social or industrial problems. It is a relatively new discipline sometimes confused with and growing out of operational research, systems research, and research and development, all of which use similar scientific procedures. The term "systems engineering" is used here because it combines most of the activity used in the other three.

The steps in the procedure can be briefly outlined as follows:

1. Define and analyze the problems arising out of the current organization.
2. Formulate theories to explain activities in the operation.
3. Synthesize or create postulated solutions.
4. Test the solutions so postulated.
5. Develop the components to go into a new system.
6. Test the altered system.
7. Establish the altered system in practice.
8. Operate the new system.
9. Analyze the system's performance.[27]

It will be seen at once that the methods of systems engineering are very similar to those of experimental jurisprudence outlined above. Using the steps of operational research set out in the margin,[28] it has a development in the engineering and scientific field parallel in time and methods to experimental jurisprudence.

The similarity of the two systems and their history have been set out at length elsewhere and need not be repeated here,[29] but it might be worthwhile to note a few of the current applications in the field of law and policy-making.

One of its greatest triumphs has been in the area of traffic engineering where law making has developed along scientific lines completely paralleling experimental jurisprudence.[30] It is significant that Underhill Moore, a law professor, worked in this field as early as the 1930's at Yale Law

School.[31] His findings were rejected by the legal fraternity but later adopted by the engineers as a complete experimental system of law making.[32] Here computers actually operate whole segments of municipal traffic administration.[33]

In another area closely connected with mechanical operations, systems engineering in all its facets was used to create the Federal Aviation Agency and successfully to direct its legal regulatory operations[34] until Nixon's minions, working in his planned government reorganization, tried to divert its policies in favor of the corporations it was supposed to regulate. Luckily, this attempt seems to have failed because it resulted in two terrible air crashes which, at this writing, are being investigated by Congress.

In its daily operations, the Federal Aviation Agency uses gaming techniques, real time simulations, and field experiments to develop operational policies and administrative regulations for the aviation passenger industry.[35] Its use of computers to control flight patterns and regulations is a delight to any lover of applied science.[36]

All of these techniques are capable of use in various kinds and levels of policy making. Take computers, for example. They are available to check the past, present, and future. As to the past, their contribution in significant statistical work is too widespread to note here. For present, they can be used as a means of controlling daily social problems[37] and, for the future, they are a device for gaming and other predictions.[38]

These and many more than the devices mentioned above are being adopted in other areas of social control.[39] The Department of Health, Education and Welfare is using scientific research not only in the familiar field of regulating food or medicine but also in studying the social impact of the present judicially based policy of integration in education.

It is clear that the case of *Brown* v. *The Board*[40] was constitutionally correct in outlawing legally enforced segregation. But although most federal government administrators and the "liberals" favor a policy of forced integration in all public schools on the ground of the equal protection clause of the Constitution, the careful studies of the Department of Health, Education, and Welfare show that such integration does little educational good to the blacks and none to the whites.[41] Additional research in the field may prove that one of the most precious clauses of the Bill of Rights has no social value as it is being now applied here as judicial and government educational policy. In fact, it may turn out to be misguided eighteenth century idealism.

The Question of Ultimate Policy

There is no doubt that experimental science can be applied to social relations to confirm or repudiate certain legal and administrative devices. In fact, it may even require confirmation or alteration of the policy behind the law, but one is still faced with the logical question of whether or not science can validate or discover "basic" legal, constitutional governmental, and social policies which are the major premises from which laws ultimately can be deduced.

To state the problem is to immediately raise the question of whether or not there are discoverable basic immutable "values," "ideals," and "social relationships" upon which the policies behind social and legal rules or regulations can be built. This controversy, which has intrigued philosophers for centuries, cannot be settled in the space available here, but a few remarks are in order.

Although law and religion have both laid claim to certainty in their constitutions, precedents, written rules, and revelations, anyone who has bothered to do any research in the field is immediately struck by the fact that "there are arguments on both sides of every case." World religious dogmas and revelations are even more contradictory than the legal cases. "Values," "ideals," "morals," and "mores" are generalities drawn from the conditions of previous simple civilizations which bear little resemblance to conditions in the science-dominated polity in which we live.[42] At their best, they may represent irrelevant observations of wise men of past generations; at their worst, they are based on superstitions like voodoo.[43] Using them as a compelling basis of policy-making is not only irrelevant to the problem at hand, it is downright dangerous. Ideals, in addition, may partake of a bit of speculation but are unreal because they have their origins not in facts of life but in speculation—usually by cloistered philosophers.

Religion is purely dogmatic in its creation of standards and rules of conduct. It should be noted that all religions are of ancient origin and conflict among themselves in almost all their details. All partake of another wordly bent. They have been a brake on the progress of the human race worldwide, and there is no reason to believe that "my faith" is the exception. In spite of these well-documented historical facts, there is the Natural Law theory that religion stands above the law and it is where the policymaker should turn for his basics.[44] Closely akin to this, and a branch of the same theory, is the belief that the validity of the law rests upon the religious beliefs or conscience of the person governed and, if law is contradictory to his conscience or his basic liberties, he does not have to obey it. This is the currently held popular belief and is written into the Declaration of Independence "that whenever any government becomes destructive of these ends, it is the right of the people to alter or abolish it." It is basic Catholic, Christian, Mohammedan, and Jewish doctrine which still is, as it was then, the rationalization of revolution. In those countries in which these beliefs are strongest, it is the philosophical and practical justification for anarchy. Just look at the developments in South America, Northern Ireland, the Near East, and even in the United States.

Closely akin to the natural law theory is the Democratic belief that the sum of the individual demands which constitutes a numerical majority of people is the proper foundation for policy-making. This has been refuted at length elsewhere. It is sufficient to say here, as spelled out at length there,[45] that, in modern complicated civilization, the individual citizen is incapable of making a valid judgment on policy matters. The majority or the sum of incompetencies is still incompetence.

All these popular sources of policy can rise no higher than hypotheses subject to verification and examination when, if ever, they are put into effect. They are best taken into consideration only as they affect popular demands. In fact, it is a proven basis of science that even scientific laws governing inanimate matter are subject to verification and change by further experimentation.[46] This is even more true when one is confronted with jural laws derived from a social experiment.[47]

Are we then thrown back on the pragmatic position that truth is what works? As Mr. Justice Holmes put it, "truth is the majority vote, there are no absolutes," and "justice is the law of the nation which can lick all others."[48] Logically, the statement that "there are no absolutes" is self-contradictory because it is stated as an absolute. Practically, in light of history, if survival is the test,[49] the nations which could lick all others have been proven wrong—their laws, ideals and fixed utopias cannot survive in a changing world. Their symbols, "the Law of the Meads and Persians which changeth not," the eternal Roman Law, as the "bright lamp of the law,"[50] the Holy Roman Empire, the Third Reich, to last a thousand years, are all dead. "The sun never sets on the British Empire" and wars "to make the world safe for democracy" are mere fading shadows. The Dictatorship of the Proletariat, the Thoughts of Mao, and free enterprise capitalism are facing mutual destruction. The Arabian confiscation of oil and the dawning of the age of hydrogen power, to name only two, are creating dislocations in our American and European solid social structure that can only be solved by a surge of new social science.

The pragmatist's statement that "there are no absolutes" should be slightly rephrased to read, "There are no *easily identifiable* absolutes." Science has demonstrated that man, like all other living creatures, needs certain environmental conditions as a basis of survival. Often called basic needs, these are a supply of water, food, air, and many others. If man's environment does not contain these basic needs, he perishes like the dinosaur. At one time, people were at the mercy of the elements to supply these needs, but this is no longer the case with highly civilized man. He can change his environment, and law and policy-making are means of accomplishing the necessary change. For example, water is a basic need. In North

Africa, and in the southwestern desert of the United States, the climate changes withholding water. The primitive people in Africa cannot survive, but highly civilized Americans use science to change policy and to institute the California Water Plan, the Central Arizona Project, and desalinization plants. The necessary water is restored and progress continues.

But power to change environment to meet one's needs may encroach upon another. The country needs food; the farmers of the Midwest meet the need with fertilizer. The fertilizer in the drainage to the rivers poisons the water of the people in New Orleans. Again both physical and social science must come to the rescue and balance the needs or purify the river, or both.

The limits within which man can change his environment without destroying himself, and the methods available to accomplish this, need to be measured and predicted. These limits are the new flexible absolutes which can be uncovered by experimental jurisprudence and systems engineering.

In addition to basic needs, there are also strong demands which men make on their legal system and environment. These demands may be for things needed or for objects which are not needed or even harmful. It is clear that demands for things needed should be granted, but the effect of yielding to demands for things not needed or even dangerous may be disastrous. Yet such demands may be so strong as to endanger the structure of society. Failure of the law and policy systems to ameliorate these demands may cause a breakdown in the social or legal system or both. A good example is prohibition. It is clear that there is no basic need for alcohol as a beverage, and that, as such it was and is, damaging to society; but the demand for it was so strong that when it was legally prohibited, prohibition had to be abolished to save the structure of the criminal law. These constant changes to meet needs and strong demands are the basic stuff of scientific policy-making.

Whether or not one policy with optimum implementation is better than another depends upon how it meets the needs and forceful demands of society. This balancing of human needs and demands in any field is a basic requirement for effective law and policy making. The present system of satisfying demands alone is not enough because yielding to demands at the cost of needs, though it brings temporary social peace, is very likely to result in stultification or fall of the civilization involved. So far, this has been the history of all civilizations. Attention to ultimate needs while still satiating forceful demands avoids this and assures continued progress of the race.

Conclusion

The task of experimental jurisprudence and social systems engineering is so scientifically to rearrange the laws and government policies that tragedies can be foreseen and prevented and progress can be continuous. Constant scientific information to create laws and to assess their effect on future social conditions is necessary.[51] If the effect of changes on the social system is studied and recorded as in steps 4 and 5 of experimental jurisprudence and step 2 of systems engineering, there can be accumulated a series of jural laws stating the relation of laws and policies to environmental conditions, which correspond to scientific laws. Because they are dependent upon complicated social conditions, they will not be the absolutes that the pragmatists are talking about, but they can form a basis for sound social engineering and policy-making.

Experimental jurisprudence and social systems engineering are two techniques, the use of which is growing. Policy-making can no longer be left to amateurs and bumbling politicians. It must be scientifically guided. Some scientific techniques are already in use. Adoption of more by all levels of government is necessary and will result in a new theory and reorganization of government, the Scienstate.[52]

Notes

1. Professor Beutel is author of three books in this field: *Some Implications of Experimental Jurisprudence as a New Social Science* (1957); *Democracy or the Scientific Method in Law and Policy Making* (1965); and *Experimental Jurisprudence and the Scienstate* (1975), hereinafter cited as: *Experimental Jurisprudence; Democracy or the Scientific Method*; and *Experimental Jurisprudence and the Scienstate*.

2. *Discretionary Justice* (1969).

3. *Id.*, p. 9, Cf., *Experimental Jurisprudence and the Scienstate*, pp. 22 ff.

4. *Am. L. Rev.* 44 (1910):12.

5. For example, see: *Experimental Jurisprudence and the Scienstate*, pp. 133 ff; *Experimental Jurisprudence*, pp. 286 ff; Cohen, Robson, and Bates, *Parental Authority* (1958); Blumrosen and Zeitz, "Antidiscrimination Laws in Action in New Jersey," *Rutgers L. Rev.* 19 (1965):191-316. There are many more.

6. See *Experimental Jurisprudence*, pp. 287 ff; and material cited in notes 7-10 *infra*.

7. Skolnick, *Justice without Trial* (1967), pp. 12 ff and authorities there cited in note 31.

8. These practices represent an important type of policy-making by a sort of common law covered by court rules. See, for example, *Ariz. Rev.*

Stat. Ann. 17 (1973), Rule 17.4 and authorities there cited. This rule-making power may be authorized by the constitution. See Ariz. Constitution Art. 6, Sec. 5, Sub. 5 (1960 Amendment) or by statute, or simply by assumption of judicial power.

9. See *Experimental Jurisprudence,* pp. 289 ff.

10. Carlin, *Lawyers on Their Own* (1962); *Id. Lawyers' Ethics* (1966).

11. See U. S. Dept. HEW, *Equality of Educational Opportunity* iii (1966); *Id.* Summary iii (1966). *Experimental Jurisprudence and the Scienstate,* pp. 293 ff.

12. *Experimental Jurisprudence and the Scienstate,* pp. 25 ff.

13. Fuentes v. Shevin, 407 U.S. 67 (1972); overruled by Mitchell v. W. T. Grant, 415 U.S. 944, 94 S. Ct. 1895 (1974).

14. Mr. Justice Stuart dissenting in Mitchell v. W. T. Grant, *supra,* 94 S. Ct. at 1913.

15. See 94 S. Ct. at 1914, n. 8.

16. *Democracy or the Scientific Method,* Ch. III at p. 75.

17. For examples of a few of these instances, see *Experimental Jurisprudence,* Ch. IX.

18. Cf. Harper, "Some Implications of Juristic Pragmatism," 39 *Int. Jour. Ethics* 39 (1929):269. Cf. also, Mr. Justice Holmes, "Constitutional rights like others are matters of degree." Martin v. District of Columbia, 205 U.S. 135, 139 (1907).

19. *Experimental Jurisprudence and the Scienstate,* pp. 68 ff.

20. Beutel, *Study of the Enforcement of the Bad-Check Laws of Nebraska* (1957); *Experimental Jurisprudence,* Ch. X ff.

21. Nebraska, Legislative Bill 427 (1971), Leg. Res. 53 (April 27, 1971), and for a more complete discussion, see *Experimental Jurisprudence and the Scienstate,* p. 273.

22. (1964), see Ch. II.

23. Simon, *The Jury and the Defense of Insanity* (1967).

24. See Kalven and Zeisel, *The American Jury* (1966), p. vii, and material there cited.

25. Simon, *The Jury and the Defense of Insanity,* Ch. 2 ff.

26. *Id.,* 66 ff., 22 ff.

27. *Experimental Jurisprudence and the Scienstate,* pp. 209 ff and authorities there cited.

28. One of the leading books on the subject outlines the steps as follows:

1. An analysis by a team of scientists in all related fields of the whole problem which the operation studied is attempting to solve.

2. Formulations of theories to explain the activities apparent in the operation.

3. Creation of new models to test the theory.

4. Experimental testing of the model and theory, either mathematically, by some theory, experimental or simulated "runs," or other scientific devices.

5. Decision to change the operation as a result of the research.

See Flagel, Huggins, and Roy, *Operations Research and Systems Engineering*; Page, *A Survey of Operations Research Tools and Techniques* (1960), Ch. 6; see also *Experimental Jurisprudence and the Scienstate,* 208 ff and numerous authorities there cited.

29. *Experimental Jurisprudence and the Scienstate,* pp. 207 ff, 213 ff.

30. *Experimental Jurisprudence,* Ch. VI, 31 Neb. L. Rev. 349 (1952).

31. See the summary and history of this work, *Experimental Jurisprudence and the Scienstate,* pp. 261 ff.

32. *Id.,* pp. 308 ff.

33. Fite, *The Computer Challenge* (1967), Chs. 7 & 8.

34. See *Experimental Jurisprudence and the Scienstate,* pp. 327 ff.

35. *Id.,* pp. 337 ff.

36. *Id.,* pp. 338-339.

37. See *supra,* notes 33 and 36.

38. See *supra,* note 36. The computers at Brookings Institute are famous for predicting economic trends as affected by law and policy.

39. For a discussion of the use of models, see Thomas, *Scientists in the Legal Systems*; Vanyo, *The Legal System, Can It Be Analyzed to Suit Scientists?* (1974) and authorities there cited at pp. 65 & 66.

40. 347 U.S. 483 (1954).

41. See *supra,* note 11.

42. See Lynd and Lynd, *Middletown* (1929) Ch. 2; Benedict, *Patterns of Culture* (1934).

43. See *Experimental Jurisprudence and the Scienstate,* Ch. II.

44. See Beutel, "Relationship of Natural Law to Experimental Jurisprudence," *Ohio St. L. Jour.* 13 (1952):67; Holmes, "Further Aspects of the Conflict Between Empiricism and Idealism," "Natural Law," *Har. L. Rev.* 32(1918):40.

45. *Democracy or the Scientific Method.*

46. *Experimental Jurisprudence and the Scienstate,* pp. 47 ff.

47. For the nature of jural laws, see *Id.,* pp. 66, 69, 75 ff.

48. Holmes, "Natural Law," *Har. L. Rev.* 32(1918):40.

49. See Harper, "Implications of Juristic Pragmatism," *Int. Jour. Ethics* 39 (1929): 269.

50. Wigmore, *A Panorama of the World's Legal Systems* 983 (1928).

51. Cf. Thomas, *Scientists in the Legal System,* Loevinger, *Jurimetrics: Science in Law*, pp. 7 ff (1974).

52. *Experimental Jurisprudence and the Scienstate.*

**Part IX
Political Science**

23 What Political Scientists Don't Need to Ask About Policy Analysis

Theodore J. Lowi

> Two main sources of irrationalism in the social struc-
> ture (uncontrolled competition and domination by
> force) constitute the realm of social life . . . where
> politics becomes necessary . . . Every rationalized
> order is only one of many forms in which socially
> conflicting irrational forces are reconciled.

> *Karl Mannheim*

The 1970s is witnessing a scramble within the discipline of political science
to be first to define the "post-behavioral era." All of these activities are a
welcome sign, all the more welcome because the post-behavioral movement is entirely positive and is in only a small part based on rejection of the
behavioral. Nevertheless, a whole generation of political scientists was
educated about a political system in which public policy was at the
periphery, to say the least.

During the behavioral period, policy, if it was invoked at all, was
reduced to issues. Few read cases or statutes or other governmental materials, except perhaps the specific documents involved in a particular study
of a single decision in a "decision-making process." Institutions, if involved in teaching or research at all, were treated merely as laboratories for
the study of behavior. Behavioral politics is strictly micropolitics; public
policy is macropolitical. Consequently, enrollment in public policy or
policy relevant courses in public law, public adminstration, "regulation of
business," "political economy," and so on, dwindled and, in many universities disappeared.

A significant case study in the prevailing outlook of political science
toward public policy was the original plan for the symposium for which this
essay was prepared. Political science as a discipline was left out altogether
from a tentative plan for the *Policy Studies Journal* symposium on "interdisciplinary approaches to policy study" on which this book is based. This
implied two things. It implied that an interdisciplinary approach to public
policy had little to learn from political science. More significantly it implied
that if political scientists were now to interest themselves in policy studies,
their primary obligation would be to learn how policy analysis is done from
all the social science disciplines *except* political science. There is much we

267

would need to know and are afraid to ask. In effect, a political scientist who would be a policy analyst must be a sociologist, or an economist, or a physical scientist, or an anthropologist, or a geographer, or some combination of these. And the members of those sister disciplines would not have to feel any obligation to become political scientists. This is, to a great extent, where we came in in the early 1950s, when it was widely felt that the study of political behavior required that a political scientist must first be a psychologist or a sociologist.

The renewed interest in policy studies should be celebrated. However, it should not be allowed to overshadow the rich existing tradition of policy studies in political science. There is an old but extremely valuable literature of policy analysis that was produced by political scientists. And even the slightest exposure to these materials will show that the political scientists who produced this kind of work had already brought a great deal from the sister disciplines into political science. Better yet, the acquisition of learning from sister disciplines goes back so far that it is no longer recognized as interdisciplinary by those who are traditional enough to engage in the older kind of policy studies. To us—and I include myself—it may turn out that the sister disciplines have more to learn from political science than the other way around.

This chapter is, first, a celebration of what political science has already achieved in the accumulation of appropriate tools for public policy analysis. Second, it will go so far as to argue that political science has very little to learn from modern economics and behavioral sociology and psychology; to the contrary, it will argue that there are some dangers inherent in borrowing prematurely and uncritically from other disciplines. Political scientists who undertake to do policy analysis before becoming bona fide political scientists are likely, I argue, to become poor policy analysts, aping this discipline, uncritically imitating that one, and developing no substantively sound theory at all.

Traditional Political Science

There are two sources of traditional knowledge about public policy in political science. One of these sources is law. The other is traditional economics, or political economy.

The economics in question was institutional or market economics. In political science the function of this kind of economics was not to stress the "impact" of policies or the manner in which governmental decisions were distributed. Rather, economics was used to bring out the most relevant sources of values and influence from society on politics. Whether it was Charles Beard and his economic approach to the Constitution, or whether it was the Marxists or the pluralists, no self-respecting political scientist was probably considered knowledgeable unless he knew a little something about the oil industry or agriculture or the food processing industry or banking—if he intended to do any work on public policies.

The role of law in political science traditionally was one of stressing the procedural and structural aspects of government. This was "public law," and it was frequently confined too narrowly to the study of the leading cases handed down by the Supreme Court. Nevertheless, even in its narrowest usages, public law was more than structure; it added substantive sense to governmental structure. In intelligent hands, it produced the ability to deal with the operative aspects of justice and injustice. There were of course questions of procedure, and few undergraduate products of traditional political science courses escaped without some knowledge of the due process aspects of government action. But operative questions of justice also came into play through legal stress on "substantive due process" as well, because it consistently raised the question of whether the government in question possessed the power to reach a problem at all. Conservatism was a strong tendency, but not inevitable. Law helped make it possible for political science to speak intelligently of antitrust, utilities regulation, dismantling holding companies, conservation, taxation. Those are real policies.

Behavioral Political Science

These two sources also make up a large part of what the behavioralists had in mind when they were reacting against the traditional in traditional political science. The behavioral reaction against the traditional aspects of the study of government was understandable and in some respects justifiable. From the level of public law and institutional economics, and from the level of political science that was respectful of those particular sources of political knowledge, it was probably impossible to deal systematically with political behavior. As in economics, it is virtually impossible to combine macropolitical and micropolitical theory. Those who wanted to study individual decisions—those who wanted to study the specific personality and other individual causal factors back of individual political decisions— would not find much usable knowledge at the level of constitution, market, industry, etc. These concepts are at such a level of society that, from the perspective of individual behavior, they were almost mystical in their quality. If they were to be appreciated at all, they would have to be broken up into elements that individuals receive and process in their own efforts to cope with their individual environment. For example, economics would have to be taken out of the macro-industrial structure and redefined as a series of individual social class, education, and income experiences. Individuals in their politics do not directly experience constitutionality and standing to sue, or agency and delegation, or statutes and administrative rulings, or collective responsibility. Therefore, it was probably inevitable that the public law aspects of traditional knowledge would have to be thrown out altogether. They in fact were thrown out, and were only brought back in through the study of the individual behaviors of judges.

Justifiable as that redefinition of economics and law may have been, something indispensable was sacrificed in the larger framework of political science in which behavioralism was only one source of theory. One might, for example, still ask whether it is possible to talk about public policy at all without some knowledge of the oil industry, without some grasp of how members of the chemical industry compete, without some sense of why and how the agriculture industry was politicized so early, without some sense why the steel industry is so uninnovative in the United States. It would have been indispensable—why not now—to know a little something about property and capitalism. It is also difficult to understand how one can speak of policy and policy analysis without some sense of law and of the laws that make big policy. Perhaps one of the worst transformations in recent years is the replacement of the terminology of law with the terminology of policy to describe the decisions that governments make to influence society. Public policy cannot mean merely the most recent single decision made by an elite, by any public or private agency. Policy must have something to do with the long-range intentions of governments and government agencies, public commitments that are going to be implemented, however crudely, with inducements and sanctions over a lot of space, time, and population. It may be more difficult to be precise and systematic about this level of knowledge, but our knowledge of this level is not improved by rejecting it in favor of micropolitical approaches merely in order to get more systematic analysis.

Post-Behavioral Political Science

The jolts of the late 1960s that led to a reevaluation of approaches to knowledge are too obvious and well understood to need any treatment here. But the main point for political scientists during this period, it seems to me, was that in all of the stress and disequilibrium, *governments had failed to perform as fully and predictably as we had grown to expect.* Now, as long as government and society were in some kind of equilibrium with each other, which would be true from the end of the 1930s until the middle of the 1960s in the United States, it would be possible to treat government as an equilibrium, to disregard it (or treat it all as a set of "environmental parameters"), and to proceed to individual and small group behaviors within that established context. But once the context itself began to fail, government in all its complexity became a series of variables rather than one undifferentiated constant. Suddenly there were thousands of students who were screaming against current political science courses and in favor of "relevance." Political science was, justifiably, accused of defending establishments. A great many political scientists were answering *mea culpa* without exactly knowing what they were guilty of. For many of them, especially those who joined the Caucus for a New Political Science, it was clear that behavioralism, or a behavioralist approach to government institutions, was incapable of handling the many problems that amounted to relevance. However, there are no doubt many others, including a goodly number of the Policy Studies Organization, who feel that they can best be relevant by bringing behavioral techniques and perspectives over into the policy context. This amounts to a return to the study of macropolitics without reintroducing some of the most important sources of macropolitical analysis. Quite the contrary. The approach to public policy from a micro or behavioralist perspective will rarely end up being the study of public policy at all.

The most significant indication, perhaps even confirmation, of this non-policy approach to policy is the extensive borrowing of behavioralists from the new economics, the economics of decision-making rather than policy-making, the economics of market structures, etc. This is not to argue that these and all the other highly formalized approaches to economic decision-making are irrelevant to political science. It is only to argue that as a prerequisite to the proper study of public policy, by political scientists, this kind of interdisciplinary borrowing will never make political science more relevant and certainly will not make it more political. For political scientists, the greatest risk of dabbling in interdisciplinary approaches for grounding in public policy analysis is loss of political perspective. It is very unlikely that we can build toward the macropolitical knowledge we need on a foundation of micropolitical and microsocial knowledge and tools of analysis. Those who already have a considerable grounding in the traditional sources of macropolitical knowledge may be able to dabble in the new interdisciplinary approaches with impunity. But those who do not start out with that larger perspective are not likely to get it at all if their course prerequisites and graduate training tie them up to microeconomics and micropsychology and microsociology before political theory, public law, institutional economics and old-fashioned political institutions.

In many respects, the recent turn toward microeconomics and other sources of formal schematics is a gigantic put-on. It is nothing but old and outmoded behaviorism insisting that it needs no retooling in order to talk policy. For many, this new concern for public policy and the eagerness to borrow right off the starting gate from all the sister disciplines is a good deal more bona fide; but the results are about the same. The political perspective is lost. What, after all, is rationality in a rational model except a set of assumptions that defines the political as irrational?

This chapter is already too long to allow for more than two or three unfairly brief examples. One very important area of recent concern to political scientists is the study of population policy. The availability of research support in this area, coupled with the gigantic amount of information available in other disciplines, has been turning many young political scientists into bad biologists. Study of the impact of welfare and health delivery decisions in communities are other areas in which political scientists can easily become laughing stocks in the eyes of real economists, real welfare sociologists and real public health experts. Whether the field is economic development in underdeveloped countries, distribution of wealth in developed countries, population control or public housing, I have not yet seen the political scientist whose work on the sociological or econometric aspect of the problem fully satisfies a well-trained econometrician, a dedicated student of the economics of public choice, or a Ph.D. in biology, epidemiology, or food sciences. In those fields, even the best political scientist can be little more than a poor amateur.

Toward a Macropolitical Perspective

The one thing that supposedly ties all political scientists together is concern about the nature, composition, and functioning of the political system—or polity, or body politic, or political economy, as personal asthetics dictates. The vocabulary does not matter; the concern is about the same. The problem arises when the political scientist tries to translate that widely shared concern into an interest in public policy. I have argued here that the worst way—and for many old behavioralists the self-serving way—to translate the general concern into the specific application to public policy analysis is to redefine policy as a decision or a set of discrete decisions made by individuals that can be studied by established micropolitical, and microeconomic and microsocial tools of scientific analysis. The best way is to insist upon understanding policy as a macropolitical phenomenon that is simply irrelevant, at least in short run analyses, to microknowledge. At this level, for political scientists, the most important questions to ask would be these—and they should be asked this way even if the tools of analysis are not yet as impressively scientific as we would like:

1. What is the policy as a *policy?* That is, what is a policy, defined not as an individual decision but as part of a long line of intention to which a government or an agency of government is committed? What is the best

way to describe the actual provisions and the ultimate meaning of a *government* decision?

2. What is the policy as a *law?* The question is put this way in order to emphasize that when one proceeds to analyze a policy beyond the surface and plain meaning of the expressed government decision, there is a better approach than merely asking whether the decision fit the formal requirements of rationality. Formalizing an analysis is a desirable thing to do, but formal economic rationality is not a relevant initial formality for the political scientist, who should already be too well aware of the severe restraints that the real political process puts upon as many as eight of every ten logically possible alternatives. Rather, the policy-as-law question is intended to put the policy phenomenon back into the traditional understanding—actually a Weberian understanding—that behind every public policy is a specific type of coercion.

3. What is the impact of the policy on the political system? Yes, political scientists should be interested in "impact analysis;" but the impacts for which political scientists can claim some analytic expertise are impacts back on the political system rather than forward toward elements of the social process. Just as the biologist may study real population change, or the engineer may study the real benefits and costs of a highway location, the political scientist might profitable and proudly ask questions the biologist and engineer would find alien. For example: What will policy alternative X do to the capacity of that government to change later to policy alternative Y, if X fails? What will a given type of sanction do to the capacity of law enforcement officers to operate, or what effect will a given type of sanction have on the actual structure of law enforcement? Will an independent regulatory approach (versus a departmental approach) reduce or increase legislative participation in future policy-making in that area? Do the new fiscal approaches to welfare militate strongly in favor of executive dominance of government decision-making? And so on and so forth.

There does not seem to be any other way to get systematically closer to the ultimate questions of justice, equity, the good life. How will the different types of policy and coercion effect the capacity of a government, the next time around, to make timely decisions? How will current policies generally affect the access of all people to the political system and the capacity of all people for defense against bad policies? All of these are macropolitical questions. A micropolitical and an interdisciplinary approach to these questions actually means neglect of the questions. And we will neglect these questions only to the peril of the discipline of political science itself. Without a fixed and determined focus on these questions and a concern for how to translate them into good analysis, political science will indeed have no reason for being; or, it will have no reason for being anything but a way station for passage toward some other field of endeavor.

24

Policy Analysis and the Political Science Profession

Phillip O. Foss

I would like to discuss two sets of ideas which I believe have some relationship to each other: the study of public policy and the status of the profession.

Policy Analysis in Political Science

According to Austin Ranney, ". . . at least since 1945 most American political scientists have focused their professional attention mainly on the processes by which public policies are made and have shown relatively little concern with their contents."[1] I would go farther and suggest that until very recently we really have been only concerned with parts of the policy process. Rather than focusing on the policy process, we have directed our attention to studies of process or behavior as if they had no relationship, or impact, on policy outputs. The discipline of political science in general has been structured by the structure of government. Thus we have studied legislative process and behavior, judicial process and behavior, administrative process and behavior and so forth with little reference to the overall policy process or to policy outcomes except as they provide feedback to the inputs of the system.

About thirteen or fourteen years ago, I introduced a new course called "Public Policy Formation" and quite frankly had a difficult time finding appropriate textual materials. As I recall, the best I could find were Dahl and Lindblom, *Politics, Economics and Welfare*, Lasswell and Kaplan, *Power and Society*, and Lerner and Lasswell, *The Policy Sciences*.[2] While all of the three were important contributions to the discipline, they were not really suitable for the approach I wished to follow. I consequently decided that I would have to write the book myself but this turned out to be one of the several books that I have not yet completed. Apparently several other people had a similar experience and came to the same conclusion because there have been several excellent studies published since that time. Among them we might include Thomas Dye, *Politics, Economics and the Public*[3] and his more recent *Understanding Public Policy*,[4] Yehezkel Dror, *Public Policy Making Reexamined*,[5] Charles O. Jones, *An Introduction to the*

Presidential Address delivered at the 27th annual conference of the Western Political Science Association, San Diego, California, April 5, 1973.

275

Study of Public Policy,[6] Charles E. Lindblom, *The Policy-Making Process*,[7] Joyce M. and William C. Mitchell, *Political Analysis and Public Policy*,[8] Austin Ranney, ed., *Political Science and Public Policy*,[9] Ira Sharkansky, ed., *Policy Analysis in Political Science*,[10] and Larry Wade, *The Elements of Public Policy*.[11]

You can doubtless add others to this listing. There have also been several studies on specific policy areas to which I shall return in a moment.

My purpose here is not to review the many approaches to the study of public policy but to point out that policy analysis in political science is of very recent vintage. It is my understanding that political scientists have always maintained that theirs is *the* policy science but until very recent years they have done very little about it. I applaud and encourage this new emphasis. It is long overdue.

Let me add that I am not talking here about gut reactions to recent events or instant stands on fragments of knowledge—which have in the recent past masqueraded under the title of "relevance." We *are* talking about knowledgeable, professional contributions to the study of public policy. As Charles Hyneman has said, "The political scientist cannot take expertise as a political scientist to the public forum except as he carries with him the fruits of scholarship."

The Political Science Profession

Let me turn now to a consideration of the state of political science as a profession. Please note that I am making a distinction between the terms "discipline" and "profession." I believe I am correct in saying that political science has the lowest professional status of any of the social sciences. It receives least outside funding for research; it is least consulted by government; and its members are least frequently employed by government—as political scientists. Economists are employed by government as economists, sociologists as sociologists, but few, if any, political scientists are employed as political scientists.

I suggest that the low status of the profession stems from two basic causes: political scientists really do not identify with the profession and our professional organizations have done little to serve their members or to enhance the status of the profession; political scientists have little knowledge and few skills that are of interest or value to anyone except other political scientists. Let me consider each of these factors in turn.

For some reason very few political scientists feel any deep sense of commitment to the profession and most of us really do not even identify with the profession. Perhaps this is because of the wide diversity of subject matter in the discipline and the variety of approaches to the subject matter.

Certainly very few of us actively promote the profession. Kissinger and Moynihan do not identify themselves as political scientists in the statements they make—and neither do the rest of us. Economists, by contrast, ordinarily preface their remarks with statements such as "speaking as an economist" or "from an economist's point of view."

With reference to the national association and the regional associations, they have done very little to enhance either the profession or the discipline except through journal publication and the annual conference. I suppose this failure of the associations is due in part to the lack of agreement as to what should be done and the paucity of resources to do anything with. We cannot expect members to endorse a substantial increase in fees when many of them feel they are not getting their "money's worth" from the small contribution they make now. So we are caught in the familiar vicious circle in which we cannot accomplish much because we do not have the funds and we can't raise funds because we haven't accomplished much in the past.

A second reason for the low status of political science is that we have traditionally had little interest or knowledge of policy matters so we have had no contributions to make of any value to policy makers. Stated differently, very few political scientists would qualify as "expert witnesses" in any of the substantive policy areas. Economics, on the other hand, has for years had experts in most of the major policy areas. An economics department of any size will ordinarily have specialists in public finance policy, transportation, public utilities, agriculture, labor, and natural resources policy. There is nothing comparable in political science. The economists are now, and have been for years, *the* policy scientists. They have become the policy scientists not only because they have actively involved themselves in policy studies but because political science has abdicated.

Policy Analysis and the Political Science Profession

In view of the considerations outlined above, I recommend that a substantial number of political scientists become profesionally involved in a substantive policy area—in addition to the more general policy approaches mentioned in the first section of these remarks. By so doing, I believe we can enhance the status of the profession and also make a significant contribution toward improving the quality of public policy decisions.

This kind of inquiry is directed not only toward the policy process but also towards what Lasswell has called "the intelligence needs of policy." As Lasswell put it (writing in 1951):

We have become more aware of the policy process as a suitable object of study in its own right, primarily in the hope of improving the rationality of the flow of decision.

A policy orientation has been developing that cuts across the existing specializations. The orientation is twofold. In part it is directed toward the policy process, and in part toward the intelligence needs of policy. The first task, which is the development of a science of policy forming and execution, uses the methods of social and psychological inquiry. The second task, which is the improving of the concrete content of the information and the interpretations available to policy-makers, typically goes outside the boundaries of social science and psychology.

In so far, therefore, as the policy orientation is focused upon the scientific study of policy, it is narrower than the psychological and social sciences, which have many other objects of investigation. However, where the needs of policy intelligence are uppermost, any item of knowledge, within or without the limits of the social disciplines, may be relevant. We may need to know the harbor installations at Casablanca, or the attitudes of a population of Pacific islanders to the Japanese, or the maximum range of a fixed artillery piece.[12]

Political scientists will typically react to such statements with cries of "I'm not an engineer" or "I'm not a botanist" and the like. Austin Ranney has made reference to these dilemmas in the following passage.

In my opinion, political scientists will—and should—be called upon to advise policy-makers to the degree that they are perceived to have special professional knowledge and skills. If all we can offer is common sense or a passion for social justice, then we have no claim to and will not receive any special attention not paid to any other citizen enjoying these admirable but widely diffused assets. And we can hardly hope to beat the subject-matter experts at their own games by becoming especially skilled hydrologists or welfare economists or astronautical engineers or whatever.[13]

We do not need to "beat them at their own game." We have a "game" of our own. We tend to become confused, I think, about the knowledge requirements for participating as professionals in the various policy areas. Let me point out that an agricultural economist need not be an agronomist; that a water lawyer need not be an hydrologist; that a sociologist who works with urban housing problems need not be an architect; and that a political scientist who studies forest policy need not be a forester.

This is not a new idea. Over the years there have been several people who have distinguished themselves with studies in specific policy areas. Perhaps most of them have worked in the field of natural resources policy. There we can mention such names as Lynton Caldwell, Henry Caulfield, James Davies, Luther Gulick, Charles Hardin, Helen Ingram, Albert Lepawsky, Arthur Maass, Dean Mann, Grant McConnell, Daniel M. Ogden, Vincent Ostrom, Robert Rienow, Geoffrey Wandesford-Smith and Norman Wengert.

However, if one moves out of the fields of natural resources and foreign policy he will have difficulty in naming five political scientists who have done significant work in any of the other major policy areas. Even in the field of race relations policy, which has received so much attention during the last few years, there has been much description and exhortation but little analysis.

One way in which political scientists can improve the status of the profession and, hopefully, the rationality of policy decisions is to become reasonably expert in specific policy areas. Are such studies to replace some of our traditional areas of concern? No, they are in addition to—not in place of. Admittedly, this is an invitation to an even more strenuous life.

Notes

1. Austin Ranney (ed.), *Political Science and Public Policy* (Chicago: Markham Publishing Company, 1968), p. 3.

2. Robert A. Dahl and Charles E. Lindblom, *Politics, Economics and Welfare* (New York: Harper and Brothers, 1953); Harold D. Lasswell and Abraham Kaplan, *Power and Society* (New Haven: Yale University Press, 1950); Daniel Lerner and Harold D. Lasswell (eds.), *The Policy Sciences* (Stanford: Stanford University Press, 1951).

3. Thomas Dye, *Politics, Economics and the Public* (Chicago: Rand-McNally, 1966).

4. Thomas Dye, *Understanding Public Policy* (Englewood Cliffs, N.J.: Prentice-Hall, 1972).

5. Yehezkel Dror, *Public Policy Making Reexamined* (San Francisco, Calif.: Chandler, 1968).

6. Charles O. Jones, *An Introduction to the Study of Public Policy* (Belmont, Calif.: Wadsworth, 1970).

7. Charles E. Lindblom, *The Policy-Making Process* (Englewood Cliffs, N.J.: Prentice-Hall, 1968).

8. Joyce M. Mitchell and William C. Mitchell, *Political Analysis and Public Policy* (Chicago: Rand-McNally, 1969).

9. Austin Ranney (ed.), *Political Science and Public Policy* (Chicago: Markham, 1968).

10. Ira Sharkansky (ed.), *Policy Analysis in Political Science* (Chicago: Markham, 1970).

11. Larry Wade, *The Elements of Public Policy* (Columbus, Ohio: Charles E. Merrill, 1972).

12. Lerner and Lasswell (eds.), *The Policy Sciences*, pp. 3-4.

13. Ranney (ed.), *Political Science and Public Policy*, pp. 17-18.

25 Policy Analysis and Political Science: Some Problems at the Interface

Thomas R. Dye

In the first issue of the *Policy Studies Journal*, Professor Yehezkel Dror called for "the application of political science to important policy problems." He correctly observed that the application of political science to policy issues was not the same as political scientists stating their personal views on these issues, either individually or collectively. He then proceeded to describe some of the requisites of a policy science methodology. Professor Dror's comments were valuable and appropriate; nonetheless, there are several important questions about the relationship between political science and policy research which continually recur in discussions about policy study.[1]

1. *Prescription and Explanation.* The first of these questions is the hoary one about the appropriate *normative* stance of the political scientist in approaching policy issues. How prescriptive can political science become without abandoning its commitment to systematic social science? Yet despite the obvious possibilities for prolonged fruitless conflict over this question, there appears to be a developing consensus that explanation must precede prescription. Not only is there agreement that explanation is a prerequisite to prescription, but there is also general agreement that explanation is best achieved through systematic analysis rather than rhetoric or polemics or introspection or dialectic. It is, perhaps, this agreement to focus concern or explanation rather than prescription, to search rigorously for the causes and consequences of public policy, to utilize scientific standards of inference in this search, and to endeavor to develop and test general propositions about public policy, that gives the policy analysis movement whatever intellectual coherence that it possesses.

2. *Advice to Policymakers.* A related question is one of the appropriate roles of political scientists themselves in the policy-making process. All scientific disciplines face the continuing problem of making their knowledge useful to society. Specifically, the policy sciences face the question of determining what their appropriate relationship with government should be. On this question there is no real consensus within the policy analysis movement. Some scholars argue for minimizing direct disciplinary links with government out of their concern about the development of scientific theory. Direct ties with government frequently mandate applied social science research aimed at providing solutions to immediate, narrowly-defined problems or remedying specific programmatic ventures. These

efforts seldom produce general scientific knowledge—at least not in proportion to the energies, resources, and money spent on them. More importantly, perhaps, is the concern expressed by many political scientists that we simply do not know enough about individual or group or societal behavior to be able to give reliable advice to policymakers. The fact that so many social scientists give contradictory advice to policymakers is an indication of the absence of reliable scientific knowledge about societal problems.

A different kind of argument for minimizing ties with policymakers is often advanced by critics of the American political system. Some political scientists do not want the discipline to have *any* connection with the government—arguing that American society and the political system is morally corrupt and that political scientists who let themselves be coopted to work within the system can only be corrupted by it. They argue that political science can only gain a "radical" perspective by functioning outside of the system, criticizing it, and pressing for radical change.

However, other scholars argue that it is probably better to provide policymakers with whatever little knowledge is produced by social science, than to have policymakers act in the absence of any knowledge at all. Even if social scientists cannot accurately predict the impact of future policies, they can at least attempt to measure the impact of current and past public policies and to make this knowledge available to decisionmakers.

The fact is, of course, that a number of political scientists do advise policymakers. They serve as members of presidential commissions, they work on staffs of commissions and congressional committees; they serve as consultants to government agencies; they testify before legislative committees; and so on. The real question is whether the policy-making process or the discipline itself should be restructured in any way to facilitate and encourage advice to policy-makers, and if so, how?

3. *Problem-Oriented versus Theory-Directed Research*. Another question confronting the policy analysis movement is the relative emphasis to be placed upon applied, problem-oriented research in contrast to basic, theory-directed research. Of course, everyone knows that good applied research contributes to theory development, and that research which is well formulated from a theoretical standpoint can have important practical implications. But it is difficult to whisk away altogether the problem or priorities in applied versus basic research. Applied policy research begins with a societal problem which is formulated outside of the discipline. Its resolution may, or may not, contribute to the development of general theories about public policy. In contrast, basic policy research generally originates as a test of some general theoretical proposition about the causes or consequences of public policy. The object is to develop a general theory which is reliable and which applies to different governmental agencies in

different policy areas. Moreover, in applied research it is necessary to give greater attention to *variables that are subject to government manipulation*, rather than to variables which cannot be manipulated by policymakers. In contrast, basic research frequently tries to explain as much of the variance as possible and gives greatest attention to those *variables which explain the largest proportion of the variance*. For example, basic research which reveals the overwhelming impact of underlying economic and social conditions on problems of urban life can only frustrate policymakers if it gives them no immediate handles for remedial action.

4. *Amateurism in Interdisciplinary Research*. There is no doubt that policy analysis requires an expansion of the traditional boundaries of political science well beyond any previous definition of those boundaries. If public policy is to be the dependent variable in our research, we must be prepared to search for policy determinants among economic, social, cultural, historical, technological factors, as well as political forces. If public policy is to be the independent variable, we must be prepared to search for policy consequences which are economic, social, cultural, historical, and technological, as well as political. But how can political scientists undertake to measure policy consequences in fields as diverse as education, health, welfare, air pollution, income distribution, law enforcement, etc? Does this not require political scientists to master concepts, methods, and measurements drawn from a wide variety of disciplines—not only in the social sciences, but also in the physical and biological sciences? And if we do so, how can we be sure that we are not abandoning whatever skills or knowledge we have as political scientists in order to become amateur economists, amateur engineers, amateur biologists, etc?

At first glance, the answer to this dilemma appears to be the interdisciplinary team research project. Certainly the idea of interdisciplinary team research on policy impact is an attractive one. But the question still remains—what special competencies do political scientists, as *political scientists*, bring to an interdisciplinary research team? Frequently the "team" ends up assigning to political scientists the task of studying the policy *process* anyhow, and assigns the task of analyzing policy *impact* to other members of the "team." How much effort should political scientists expend in training themselves in the concepts, methods, and measures of other disciplines in order to undertake policy impact research? Of course, every political scientist will have to answer these questions for himself, and it is likely that eclectism will continue to characterize our discipline as a whole. But it is important to understand that policy research does raise questions about the boundaries of our discipline.

5. *The Multiplicity of Concepts and Approaches*. The policy analysis movement, and political science generally, is confronted with a bewildering variety of conceptual models and approaches to research. Rational

models, incremental notions, group theories, systems models, power and elite concepts, and other policy-relevant ideas compete for our attention. Actually these approaches are not competitive, in the sense that any one could be judged "best." Doubtlessly most policies *are* a combination of rational planning, incrementalism, interest group activity, systemic forces, elite preferences, etc. However, this theoretical eclectism frequently interferes with scholarly communication—policy researchers "talk past" each other. More importantly, this multiplicity of concepts and models impedes efforts to cumulate reliable research findings and develop a general theory of public policy. No one seriously contends that there is any "one best way" of conceptualizing public policy. Each type of model, and variation thereof, provides a separate focus on public policy and assists in explaining different aspects of policy causes of consequences. But diversity in conceptualization also has its drawbacks—it results in a great deal of noncumulative research and it inhibits effective communication among researchers.

6. *The Diversity of Subject Matter*. There is some danger that the study of public policy is really the study of *everything*, and that there are really no common concerns of researchers working in different policy areas. The first issue of the *Policy Studies Journal* dealt with environmental policy, civil liberties policy, economic regulation policy, electoral policy, foreign policy, civic policy, educational policy, poverty and welfare policy, as well as comparative public policy; other areas of expressed interest include housing policy, health policy, race relations, manpower policy, tax policy, and urban policy. Is there sufficient commonality of interest—theoretical, methodological, or substantive—to justify serious intellectual interaction among scholars concerned with such widely divergent subject matter? Perhaps this diversity of subject matter would not be an obstacle to the development of a policy science *if* there was a common theoretical or conceptual thread in policy study. But, as we have already suggested, this does not seem to be the case.

These remarks are certainly *not* meant to discourage the development of the policy studies movement in political science. But it seems prudent to recognize some of the questions which may impede progress toward a coherent cohesive intellectual movement.

Note

1. One such discussion was the Conference on the Measurement of Policy Impact at Florida State University May, 1971, supported by the National Science Foundation. Many of my observations are drawn from this Conference, which included discussions on the following topics: For-

mal Choice Models in Policy Research (William C. Mitchell); Impact of Outcomes on Demand and Support (Herbert Jacob); Evaluative Criteria in Social Policy (Julius Margolis); Energy Policy and Environmental Protection (Robert Lawrence); Federal Air Pollution, Some Thoughts on On Effects and Feedback (Charles O. Jones); Policy Impact Analysis, A Suggested Research Strategy (Thomas J. Cook and Frank P. Scioli, Jr.); Problems in Measuring the External Costs and Benefits of Public Programs (Lawrence L. Wade); On the Measurement of Dependent Variables in Policy Impact Research, Some Effects of Reliability on Validity (David C. Leege); Measuring Unnecessary Delay in Administrative Proceedings, The Actual Versus the Predicted (Stuart S. Nagel); The Redistributive Dimension of Public Policy (Brian R. Fry); Systems Analysis by McNamara and Easton, A Proposal of Marriage (Ira Sharkansky); Social Science Research and Public Policy (Robert Lane). Copies of the Proceedings of the Conference on the Measurement of Policy Impact are available free on request to Thomas R. Dye, Department of Government, Florida State University, Tallahassee, Florida 32306.

26 Social Science Research and Public Policy

Robert Lane

First, I am going to talk about policy analysis—what happens when the government intervenes in a social system. Public policy analysis is applied social science in several senses: first in the identification of the need to which the policy is addressed, second in the inquiry into the consequences of government action, and third in the evaluation of public programs.

If it is true that public policy is applied social science, why is it that in Washington and the state capitals the presence and influence of social scientists is so small? I would argue that there are several reasons. One is that current social science with its more precise measurement capacities frequently loses some of its potential audience. It does not have some of the congenial properties and progressive spirit that early social science had. In the earlier era it was easy to talk in terms of what ought to be done, to talk in terms of moral norms. But you can start on a different track once you measure systematically the causes and consequences of public policy.

For example, when you engage in research on the causes and conditions of educational improvement, you are beginning to tread on some toes. It would be easy for a liberal to urge self-determination in educational systems. But, a social scientist may run across findings that one of the most important conditions of better education is that culturally-deprived learn more and better if they are in a context of the culturally-advantaged. Immediately you have a conflict with a "progressive culture," and that conflict loses for social science some of its support. You lose even more, for example, when you discover that teachers' salaries have no relationship to improved education. Here people begin to wonder about the methodology of the Coleman Report. We are working with a set of methods and tools that are uncongenial to lawyers who are dominant in the policy process, so you have lost some rapport which was not the case when it was a verbal argument.

I am saying that contemporary social science in its policy analytic role has some properties that make for new kinds of conflicts. At the same time, of course, it has somewhat more reliable knowledge. Indeed in Washington I think there are two religious movements. One of them is the social indicator movement and the other is the program evaluation movement.

The above comments were tape recorded from a largely extemporaneous talk by Robert Lane at the NSF Conference on Measurement of Public Policy Impact at Florida State University in May 1971, before the establishment of the Policy Studies Organization.

These movements are pursued with real missionary zeal. So it is wrong to say that there is no support for behavioral policy analysis. Indeed, one can compare program evaluation with the General Accounting Act of 1920 which made for precise accounting funds. As Moynihan says, under GAO control the money may be wasted but you are pretty sure it is not being stolen. Now Ribicoff has introduced for the General Accounting Office a program evaluation bill. This is a rather neat cycle in the sense that it is now fifty years later that Congress is proposing to not only make sure that the money is spent for purposes intended, but also to make sure that the purposes intended are served.

If it is true that policy analysis is applied social science, we must conclude that the training function for this purpose is badly done. Now, of course, the function of conceiving of policies is really a generalist function and liberal arts training is certainly the first ingredient. But it is just as important to think about implementation. It is no more technical to have some kind of consideration of the knowledge into action problem than to weigh competing values. The liberal arts function probably misses an ingredient here which would be very useful. The specialist function comes packaged in disciplines, and consequently the interdisciplinary needs are very great. Here the various research and policy institutes seem to be making a major contribution.

I think it is desirable for a political scientist interested in environmental politics to learn enough engineering to know about particulates in the atmosphere. As an old hand at stealing from another discipline, I can testify that you can learn quite a lot, or seem to know quite a lot, about neighboring disciplines when you pursue a particular purpose. Talking to people within those adjacent disciplines is very useful. It is not out of the question that we could learn enough engineering, enough biology, as well as enough economics, so that we can master some small domain. Do not lean too heavily on it, but enough to be able to judge what is reliable and what is not. I think that this is another function of training for policy analysis which is moving ahead but not with the degree of urgency or tension which I think the discipline should encourage.

I also think the research function deserves some attention. For most of us the standard paradigm is the dissertation. It involves relatively small data collections that one man can manage. This is the way we train our students. But I think for policy analytical functions it is too small in scale. We should encourage larger-scale, team research. The need for training to address the major problems in a major way with large bodies of data is undeniable.

Further, I think the extraordinary thing about our federal evaluative studies at the moment is that they are going away from correlational analysis and seeking to make social experiments. That is to say, they want to try one thing in one group of cities and another thing in another group of cities and see what the difference is. We have always complained that social science is not sufficiently experimental. Well, here is an opportunity to make it experimental. We should put ourselves into this effort in Washington.

There have been a number of studies of what should be done to improve the social science capacity for helping government: Knowledge into Action, a couple of conferences by Brookings on behavioral science in legislative programs, and another by the Department of State on research and foreign policy. Most obviously, they want federal departments and agencies to have inhouse capacity for social scientific analysis, and when they do not have it or cannot find it, to enter the inhouse training fields and/or give educational leaves to their staff so they may get trained in that way. The President's Science Advisory Committee and Office of Science and Technology should have more social scientists on them. Another interesting recommendation is that the president and Congress should prepare annually a statement of long-range research needs. This would be a kind of "state of the union" or "state of the economy" message, or maybe a "state of knowledge" or "state of our ignorance" message. That would be a very interesting thing. It need not be all that big or all that public. But some kind of appraisal in advance of needs for more information would be a very interesting thing.

Some of the other recommendations are that there be more money for social scientists, and that the government and scientific community should establish better liaison. There is also a proposal for a kind of early alert system; when you are going to have a legislative hearing people should know about it a couple of months in advance and should be able to prepare research. Hearings do make a difference, because congressmen learn through their ears when they haven't got time to read something. They will remember what is said much more easily than what is presented to them in some kind of memorandum. Early alerts and better social science representation and more thoughtful, better preparations would be very useful.

There was also a recommendation that appropriate professional associations and concerned universities inform their interested members and constituents about researchable questions generated by public policy problems. The capacity of a professional association to do something in this area is an important and difficult consideration.

There are some other suggestions—the "council of social advisors" keeps coming up. One alternative to this is that the Council of Economic Advisors should include more social scientists as non-economists and behavioral scientists. This alternative might also include some natural scientists. Another suggestion is that the Library of Congress should establish a set of rotating professorships for social and behavioral sciences to advice members of Congress and the staffs of congressional committees. Then, there are the national institutes for advanced research and public policy. There are at least twenty-five social problems research institutes throughout the country. The Urban Institute in some ways was in response to suggestions of this kind. Another interesting suggestion that has been made is that the final reports of all studies with policy relevant implications have set aside funds for implementation.

Let me speak a moment on the capacities of the professional associations for doing something about the knowledge into action problem. It is a complicated matter. The constitutions of some associations talk about their public welfare responsibilities; ours does not. The psychologists', the geographers', and the statisticians' do, however. The historians have a curious relationship: they are required to submit their annual report through the Smithsonian to Congress.

A word or two about the various social science associations. I have some data from a little survey on membership growth over the last few years, the decade 1960-1970. They have all increased, the statisticians least, by only about a third; the psychologists only by about 66 percent. Most of them—historians, sociologists and others—have about doubled, except for political science. Political science has increased over this decade by 176 percent, the largest growth of any of them. We think about ourselves as an organization about half the size that we actually are. Our capacities for policy inputs and specialized analysis is that much greater; plus our political muscle is a little bit more than it appears to be. Finance, I am sorry to say, is a strike the other way. Our budget has not increased as rapidly as many of the other social science associations. The physical sciences get about $800 million from all government sources; life sciences about $500 million; psychologists, alone about $55 million; all of the social sciences, about $72 million; of which ours is less than $3 million.

The internal politics of professional associations sometimes makes policy research difficult. Of course it depends on what you are proposing to do. There are those who take the position that you should have nothing to do with the government because it is corrupting. They believe our only function is to stand back, to gain a perspective for radical comprehensive critique. On the other hand, there are those who say that whatever you can do in some small way to improve the quality of housing, upgrade education, reduce poverty, reduce inequality, even within a Republican administration, makes somebody better off, so we just try to do so. What I find distasteful is that any body should want to deny the other side's position and say that we collectively, should do all one and not the other.

Now, what I would like to propose is that the American Political Science Association endeavor to provide some kind of an information brokerage system on policy matters. This would include information about research needs and government people who are looking for information on legislative staffs, committee staffs, HUD, HEW, etc. On the other side, it will be matching those needs with the research capacity, the research findings, information about who is doing what. This brokerage function can only be performed by some agency that knows who has what kind of expertise. The National Associations, better than SSRC, better than NRC, are able to perform this function. I would think the APSA ought to have some kind of a newsletter which provided this brokerage function. It might very well also include information on training needs and training capacities. The Association would be an appropriate place to house this.

One of the choices that members of our Association should have is whether to avail themselves of such a service. Without it, a kind of pluralistic ignorance prevails. I think it is to improve the choice capacities and not to diminish them that we should have such a service. It might be argued that it is not our traditional role to do this. But, it seems to me that it is part of the tradition of information and communication of the Association. Have we the capacity to say anything about public policy? I think we do. It is most important not to oversell, but we do not have to oversell. We can simply say rather humbly what we do not know; that is to say, we can identify areas of ignorance as we identify areas of knowledge.

Association involvement could democratize what is currently a set of baronies in the policy advisory field. It has always been the case that some distinguished political scientists have influence in Washington, like Kissinger, or Moynihan. They, in a way, are most likely to resist Association involvement. A good way to democratize this influence is to spread it out so that everybody knows where the inputs are needed. The Association can provide a brokerage function with full and open information about policy-relevant research needs and capacities. It is quite important that this be governed by a committee with a full range of political representation so that there is some kind of reassurance that it is not people with particular ideological commitments who are being brought into the picture.

Indexes

Index of Names

Index of Subjects

Academic evaluation research, 17-19
Accountability, 14, 143-145
Addiction, drug, xii
Administrative agencies, xiii, xiv
Advising policymakers, 281-282
AFL-CIO, 136
Agencies, administrative, xiii, xiv
Agriculture, 29, 277
Air rights, 77
Alcoholism, xii
Algebra, 211-220
 Matrix, 211, 221
Allocation of resources, 65-66
American Civil Liberties Union, 94
American Journal of Sociology, 4
American Political Science Association, 290
American Political Science Review, 211, 212
American Psychological Association, 119
Amisuc curiae briefs, 119
Analysis, causal, xii, xiii
Analysis, deductive, xiii, 89, 91
Analysis of variance, 29
Analytical techniques, 221
Anthropology, xiii, 57, 149-162
 Historical development, 4-5
 Political, 151
 Social, 151-161
Applied mathematics, 211-220, 221
Applied social research, 6
Applied sociology, 51-54
Asia, 4
Assessing social policy, 33-43
Association of American Geographers, 163
Attitudes, political, 214-215
Axiomatic reasoning, 91

Bay of Pigs, 126, 127, 132
Behavior, political, 214-215
Behavioral models, 52
Behavioral political science, 269-270
Behavioral research, 85
Behavioral studies, 54
Benefits, marginal, 75
Berlin, 164
Biological science, xiii
Biology, 227, 234-235
Biomedical technology, 234-235
Brandeis Brief, 113
Brandeis University, 58, 113-114
Briefs, amicus curiae, 119
Britain, 3, 4, 5, 152, 153, 164
 Labor Party, 5

British Empire, 4, 258
Brookings Institution, 289
Brown v. Board of Education, 113, 114, 256
Budgeting, program, 138
Building of coalitions, 85
Bureaucracy, 36, 37, 94, 95, 139, 179, 185
Business management, 138

Calculus, xiii
California, 38, 80, 82, 137
California, University of, 99
California Water Plan, 259
Campbell's "Experimenting Society,"
 108-109
Canonical correlation, 213
Capitalism, 67
Caucus for a New Political Science, 271
Causal analysis, xii, xiii
Causal models, 52
Causal relations, 49
Census development, 3
Central Arizona Project, 259
Central Intelligence Agency, 126, 251
Change, social, xii, 160
Chicago Jury Project, 254
Chicago, University of, 58
Child development, 115
Choice, collective, 67, 78-81
Citizen participation in policy decisions,
 177-183
Civil liberties, xiv
Classical rational choice, 66, 89-102
Clinical evaluation, 11
Coalition-building, 85
 Minimum winning, 79
Cold War, 5
Coleman Report, 287
Collection of data, 38
Collective choice, 67, 78-81
Collective goods, 76
Collective rationality, 92
Columbia University, 6, 58
Commission on Behavior Modification, 119
Communications, 5
Communists, 34
Community control, 80
Community power, 135-136
Comparative study, 158-161
Comprehensive evaluation, 13-15
Computer science, xiii
Concept of social planning, 58-60
Concurrence-seeking tendency, 126

301

About the Contributors

Michael Barkun is professor of political science in the Maxwell School, Syracuse University. He holds a 1974-75 Senior Fellowship from the National Endowment for the Humanities. Professor Barkun is engaged in research on the relationship between massive disaster and the rise of millenarian movements. His books include *Disaster and the Millennium* (Yale University Press, 1974); *International Law and the Social Sciences* (Princeton University Press, 1970); and *Law without Sanctions* (Yale University Press, 1968).

Ilene Nagel Bernstein received her undergraduate training at Alfred University and Hunter College, and her doctoral training in Sociology at New York University. She is an assistant professor in the department of sociology at Indiana University. She has coauthored a monograph with Howard Freeman, *Academic and Entrepreneurial Research: The Consequences of Diversity in Federal Evaluation Studies* (Russell Sage Foundation, 1975), and published several articles on evaluation research methodology. Besides her work in evaluation, her research interests include the sociology of science, and criminology.

Frederick K. Beutel is professor emeritus of University of Nebraska and occasional visiting professor of law at Arizona State University. He has wide experience as counsel and administrator in federal and local government and is author, among others, of *Some Potentialities of Experimental Jurisprudence as a New Branch of Social Science* (1957), *Democracy or the Scientific Method in Law and Policy Making* (1965), *Operation of the Bad-Check Law of Puerto Rico* (1967), and *Experimental Jurisprudence and the Scienstate* (1975) and numerous articles in the field of jurisprudence and public law.

Donald T. Campbell is a professor of psychology at Northwestern University, Evanston, Illinois. He received the Ph.D. from the University of California, Berkeley, in 1947. He has also taught at Ohio State University and the University of Chicago. Dr. Campbell is best known for his methodological articles on validity of measurements and on the design of experiments in field settings. He is a member of the National Academy of Sciences and currently President of the American Psychological Association.

Gene Coggshall is the administrative assistant to the Cornell University Program on Science, Technology, and Society and a part-time instructor at

309

Ithaca College. He has been a technical writer with ITT World Communications.

Thomas R. Dye is professor of government at Florida State University. He is the author of *Understanding Public Policy, Politics in States and Communities, The Politics of Equality, Politics, Economics, and the Public,* and coauthor of *The Irony of Democracy, The Few and the Many,* and *Politics in the Metropolis.* He has taught at the University of Wisconsin, the University of Georgia, and Bar Ilan University, Israel.

Robert Ferber is research professor of economics and business administration and director of the Survey Research Laboratory at the University of Illinois. He is also coordinating and applications editor of the *Journal of the American Statistical Association.* In these respects and in various consulting activities, Professor Ferber has been involved in the application of statistical techniques to public problems in a number of the social sciences. Books and articles by him have appeared in many different journals, principally in economics, statistics, and the business areas.

Phillip O. Foss is a professor and past chairman of the political science department at Colorado State University. He was president of the Western Political Science Association in 1972-73 and a consultant to the National Academy of Sciences. Professor Foss's publications include *Politics and Grass* (1960); *Politics and Policies: The Continuing Issues* (with Duane W. Hill, 1970); and *Politics and Ecology* (1972).

Howard E. Freeman is director of the Institute for Social Science Research and professor of sociology at UCLA. Prior to coming to UCLA in 1974, he was Morse Professor of Urban Studies at the Florence Heller Graduate School for Advanced Studies in Social Welfare at Brandeis University. During 1972 to 1974, he served as the Ford Foundations' social science advisor for Mexico, Central America and the Caribbean. Professor Freeman is the author of *Social Problems: Causes and Controls, Social Research and Social Policy, Entrepreneurial and Academic Research* and *The Clinic Habit.* He is the coauthor of *America's Troubles, The Social Scene, Handbook of Medical Sociology* and *The Dying Patient.* Professor Freeman has contributed many articles on medical care, mental health, and social problems to academic journals, as well as written widely on the relationship between social research and social policy.

Martin P. Golding is professor of philosophy at John Jay College of Criminal Justice, City University of New York and Adjunct Professor at Columbia University. He is the author of the recently published book *Philosophy* *of Law* (1975) and the editor of a book *The Nature of Law* (1966). He has published articles on legal and social philosophy and ethics, including articles on judicial decision-making, human rights, and ethical issues in biological engineering and population policies. Professor Golding is the Secretary-Treasurer of the American Society for Political and Legal Philosophy and a Fellow of the Institute of Society, Ethics and the Life Sciences.

Irving Janis is a professor of psychology at Yale University. His current research is on social psychological aspects of decision making, effective counselor-client relationships, and psychological stress. A number of his publications are relevant to his chapter in this volume, including "Group Identification under Conditions of External Threat," in Cartwright and Zander (eds.), *Group Dynamics: Research and Theory* (1968); *Victims of Groupthink: A Psychological Study of Foreign-Policy Decisions and Fiascos* (1972); "Vigilance and Decision-Making in Personal Crises," in Hamburg and Coelho (eds.), *Coping and Adaptation* (1975); and (in collaboration with L. Mann), *Decision Making: A Psychological Analysis of Conflict, Choice and Commitment* (in press).

Ernest M. Jones is professor of law at the University of Florida at Gainesville. He has a professional interest in legal policy studies and has been active in law and social science movements.

Alfred J. Kahn is professor of social work and teaches social policy and social planning at the Columbia University School of Social Work. Dr. Kahn has served as consultant to federal, state and local agencies, to voluntary organizations and to foundations concerned with: the planning of social services, income maintenance, child welfare, related programs, international collaboration, and social policy generally. He is the author of *Theory and Practice of Social Planning* and *Studies in Social Policy and Planning*, as well as *Social Policy and Social Services* (Random House).

John Ladd is professor of philosophy, Brown University. From 1956 to 1969 he served as secretary-treasurer of the American Society for Political and Legal Philosophy. His writings in the area of social philosophy include *The Structure of a Moral Code* (Harvard, 1957), a translation of Kant's *Metaphysical Elements Justice* (Bobbs-Merrill, 1965), *Ethical Relativism* (Wadsworth, 1973), and several articles in *NOMOS*. Especially relevant to the present topic is "Morality and the Ideal of Rationality in Formal Organizations," MONIST, vol. 54, no. 4 (October, 1970).

Robert E. Lane is a professor of political science at Yale University. He has been president of the American Political Science Association (1970-71) and the Policy Studies Organization (1973-74). His publications include *The Regulation of Businessmen, Political Life, The Liberties of Wit, Political Ideology, Political Thinking and Consciousness, Political Man.*

Daniel Lerner is Ford Professor of Sociology and International Communication at the Massachusetts Institute of Technology. He has been a visiting professor at universities throughout Europe, the Middle East, and Asia. Among his major books are *The Passing of Traditional Society, The Policy Sciences, Psychological Warfare Against Nazi Germany,* and *Euratlantica: Changing Perspectives of the European Elites*—all of which are available in paperback. Professor Lerner's writings have been translated into most of the world's major languages.

James P. Levine is an associate professor of political science at Brooklyn College of the City University of New York. His dissertation from Northwestern University on the impact of obscenity law on booksellers won the Corwin Award for the best doctoral thesis in the area of public law given by the American Political Science Association. Professor Levine has published articles on the legal process in *Syracuse Law Review, Wisconsin Law Reviwe, Law and Society Review, American Behavioral Scientist, Urban Affairs Quarterly,* and *Polity.* His current research is on the role of the public in crime prevention; this work will be published in a book to be completed in August, 1975 tentatively entitled *In Memory of Kitty Genovese: The Public Role in Crime Prevention.*

Theodore J. Lowi holds a John L. Senior Professorship of American Institutions in the department of government at Cornell University. His publications include *The Politics of Disorder* (1971); *The End of Liberalism* (1969); *Private Life and Public Order* (1967); *At the Pleasure of the Mayor* (1964); and *Legislative Politics U.S.A.* (1962, 65, 72).

Duncan MacRae, Jr., is William Rand Kenan Jr., Professor of Political Science and Sociology at the University of North Carolina, Chapel Hill. He has previously taught sociology at Princeton and Berkeley, and sociology and political science at the University of Chicago. Professor MacRae has published a number of articles on the foundations of policy analysis and in 1974-75 is President of the Policy Studies Organization.

Eugene J. Meehan is professor of political science and fellow of the Center for Community and Metropolitan Studies at the University of Missouri, St. Louis. His publications include *Public Housing Policy: Myth versus Reality* (Rutgers University Center for Urban Research, 1975; *Foundations* *of Political Analysis: Empirical and Normative* (1971); *Value Judgement and Social Science* (1969); *Explanation and Social Science* (1968); and *Theory and Methodology of Political Analysis* (1965).

D. J. Montgomery is professor of physics and research professor of engineering at Michigan State University, from which he is on leave as Fulbright Researcher and Guest Professor, Department of Macroeconomics, Univeristy of Augsburg. In recent years he has devoted himself primarily to studying the social consequences of technology, and has developed courses and written papers on matters related to technology assessment.

Michael C. Musheno is an assistant professor of political science at Brooklyn College of the City University of New York with major research and teaching interests in criminal justice and urban policy analysis. He is currently the coprincipal investigator of a large policy research grant from LEAA focusing on the role of the police in handling non-criminals, particularly public inebriates, and is the acting director of his department's Center for Political Research. Along with Palumbo and Levine, he is the coauthor of a monograph, "Evaluating Alternatives in the Criminal Justice System."

John O'Loughlin is assistant professor of geography at the University of Illinois at Urbana-Champaign. He is presently chief investigator in a traffic and transportation study of the Urbana campus and is the author of "Malapportionment and Gerrymandering in the Ghetto," a policy study for the Association of American Geographers' Metropolitan Analysis Project.

Dennis J. Palumbo is professor of political science and director, Urban Administration and Information Science Program, Brooklyn College. His publications include "A Systems Analysis of Local Public Health," *American Journal of Public Health,* "Predictors of Public Policy; The Case of Local Public Health," *Urban Affairs Quarterly;* "Power and Role Specificity in Organization Theory," *Public Administration Review;* "Professionalism and Receptivity to Change," *American Journal of Political Science*, and *Statistics in Political and Behavioral Science.* Professor Palumbo has done research under grant support in public health policy and evaluating alternatives in criminal justice.

Warren J. Samuels is professor of economics at Michigan State University. He is editor of the *Journal of Economic Issues,* and is the author of *Pareto on Policy* (American Elsevier, 1974); *The Classical Theory of Economic*

Policy (World, 1966); "An Economic Perspective on the Compensation Problem," *Wayne Law Review*, vol. 21 (November, 1974); "The Coase Theorem and the Study of Law and Economics," *Natural Resources Journal,* vol. 14 (January, 1974); "Interrelations Between Legal and Economic Processes," *Journal of Law and Economics,* vol. 14 (October, 1971); and articles in the theory of public utility regulation and the history of economic and legal-economic thought.

Serena Stier is a clinical psychologist, trained at U.C.L.A., who has moved into the policy studies area as administrative officer for policy studies at the American Psychological Association. One of her major responsibilities in this position is staffing the APA Commission on Behavior Modification. In addition, Dr. Stier serves as liaison to many groups concerned with developing a working relationship between law and psychology. She has made national presentations and published papers in the areas of family therapy, child advocacy, and law and psychology.

Jack Thomas is Associate Dean of the College of Education, University of Illinois at Urbana-Champaign. His primary interests include the analysis of federal policy on educational research and development, and the application of administrative science findings to educational problems. His teaching area is "higher education management." Dr. Thomas has undertaken policy oriented consulting assignments for the Urbana, Illinois Public Schools; the California Department of Education, and the USOE. Before coming to the University of Illinois, he served as the administrative officer for Stanford University's Center for Research and Development on Teaching.

L. L. Wade is professor of political science at the University of California, Davis and is the author of *The Elements of Public Policy,* 1972 and the coauthor (with R. L. Meek) of *Democracy in America: A Public Choice Approach,* 1975 and (with R. L. Curry) *A Logic of Public Policy,* 1970 and *A Theory of Political Exchange,* 1968. Professor Wade is a former NSF Fellow at the London School of Economics and Political Science (1971-72) and a Senior Fulbright-Hayes Scholar at Waseda University, Tokyo (1974).

Paul M. Wortman is associate director of the Northwestern University Evaluation Research Program and an associate professor of psychology. For the past three years he has been involved in the evaluation of many programs in the fields of education, health care, and mental health. Dr. Wortman is working with his colleagues to develop new techniques of analysis and to test them by performing secondary analyses of educational data. A primary focus of this research is the policy relevance of evaluation methods. His most recent publication in this area is "Evaluation research: A psychological perspective" which appeared in the May, 1975, issue of the *American Psychologist*.

About the Editor

Stuart S. Nagel is a professor of political science at the University of Illinois. He is the coordinator of the *Policy Studies Journal* and the secretary-treasurer of the Policy Studies Organization. He is the author or editor of such books as *Policy Studies in America and Elsewhere* (Heath, Lexington Books, 1975), *Improving the Legal Process: Effects of Alternatives* (Heath, Lexington Books, 1975), *Environmental Politics* (Praeger, 1974), *The Rights of the Accused: In Law and Action* (Sage, 1972), *Law and Social Change* (Sage, 1970), and *The Legal Process from a Behavioral Perspective* (Dorsey, 1969). Dr. Nagel has held fellowships from the LEAA National Institute, Yale Law and Social Science Program, National Science Foundation, Russell Sage Foundation, Center for Advanced Study in the Behavioral Sciences, Social Science Research Council, the East-West Center, and the American Council of Learned Societies. He has been an attorney to the U. S. Senate Subcommittee on Administrative Practice and Procedure, Office of Economic Opportunity, Lawyer's Constitutional Defense Committee in Mississippi, and the National Labor Relations Board.